TRAVELING
OFF THE
X

by
JO PATTI MUNISTERI

DEFIANCE PRESS
& PUBLISHING

Traveling Off The X

ISBN-13: 978-1-948035-80-4 (Paperback)
ISBN-13: 978-1-948035-81-1 (eBook)

Published by Defiance Press and Publishing, LLC

Bulk orders of this book may be obtained by contacting Defiance Press and Publishing, LLC. www.defiancepress.com.

Public Relations Dept. – Defiance Press & Publishing, LLC
281-581-9300
pr@defiancepress.com

FOREWORD

Traveling Off The X refers to the concept of getting out of the line of fire, moving off the target area (the "X") be it physical, emotional or even spiritual danger.

Each chapter in this book contains at least one situation where there is present or possible physical, emotional, and/or spiritual danger. How the different people in different places manage to travel off the "X" in their particular circumstances is the common theme for this work.

This is a work of non-fiction; however, the names in some chapters have been changed or omitted for the sake of privacy and security.

The time frames are, out of necessity, compressed. What in reality took days, weeks, months or years in real time was consolidated or shuffled for the sake of clarity.

I hope this book reaches and benefits those who have experienced hardship and suffering in life as well as those who are curious about parts of the world which are less traveled.

"All journeys have secret destinations of which the traveler is unaware."

– Martin Buber

ACKNOWLEDGEMENTS

Throughout my life many people have supported my writing and my professional and personal struggles.

First, I would like to thank my friend, colleague, and editor Randi Perlman. There are not enough words to express my gratitude.

Second, I would like to sincerely thank my former trainer and friend, Colonel Richard E. Swisher (Ret.) In challenging situations, no matter where I was—both professionally and personally—Rick made himself available for sage advice.

To all my friends and colleagues who supported me over the years, but for whom privacy is paramount … thank you!

To my family members who also value their privacy but who know who they are and who gave of their time and love to encourage me, I hope they know how much they are loved and appreciated, too.

To my daughter Sequoia and her husband John, I hope this book is a guide to deeper understanding, love and peace.

DEDICATION

This book is dedicated to my dear friend, colleague and teammate, Lisa Marie Akbari.

Lisa was born in Bridgeport, Alabama, USA on November 9, 1980. Lisa graduated with a master's in international psychology, from the Chicago School of Professional Psychology (2012-2014). She completed a master's degree and did PhD Coursework in Clinical Psychology at the University of Wyoming (2003-2008). She received her bachelor's degree with Honors from the University of Nevada (2000-2003).

Lisa served in the US Coast Guard and was a Department of Army Civilian (DAC) with the Human Terrain System. She certified as a US Army Social Scientist and Combat Analyst from Ft. Leavenworth, Kansas, USA. Lisa worked as an independent contractor for a number of US companies and Non-Government Organizations (NGOs) overseas. She and I worked together for a USAID project contracted out to Checchi Company, Ltd in Afghanistan in 2015.

Lisa was fatally shot on the night of December 20, 2015, in Kabul, Afghanistan.

TABLE OF CONTENTS

1. BOATING IN BUCHAREST – ROMANIA

This journey requires me to land behind the Iron Curtain of the Soviet Union and travel by myself for sixty days. I am to use at least five different means of transport other than airplanes. My plans include traveling by bicycle, train, hydrofoil, boat, by foot and by horse. I need to remain as low key as possible, blend in with the local population, and report back in written form before presenting to a small group at the United Nations upon my return. My expectations for this trip are meshed with the responsibilities placed upon me by winning a travel grant. I am the first female selected by the all-male Circumnavigators Club.

My mentor, Ray Dinsmore, President of the Foundation which has awarded the funds, is at the airport. He gives me two letters to carry with me. One is addressed to my first contact in Romania, and the other to someone I will meet when I get to Moscow. A few months ago, when their representative, Mr. Dinsmore came down from New York to meet me at Georgetown University, I had just turned twenty. I'm not sure how old he is but since he is retired, I'm assuming he is over sixty. He reassures me that I will be fine and to remember to stop, take a deep breath and pause for a moment when I feel nervous. He arranges for a photographer to come snap a picture of me at Kennedy Airport shortly before I have to check in with Pan Am airlines.

Looking through the wall-sized glass window at the airport, I can see the outside and myself and I smile remembering his advice. I inwardly vow to make this trip a success for his sake. He took a chance recommending me.

It will be at least a twenty-six-hour trip stopping in three different countries before landing in Bucharest, Romania. Nicolae Ceausescu is at the height of his power as a leader in the Soviet communist country. I've been warned to be careful whom I speak to, who meets me and who I get in a vehicle with. There are no cell phones, no internet and few functioning pay phones.

Figure 1. Jo Patti Munisteri – Kennedy
International Airport, New York 1973

I'm painfully aware that my American clothes and matching shoes
stick out as I exit with my backpack and large purse. The airport in
Bucharest doesn't feel air conditioned. The air is heavy with cigarette
and cigar smoke. I see a white sign with my name spelled incorrectly
but still recognizable. A woman is holding it. I didn't expect my guide
to be a woman.

We greet each other and she shows me her ID. Her English is excellent. She's the interpreter for the United States wrestling team. They will be in the capital for a few days.

Luminista is Romani, with long black hair, a strong-featured face and piercing brown eyes. She ushers me out to the crush of people and vehicles at the entrance, then points to a car with a driver. She insists on carrying my bag even though she must be at least twenty years older than I.

When I glance out the car window, I see a world of gray, grim people and buildings. It is June in the summer of 1973.

I try to concentrate, find some bearings in the landscape, breathe deeply and listen as Luminista—her name means "little light,"—names streets, historical buildings and highlights of her city. Every few minutes she switches to Romanian and speaks to the driver in spitfire-like sentences. I feel inadequate knowing only French and a little Italian. Luminista will be my guide, my interpreter and my protector for the first week.

Driving into the capital, I feel as if I am going back in time. This place looks as if it hasn't recovered from World War II yet. People walk wearily. There is apprehensiveness in their bodies and in the atmosphere. Many are wearing worn out shoes or sandals. This is my first encounter with a communist country and people. There was so much praise lavished on "the equitable system of communism" when I was in America. It was touted as a "paradise for workers." I am not impressed.

As we pull up to a shabby looking guest house, Luminista pays the driver and helps me with my bag.

"You will stay here, my dear. Rest now and I will come by at 7:00 p.m. We will go to dinner in a restaurant I know. There you can change money. You have US dollars, yes?"

"Yes," I nod. A creeping fatigue, jet lag is starting to permeate my mind and body.

"See you later, thank you again, Luminista."

"Ciao, Joann … a." She waves as she springs down the front steps.

I lug my bags up to reception, check in and collapse on the very hard mattress. Lying completely horizontal after sitting upright on planes for two days is heavenly. The only item I unpack is my small, plastic wind-up alarm clock. I set it for 6:00 p.m. and easily drift into dreamless sleep.

"Ciao Joann … a" Luminista greets me with a closed-mouth smile at reception. She is dressed in an intricately embroidered white blouse and deep red-colored, dirndl-style skirt. I imagine it must be a traditional design and comment on how lovely she looks in it. She raises her eyebrows as if she is not sure I mean my compliment.

"You have your dollars to change?" Lumnista asks.

"Right here." I indicate a place in my purse. I am hesitant to show her how much I have.

"Oh, this is for you, too." I hand her the letter Mr. Dinsmore gave me at the airport in New York.

"Ok, first we go to change money before we eat. Come this way."

I walk beside Luminista on the uneven sidewalks. The sun is still shining. People are out promenading after work. I showered and changed into more casual clothes. My own long, dark hair and features fit in here. Almost no one takes a second look at us until we approach the "Bureau de Change." Luminista apparently knows the man behind the desk and chats to him before she instructs me to bring out my money. I have smaller bills and give him five $20.00 notes. He grunts as he counts and trades them for Romanian *leu (XX)*.

"Multumesc." We each say as a "thank you" before departing. In the foyer I ask Luminista how much I owe her for the ride from the airport.

"No, I pay that, don't worry," she assures me. I decide not to press her.

We pass from the more official looking part of the city to a quarter that is more a marketplace with stalls, cobblestone streets and basement businesses.

Luminista pauses at a sidewalk café and nudges me inside. A group of musicians rest on a small platform back from the tables and the smells of lamb cooking. An older man struts forward to meet us.

He recognizes Luminista and cases me with his eyes as they speak in a language I have never heard. We follow him to a table inside.

As soon as Luminista starts to speak to me in English, patrons from other tables turn their ears to us. We lower our voices.

"They have very delicious food here. You will try real Romanian food."

"Is there anything you would recommend?" I ask, puzzling over the menu.

"*Sarmale*(cabbage rolls with meat and cheese) are very good."

"Fine, we can start with *sarmale* then." I was hungry but careful only to order cooked foods in case my stomach rebelled.

Patrons who had finished their meals were smoking at the inside tables. I felt my throat tighten. The musicians began tuning up their violins, guitar, mandolin and accordion. The whole room started to hum.

"Tonight, is special night for music," Luminista explained. "You will hear traditional Roma music ... you call us, Gypsies I believe."

"Lulu!" The man at the microphone looked directly at Luminista.

"My friends call me Lulu, dear. You can call me Lulu, too. It is easier than Luminista, no?"

"As you wish. Actually, I like both your names."

Luminista gave a graceful gesture of recognition with her right hand to the man at the microphone. He nodded and turned to count out the opening rhythm for the group.

The violins began a melancholy strain as the singer closed his eyes preparing to join in on a higher note sliding a wailing phrase up and then down the scale. The guitar strummed a beat and the melody spun into all the instruments until the singer began another beat by clapping his hands.

I was mesmerized, but my feet still kept time. Lulu grinned between bites of her bread dipped in olive oil. The tempo and volume increased as we tasted our *sarmale*.

In songs that followed, patrons hummed or sung along until suddenly we heard a crash. Raucous voices outside swelled in another crescendo. Two men started to fight right in front of the restaurant. No one moved to stop them. One of the men threw a chair which just missed the window near us.

"I think we should go. Let's get the check now," I insisted.

"Better we wait, the fight will be over in a few minutes. Is normal here."

Luminsta carried on eating her dinner as the music continued. I was at the mercy of her decisions.

Before I left America, I had been given a briefing at Georgetown University by three different security 'experts' which included what situations to "avoid at all costs." This was definitely one of them. I didn't know the language; I didn't know how to get back to the hotel and I had no other contacts or people who knew me. I was stuck and she knew it.

I couldn't finish my *sarmale*. In less than six hours behind the Iron Curtain I was already in a risky situation. I was on an "X." I scanned around for exits.

"Ca va?" Luminista switched to French. I stared at her a moment before replying.

"Ca va bien, merci."

I watched as Luminista finished her glass of wine and savored the last bites of her meal.

As she predicted, the fighting wound down. The men who were fighting were restrained by comrades holding each away from the other. One of the men was escorted down a side street. At a nearby table, men laughed as they ate. No one appeared to be concerned ... except me.

"Demain matin ..." She continued. Luminista would pick me up in front of the hotel tomorrow morning at 8:00 a.m. sharp. We would be joining the US wrestling team for their bus tour.

Luminista raised her head in the direction of the waiter, and he brought us the check. I paid for both of us. She gracefully accepted. We pushed our chairs back from the table.

"What is this part of Bucharest called?" I inquired as we walked.

"Centrul vechi Bucuresti (the old Bucharest), one of the few sections that that bloody man was not able to destroy."

I sensed her anger at the known Stalinist, Ceausescu, but I was given strict instructions not to engage in discussions about politics or current leaders.

"Let me show you a place that foreigners do not go, my dear."

Luminista quickened her pace and steered us down an alleyway. There were no streetlights and few people. My inner voice was trying to speak to me, to warn me, but my feet kept pace with hers.

We stopped before a plain door. There were no windows, but I saw a light seeping from under the entrance. Luminista knocked firmly. We heard footsteps lumbering toward the door.

An elderly man with a long white beard, a pale face and bushy gray eyebrows opened the door slowly. He squinted at us, then turned his head from side to side scanning the street to see who might be looking, before he let us in.

We walked down a dimly lit corridor to a series of open exhibition rooms. A young man was standing guard by the first room. Luminista nodded to him as we entered the large open space. We caught each other's eye. He seemed to be surveying my inner landscapes and I felt drawn to him for some reason. No words yet, just an energetic cord connected us. Luminista was absorbed in a huge canvas across the room.

"Ah, this one is so full of power! Do you see, Joann ... a?

For the first time I took a minute to view the art hung tentatively on the large walls. Each one was painted with only three colors: black, white and red. The brush strokes were masterful and the way these three colors were used was different for every painting. In one, the canvas was painted red, and the figures were in black, and outlines of white were used for objects. In another, the canvas was painted black, and the figures were in red or white.

"Why only three colors? Is this the artist's signature style?" I inquired.

"No, not precisely. Most artists are *only permitted* to use these three colors. It is part of the communist party dictate for artists. The subject matter is also dictated. Artists may only display paintings, drawings or collages of "acceptable" themes. But if you take your time and look closely, you can see between the lines of the colors, what the artist intends, no?"

I looked around the room, careful to avoid the young man's gaze. The paintings seemed to shout. The figures were in agony. The restriction in use of color and subject let loose repressed sufferings. I was astonished.

Luminista was watching me closely. My eyes began to tear. I became embarrassed and turned to the back wall away from their eyes.

"Yes, my dear. I knew you could 'see.' Are you sure you are not Roma?"

The older gentleman spoke in a raspy voice to Luminista. For once she hesitated.

"There are others coming soon. We should go or they might ask questions about you. This is not a place for tourists or outsiders. Sorry, dear. This is the way here. Plans must change."

The younger man walked over to us. He bent to whisper something to Luminista. She took a fleeting glance at me as she answered him, and he nodded. The three of us made our way to the outer door.

"Sunday, ok?" He startled me by speaking English.

"Ok, I guess." I regarded him closely.

"Cismigiu Park by lake. Two o'clock. Lulu will say you how. My name is Stefan."

I inhaled slowly. "My name is Joanne. A pleasure to meet you."

He ushered us out and Luminista hurried along until we reached the main street.

"Please tell me," I entreated, practically breathless from the pace Luminista had set.

"He is interested in you, but be careful. Others will watch and I cannot be with you on Sunday. Stefan speaks a little English but understands more. Do you want to meet him?"

I paused by the streetlight and considered. Going by myself without an interpreter or official escort to meet a strange man was not prudent, yet part of me was intrigued.

"Do you know him? Is it safe?" I asked, trying to keep my breathing even.

"Yes, he is safe. Stefan is a student at the Institutul de Arte Plastice Nicolae Grigorescu, he is a talented sculptor in his last year. I think it's alright if you meet for a few hours. We will speak more tomorrow."

"What are we doing tomorrow?"

"In the morning we go with the USA team on the bus for tour. Then we go together to the salon. This is the best place to really hear what women have to say. I know the owner."

Luminista knew my grant involved recording and analyzing the perceptions of women who lived behind the "Iron Curtain," then comparing these to those of women in the USA. It was an ambitious undertaking, but one member of the Circumnavigator's Club insisted. I changed my project to one which concentrated on women since I was the first female to be chosen for their travel fellowship. Maybe this all-male club was curious about the women of the Soviet Union. Probably.

We had reached my hotel entrance.

"Thank you, Luminista. I will be standing on these steps ready at 8:00 a.m."

"Very good, my dear. Hope you enjoyed your first night in Bucuresti!"

"Oh, yes I did. Good night, *multumesc*."

"You're welcome. *Ciao.*"

Luminista stayed and watched me until I was in the front lobby.

In my room I let down my guard and fell asleep trying to close my nose to the smell of cigarettes in my "nonsmoking" room. I learned there really is no such distinction in Romania. Most people completely ignore the signs. When many laws are unjust, many people find a way not to obey.

"Ciao." I greeted Luminista with a smile and kiss on both cheeks. We acted like fast friends walking arm in arm to a waiting car and then onto a chartered bus full of young, fit, energetic American wrestling competitors. This was a different world from the outside. Luminista and I sat in the front seats so she could stand and face the group to give her tourist guide narration as we drove. She was charming, articulate and informative. The guys mostly paid attention and were on their best behavior. We stopped to walk around the *Muzeul Taranului Roman* (Peasants Museum).

Soviet dominated countries made great efforts to emphasize how their system was different than the previous feudal ones. They placed these kinds of museums near or in the capital cities and carefully exhibited the worst portrayal of 'lower class' life as a way to propagandize the "better communist system" they were now subjected to, under whichever puppet leader had been chosen for them. But life was grueling for most people and hadn't improved significantly for Romanians, especially not for Roma, according to Luminista. She should know.

"You may use your cameras, gentlemen, if you wish to take photos."

The team posed taking pictures in front of instruments of torture and weapons displayed. Every time we entered another room, the museum guard on duty would turn on the lights and as we left, turn them off again. I supposed they were conserving electricity and had a tight budget. It was not something I observed in any western countries in their capital city museums. Walking in these rooms reminded me of other times in other galleries.

We moved to London when I was seven and lived there for about eighteen months. My parents took us to museums and castles in England, France and Italy since they impressed upon us it might "be your only chance" to travel outside the United States. After returning to New York for a few years, we moved to Texas when I was eleven. There, too we were compelled to visit every possible art museum and gallery the city of Houston hosted. My siblings and I spent hundreds of hours in museums and libraries. It was a place where all six of us children had to be quiet and slow down. My mother could keep track of us easier in those spaces. Most museums didn't charge an entrance fee in those days. The arts in Houston were generously supported by the Hogg family. I wondered what type of cruel parents would name their daughter Ima Hogg? The libraries were always free.

When I relocated to Washington, D.C. for my studies at Georgetown, one of the first places I sought on a free weekend was the Smithsonian, followed by a leisurely afternoon at the Freer gallery. I felt connected to history, art and human achievement in those museums.

After walking around the old palace in Bucharest and eating bagged lunches at the main square, it was time for them to go to practice. We drove to a large community sports center. The guys were eager to get on the mats. I accompanied them with Luminista. We had a chance to look inside the main gym before getting back on the bus. The sports center was run down, paint peeling off the walls, worn mats and ropes, but it was organized for easy access to weights and machines. There were both girls and boys in the gym and none of the lockers had locks. I guessed they didn't have problems with theft there, unlike in my own country.

"Now, to the salon." Luminista seemed as eager as I was to spend some time getting fussed over by other women. My body was still adjusting to the time, temperature and culture change.

The "Salon Chic" was anything but chic. The floor tiles were a mustard yellow color, the chairs a fake black leather. It had an ammonia chemical smell which burned my nostrils. There was a large open room with about twenty stations where women were cutting, coloring and styling hair. While the clients soaked their feet, someone knelt beside them and trimmed their toenails and applied polish. Women were chatting to their stylists and some to each other. A youngish woman with long, dyed, straw colored hair wearing high heels greeted us at the cash register in front.

Luminista had arranged everything. We were escorted to adjoining stations in the back. When I saw the dirty water in the plastic tubs, I had second thoughts about taking off my sandals. I never wore nail polish and didn't want to start now. However, I was in a tricky situation. I might offend both Luminista and the salon staff if I just sat there without purchasing any of their services. I swallowed hard before dipping my bare feet in the warm sudsy water.

"Is it always this busy?" I asked in a low voice. Luminista was enjoying her time here already. Her face was relaxed, and she was picking out a deep red polish for her feet and her hands.

"In the afternoon, yes. The location is good, near to government offices. Women take a long lunch, maybe three hours from work and sit here, talk, get more beautiful and can walk back to work."

She explained that once you have a government job, it is almost impossible to be fired unless you are indiscreet about political views contrary to the government. No one works very hard, she told me. It is better if you don't work hard and make it difficult for everyone else. They can take long lunches, long vacations and long breaks. They only hire their friends who will do the same. Everyone inside their circle is content. This is the machine.

Over the next few hours Luminista both spoke and listened to the women in the salon. I watched, waited and wondered. She would translate for me after we left.

"Do you like?" Luminista proudly presented her newly polished nails. I giggled. She seemed satisfied.

When we exited, I inhaled and exhaled deeply. The chemical smell lingered in my lungs. Luminista sensed my discomfort.

"Come, I take you to a place with beautiful perfumes, eh?"

How could I resist. We wound our way to another part of the city. Luminista had boundless energy, so we walked everywhere. I enjoyed her company but continued to stay alert wherever we went. I could blend into Romanian society when I was with her except for my shoes. Shoes can be a giveaway. Mine were a western style not seen in the Soviet controlled Bucharest. Once again Luminista walked me back to my hotel before wishing me well for the next day and setting a time for our Monday excursion.

On Sunday, I followed Luminista's instructions and found my way to Cismigiu Park. This was the first trip on my own in Romania. I was excited.

The park was full of people walking, sitting on the grass, having picnics, playing their version of football (soccer) and playing chess.

Stefan saw me first and came over to me. I sensed he was nervous.

"*Ciao*, Joanne. Nice to see you."

"Nice to see you, too, Stefan."

"We go to the boats now. Better to talk there, okay?"

"Ok."

Stefan led me to a place where they rented rowboats. Each boat was painted a different pastel color and contained heavy oars. I was much more adept at paddling canoes than I was at rowing, but Stefan was determined to row the boat. He offered his hand. I took it to step down into the skiff.

Stefan was a skilled rower. We were gliding on the park lake passing couples and families in other boats. I began to feel more at ease and tried to make conversation.

"Do you have family here in Bucaresti, Stefan?"

"Yes, my parents and my sister. She is married and have one son. You have sister and brother?"

"Oh yes, I have one sister and four brothers. I'm the eldest."

We exchanged basic knowledge about ourselves. Our words seemed to flow in a rhythm with the water. I sensed Stefan wanted to tell me more but didn't have enough English to communicate. We somehow sensed each other's energies and were comfortable in silence for minutes at a time.

Stefan steered the boat under a bridge and then hauled in the oars. He rested his arms for a moment and smiled.

"I want to go to America, Joanne. You help me?"

My eyes grew wide. This was not what I expected. I didn't want to risk hurting his feelings, but I also needed to make my position clear.

"Stefan, I'm sorry but that is not possible for me. I must travel alone and *cannot* take anyone with me."

"You no understand. I cannot stay here. You see, to speak we must go in boat. No freedom here. I am artist. I need freedom to paint ... to live!"

Part of my heart was deeply moved. I wanted to help him somehow, but my brain controlled my emotions and reminded me of the burden I had as the first "girl" to win the Circumnavigator's fellowship. There was no room for personal involvement or any mistakes on this trip.

"You're right, Stefan. I don't understand. It must be hard for you."

"Please. You can take me in your car. You go tomorrow?"

"So sorry, Stefan, I can't, there is no room. Besides, we're only going to Transylvania. We are not going out of Romania."

"You take me in your trunk. Take me out of Bucaresti." Stefan was persistent. I wondered how he knew my itinerary and then realized Luminista could have told him. Maybe she knew he needed to leave Romania and set me up.

Figure 2. Cismigiu Park, Bucharest, Romania

I decided I would try to find a ride with some of the Americans rather than rely on Luminista for transport after next week. I would get to Hungary on my own. Budapest was my next destination.

"Stefan, let me ask some other people if they can take you, but I can't. It's not my car. It's against the rules I have to follow."

Stefan looked steadily at me. He looked crestfallen for a second, but he resumed rowing while changing the subject.

We floated into the dock. Stefan hopped out to tie the boat, then helped me up to the shore. There were a number of people looking at us as we disembarked. I felt conspicuous.

"Come drink coffee, ok?" He offered.

"Alright. Is the café near the park?"

"In the park." Stefan slowed his walking pace to mine.

We sauntered over to a place that was more like a cafeteria than a café. Stefan knew his way around and found a table.

"Wait here, please. I go take coffee."

"Thank you. I'll just sit here then."

Stefan nodded. He walked resolutely to the line of people waiting to give their orders for food and drinks. I reflected on my first days in Romania. All the stories of "greater equality" and the "promise of communism" we were bombarded with in college and by various forms of media, vaporized in the reality of being in an actual Soviet communist country. "Modern" Soviet Romania and the other eastern European countries including Russia, (as I would soon find out), were far behind America in every respect from what I could discover. People were stressed, service was slow, standards were haphazard, lines were long, buildings were dilapidated, equipment was antiquated, streets were grimy, and scarcity was common.

An older couple sitting at the next table, who were evidently foreigners, kept looking at me. The man cleared his throat, and the woman began to speak in English.

"Excuse me dear, but you do speak English, don't you?"

"Um, ... yes." I couldn't quite place their accent, but it sounded British.

"Are you here visiting family or on holiday?" The woman leaned into my table.

"On holiday." It felt easier not to explain my actual purpose for this trip.

"Do you speak Romanian?" the man inquired.

"No, just French and English."

"Then how do you communicate?" The woman seemed surprised.

"Oh, he speaks some English and I have another friend here who can translate."

I considered making an excuse to go over to find Stefan. It was better not to engage in conversations with strangers under the circumstances.

"If you wish, we can translate for you. Here he comes now." The woman was quite pushy.

"That's alright, ma'am. Thank you, anyway."

Stefan returned carrying two white cups of coffee. He had a few cubes of sugar as well.

The man started speaking to Stefan in Romanian. The woman interjected phrases in Romanian from time to time, as well. I sipped my drink slowly.

"Oh, he says you're from Texas, is that right?"

I nodded between sips. The couple were intensely interested now.

"You're here on your own? Is that right? How brave!"

"No," I replied. "I'm not really on my own." I couldn't explain my grant to these strangers.

"Excuse me, but we really can't stay long." I rose from the table. "It was nice meeting you both."

Stefan understood and thanked the couple as well. We held our cups of coffee and purposefully walked toward a public bus stop.

"Stefan, thank you very much for the boat ride and for the coffee."

"You are welcome," his voice softened. "You are my guest."

We found a spot to sit and wait for the bus back into the city. Stefan was quiet. I took my time finishing my coffee. Other folks joined us waiting for transport.

The bus I was supposed to catch finally arrived.

"You don't have to come with me Stefan. I know my way back and I know you live on the other side of the city. Please, don't worry about me. I will get back just fine."

"I see you again?" Stefan asked earnestly.

"I hope so," I said stepping up into the bus. "*Ciao and mutelmesc!*"

Stefan raised his eyebrows and partly smiled at my attempt to speak Romanian. The bus driver shut the folding door.

I watched Stefan from my seat by the window.

Stefan stood watching me until the bus drove out of sight.

We were never to see each other again.

2. SCORPIONS AND SPIDER MONKEYS – BELIZE, GUATEMALA

"**I** have an idea how you can get your last few credits to graduate Jo, while traveling and scuba diving. Sound good?"

My friend "Little John" gave me a mischievous smile. He always had lively ideas. "Go on ..." I encouraged.

"There are two scholarships for seniors from Georgetown to join an expedition sponsored by the AUIE (Association of Universities for International Education). Here's the brochure I picked up. I think we both have a chance. We only have to pay for our own gear and any extras."

I examined the glossy pages of the brochure. The photos were stunning and inviting. We could meet all the basic requirements for this "Terrestrial and Marine Expedition in Belize, Guatemala and on Glover's Barrier Reef in the Caribbean. Two months of field research on land and sea."

"Worth a try. Let's get started. We only have about a week before the deadline. It looks like we might have to pay for the scuba certification course as well but it's not that much."

"Already sourced that, Jo. The pool part we can do here and the open water we can do in Delaware. It'll be cold but it's not that far."

"Alright, I can take extra shifts at the Center Café, write some term papers for cash. I'm in!"

Little John and I were in different schools at Georgetown. He was in the main College and I was in the Foreign Service school. He was graduating with a pre-med major. I was in International Relations with a minor in Ecology. We were both from first generation Italian immigrant families and we lived with four other Georgetown seniors in a private house near campus. Although he didn't "come out" until later in his twenties, John was great friends with lots of girls, but he was not attracted physically to us, which made him a "safe" companion in any situation. We could be honest with each other, too. Little John was so named because he was short, but he had a giant heart.

We were notified of our selection for the field expedition in Central America within a month. Both Little John and I were chosen. We passed the PADI course and the open water section. We spent hours in the library researching the areas where we would be conducting studies. There was no world wide web in 1974.

After our graduation ceremony, I introduced my paternal grandparents and my father to my housemates. My mother never supported my personal achievements that she didn't attend. Fortunately, my grandparents did. They especially liked Little John. When they heard our plans and saw how we prepared, they wished us "good luck" and my grandparents slipped me a little extra cash. My grandfather handed me a beautifully wrapped present from both of them. They encouraged me to open it before they left to "make sure it fits." When I opened the box, I was overcome with gratitude. They had bought me a handsome pair of binoculars with three magnification settings. There were two different types of straps, lens caps and a rugged case.

"These are waterproof, dear. We consulted the *Audubon Society Guide*."

"They are perfect. I'll take very good care of them. *Grazie mille!*"

My grandparents had been public high school teachers in Brooklyn before they retired. My grandmother (Inez) had come back from Italy as a widow with my father and his older sister, my aunt Lauradele. Inez married Peter Munisteri in New York. They raised three children and put them all through private universities in the States. They didn't make a high salary or receive a large pension. Their gift meant a sacrifice of their own finances and it meant a great deal to me.

We packed our backpacks, re-packed them at least three times to cast off any extra weight, then practiced our Spanish. When we arrived at the airport, we thought we were ready.

TACA (we renamed them 'take-a-chance airways') was the sole commercial airline going to Belize. We took off, only to fly for about an hour and then return to the New Orleans airport. There was some sort of mechanical problem. We waited for hours before we finally re-embarked and landed in Ladyville at the Belize City International Airport. We had entered into an entirely different world of the Americas.

The British had at one time colonized this country. They still had bases there in 1974; the language they spoke was Creole. It was a distant cousin to English.

Figure 3. Inez Patti Munisteri, Peter Munisteri and author at Georgetown University, Washington, D.C. photo by Joseph Munisteri USA 1974

Little John and I passed through customs and met a group of other graduate students from various parts of the US and Belize. Fortunately, they all spoke English. The lead professor handed us prepared sheets of instructions as we piled into open bed trucks in the humid heat. We were excited and curious, but as we realized while chatting with our new colleagues, we had not only signed up for an expedition—we were on a "survival" expedition in Central America. We would soon grasp the difference.

Our first studies were ornithology and etymology with Sergeant Dora. She was a retired British Army Sergeant, a widow who lived in the outskirts of the city with a number of large reptiles and exotic birds. We boarded in old army barracks, six women in one room and the other twenty-five men in five other rooms. The barracks were just canvas tents over a raised wooden platform. Shower blocks were outside. We were issued mosquito nets, kerosene lanterns, large butterfly nets for catching specimens, and spiral notebooks. The other four women were graduate students from different mid-western colleges. We introduced ourselves as we rolled out our sleeping bags and began to unpack.

We had been warned not to drink the water but to use filtered water to fill our canteens and brush our teeth. On our required list was Lomotil for when we got "the runs." We also brought insect repellent and moleskin. We were going to be on our feet outside for most of the daylight hours.

Our first wake-up call was at 4:00 a.m. Sergeant Dora wanted us to greet the dawn, binoculars in hand to spot the various birds we were to follow.

Sergeant Dora was a no-nonsense, hardy woman who was an expert at tracking, noting detail and identifying species. No one was late to her class. Learning how to use binoculars efficiently takes time and training. Sergeant Dora impressed upon us the fine art of focus with and without our binoculars. She also insisted on using the correct scientific descriptions.

"That would be buffy streaks, Michael, not just streaks."

She urged us to scout for females of the species since they were more difficult to describe and didn't sport outrageous colors.

"Spotting the males of the species is too easy!" she declared.

We ate our breakfast whilst sitting on the buttress roots of Kaway trees. They formed a sort of thin wall. We hopped off, washed our tin kits and clambered into the jeeps.

Sergeant Dora brought us to a rivulet where thousands of Jesu Cristi lizards were "walking on water." Biting Caddis flies buzzed around us. She wore rubber boots and boldly waded into the water, ignoring the flies as we watched her from the shore.

"Isn't this remarkable!" she exclaimed holding one of the flies gingerly between her fingers. It had an iridescent green tail and large bug eyes.

"Come on then, catch your first specimen of the day. Off you go."

I spied Little John walking into the water. His glasses were fogging up and he had to stop and wipe them. He probably couldn't see me. I waded in to join the great catch. The water was warm.

"Aren't there aquatic snakes and alligators here, too?" I asked.

"Probably," Little John replied. "Good thing we have our hiking boots on. Stupid that we get them wet first thing. It's a damn humid climate. They will take at least a day to dry out and I only brought one pair."

"Got one!" A tall grad student named Dave displayed his Caddis fly to us.

"Well done. Now find another," Sergeant Dora pressed us.

After a half hour in the water, our own sweat soaked through our clothes. We were sopping wet when we waded back to shore. Sergeant Dora was beaming since we were all successful. We sloshed back to a building where chairs, tables and microscopes were set up as a makeshift laboratory.

"Get out your notebooks. Draw and label your creature and see if you can find your Neotropical Trichoptera. The catalogue is here on my desk. At present there are over three thousand known species. Perhaps you will find a new one, you never know ..."

The rest of the morning was devoted to setting up our microscopes and finishing our first field notes. At lunch we assembled outside for instructions before being served rice, red beans and stewed chicken. Siesta time was allowed after lunch. We took off our wet clothes and hung them on makeshift clothes lines. The wind was up. By dinner time they had dried although our hiking boots were still moist.

Doc Pippen, the lead professor and a PhD in terrestrial biology, gave a lecture out in the open before dinner. He was not an inspiring speaker. There were numerous distractions in the lush landscape. It was easier to write while listening since he maintained a slow, steady pace talking and gesturing. Little John sat next to me so we could compare notes over the next three hours. From time to time, we would look up and see varicolored snakes slithering over the lianas, above our heads.

"Tomorrow morning ..." Sargent Dora barked. "Be prepared with your butterfly nets after breakfast. We will be doing pair sweeps— two hundred strokes a quadrant for each pair. Be sure to dress in long sleeves and long pants. Any questions?"

The tall grad student from Indiana named Dave came up behind us. "I have a question," he said in a low voice so only we could hear.

"Where do we buy Belizean rum? I hear the Travellers Liquor-Gold rum is the best. Want to go with me into town tonight?"

"How do we get back to Belize City? We're miles away," I said.

"Well," he answered. "Those local boys in our group have a car and they know the way. Want to come along?"

"What time?" Little John chimed in. I guessed we were going.

"Right after dinner. Meet us by the ablution blocks and no need to mention this to anyone else. We don't have room in the car."

We nodded and made our way back to our separate barracks. I had one casual skirt and blouse with me, but at least they were dry. After dinner I changed and met up with Little John, Dave and the two Belizean grad students. We piled into their car and sped off.

We pulled onto a street with a number of small stores and one nightclub in a seedy side of town. A few women stood outside soliciting. British soldiers hung around in various states of drunkenness. The women glared at me although I wasn't any competition. I felt very uneasy. The Belizean guys told us to ignore them. They collected our dollars and went inside with Dave to buy the rum.

Dave came back to the car. "Wow, liquor is cheap here." He gave one bottle to Little John and kept two for himself.

"We should get some coconuts and pineapples. Make a real Caribbean drink." The Belizean guys returned with cigarettes and started the car.

"Where do you want to go now?" The driver evidently knew Belize City.

"We can go to a nice club where we can make our drinks and dance. Ok?"

"Dance ... oh yeah, let's do that." I did love to dance and see how other cultures danced. I figured with an escort of four capable men, I shouldn't have any trouble. I wasn't planning on drinking much. I'd never tasted rum. In Texas, my friends would drink beer, cheap wine or maybe some Scotch or Tequila. Weed (marijuana) was cheaper than alcohol.

The Coconut Grove was a club with an outdoor terrace and raucous live music. We sat outside while Dave and the boys went to buy coconuts and pineapples. The Belizeans had a hammer to crack the coconuts expertly. Dave brought out a knife to cut the pineapples. They passed around straws so we could mix our drinks. They tasted sweet and smooth. I had no idea how strong the rum was until I got up to dance.

"Whoa, Dave. That rum is powerful. Let me get my bearings, ok?"

"Here, eat another slice of pineapple. Good, now hold onto my arm."

Little John laughed and joked with the Belizeans as Dave directed me to the dance floor. The club had blinking neon lights and a crowd of young and middle-aged dancers gyrating to the Caribbean beat. It was a friendly throng full of energy. We were getting to know Belize with our feet and getting to know each other. After a few dances I was breathless and indicated it was time to rest.

When we returned to the terrace, two Honduran women had come to chat with the Belizeans and Little John. They made room for us to sit down and introduced themselves. Little John offered them drinks. Everyone seemed to be mildly buzzed. One of the Honduran women asked Little John to dance. One of the Belizean guys, the driver, asked the other woman to dance with him. We watched them leave, then sat back to look out over the city street.

It was already after 10 p.m. We had to be back before midnight. Dave poured himself and our Belizean friend another drink.

"Want one, too?" he asked me.

"No, thank you Dave. I need to be able to function tomorrow."

"Yea, but tomorrow is our last day in Belize before we head out to the jungle and on to Guatemala. Last chance for a real mixer. You sure?"

"Alright, but mostly coconut milk and just a little rum this time." Dave mixed the drink in the coconut and cut off two large slices of pineapple.

We three toasted. "To new adventures!"

We bid farewell to the Honduran ladies before we headed back to Sergeant Dora and our barrack beds. I crept in as quietly as I could and fell fast asleep.

Four o'clock came way too early the next morning. Sergeant Dora was in fine form, but my head was throbbing. I couldn't wait for coffee and breakfast.

"Where were you last night?" Nancy, one of the other women in my barracks, questioned me before breakfast. I hesitated before telling her.

"We went into town, but I'd appreciate it if you didn't say anything to the others. We only had room for three of us. Sorry, maybe next time?"

"No problem. I wanted to know if you would be my pair for this afternoon doing the butterfly sweeps. Are you up for it?"

"Yup, I'm down for it. Have to cover up completely with all those biting insects. We are goin' to be swimmin' in our sweat, eh?"

It was scorching work doing two hundred sweeps per quadrant. After hours in sweltering heat, both Nancy and I started doubling up. Each swing right to left and left to right was supposed to be one sweep, but by the end of the afternoon, we made each swing each way count as one. We collected enough specimens to keep us busy for weeks, inspecting them under the microscope, comparing them to catalogued species and noting details.

We couldn't wait for a shower. We grabbed hoses outside the dining hall and sprayed each other. The water was blessedly cool.

We hung our clothes out on a branch and changed into our bathing suits for the rest of the evening. All of our gear had to be packed and ready to go by five o'clock the following morning.

The jeep ride was along primitive dirt roads into the jungle. It was bumpy but we didn't mind. Little John, Nancy, Dave, two of the Belizean boys and one Professor Green, rode together. The Belizean guys took turns driving. The plan was to journey to Tikal, Guatemala stopping at two outposts which had small wooden cabins. We wouldn't have to set up tents to do our research for the first weeks.

We pulled into the first outpost before twilight. The cabins could only fit three comfortably. I chose the one nearest the shower block. The two Belizean guys and Dave bunked together while Little John found two grad students from California to room with. We were all sunbaked and dust caked from the journey. Doc Pippin tasked each cabin with duties for meals and clean-up for the next few days. He and the other two professors were adept at supervising. A few local men maintained the camp and did the cooking.

The next day we were to spend recording more details about the specimens we recovered. We needed to sweep more quadrants in the areas that were once used for slash and burn agriculture. The fallow fields had been sprayed twenty years before with Agent Orange, and the effects were still visible. AUIE was tasked to do research on the soil, flora and fauna in the area as a follow on from their initial findings in the 1950s.

We were employed, but not paid, by the Dupont company to do this field research before we reached Tikal. The grant covered our expenses in country. In exchange we exposed ourselves directly to Agent Orange by collecting and processing the samples. The effects on humans in the areas, and all the members of our team, would not be fully known until years later.

On the outskirts of the Mayan ruins in Tikal were farming areas where Agent Orange, Agent Blue and other dioxin agent "herbicides" and defoliants were sprayed during the CIA (Central Intelligence Agency) effort to topple the Arbenz government in Guatemala. This was in the 1950s, after President Juan Jacobo Arbenz Guzman announced a new agrarian reform plan which included nationalizing the US based United Fruit Company.

US Secretary of State, John Foster Dulles was beholden to bank interests and US banana investments. He cued the CIA to "intervene." It was an engineered take-over meant to appear as if it were an inside coup by Guatemalan nationals angry because of Arbenz "Communist ties." The accusation was false, but it stuck. We know from documents and testimonies that it was actually the CIA staging the "coup" against Arbenz using their own assets. Arbenz was forced to resign and go into exile. In 1971, he supposedly drowned in his own bathtub, while living in Mexico City where he had been granted asylum.

Guatemala has not had a stable government since Arbenz. The lands where Agent Orange was tested are poisoned for decades after being saturated. Upon seeing these chemicals were so "effective," the US government continued using them in other areas of the world. The heaviest use was in Vietnam.

About 50 million liters (13 million gallons) of Agent Orange—containing about 170 kg (375 pounds) of dioxin—were dropped on Vietnam from 1961-1971. Agent Orange was one of several toxic herbicides used in Vietnam after being tested in Central America. Others were labelled: Agents White, Purple, Blue, Pink, and Green. The names derived from color-coded bands painted around storage drums holding the herbicides. The US Department of Defense called this chemical bombing plan *Operation Ranch Hand*. It went on for a decade.

The company that manufactured all the multicolored "Agents" was Dupont. In 1974, there were already thousands of US military veterans and their families, who suffered from the effects of these "Agents." They were in the process of suing Dupont.

When we were chosen for this field expedition, there was no open-source document outlining the possible side effects from exposure to Agent Orange. We were sent to the areas where these defoliants were already in the soil and ecosystems for one generation. The Dupont company—via the AUIE universities—wanted raw data and research *before* the class action court case came to trial.

Dupont had an army of lawyers and their own "research" they could manipulate to stall those trials. Veterans were already dying every year from the effects. Their children were born with birth defects. Lingering toxins caused fast growing cancers and other withering diseases in conjunction with nasty skin conditions. One of the other reasons for calling D 2,4,T "Agent Orange "was because of the liver being adversely affected. Victims of the poisoning would turn an orange/yellow color similar to those afflicted by hepatitis, also known as jaundice.

Dupont didn't want the general public to know they were continuing to wage ecocide. The Veterans Administration (VA) denied the "disabilities" associated with exposure to Agent Orange because to do so would be to acknowledge that essentially chemical warfare had been waged and sanctioned under Presidents Lyndon B. Johnson, Richard M. Nixon and into the Gerald Ford administration. We only discovered these heinous acts, long term side effects and policy decisions years after these men were no longer in politics. We didn't know it, but we were specially selected human guinea pigs.

We sat at long wooden tables in an open-air dining area with our kerosene lanterns and microscopes. There was no electricity. Between our flashlights and the lanterns, we strained our eyes to discern the characteristics of our specimens. Most of the insects were damaged after our butterfly sweeps by the rough jeep journey and hasty packing.

"Can an insect have eleven legs?" I joked.

"Must be a new species," Nancy teased.

However, a number of diligent students in our group even fancied they'd discovered new species in their sweeps.

It was a competitive atmosphere in every way: physical strength and endurance, mental ability for problem solving, academic knowledge and wit. There was also intense sexual friction. As part of a small number of females, the odds were in our favor. It was instructive to note how quickly our group devolved into primitive behaviors once we were out in the jungle.

Our last night before packing up and moving on again, one of the largest male grad students, a college football linebacker named Wes, decided it would be a beneficial team building exercise for us to divide up into two teams and engage in a tug of war over the open sewage ditch. He deliberately chose the least athletic and rather annoying male in our expedition to be the captain on his end. I privately nicknamed him "Piggy" because of the similarity between him and the character so named in *Lord of the Flies*.

The other team captain was the stockiest Belizean guy named Jude. He chose one of the stronger mid-western guys for his lead. I could already guess what they planned. I wasn't upset to be chosen last. Of all the females, I was the shortest and the thinnest, not useful in a tug of war where brawn, weight, height and strength were the key to winning.

One of the cooks was enlisted to be the referee. He counted us down to start the game. "*Uno, dos, tres* ... go!" It wasn't to be much of a contest. The whole tug of war lasted only about six minutes and Piggy was pulled deep into the sewage ditch. He must have known his fate before we began.

None of us girls were pulled in luckily. It was a vile smelling, foul morass, and the other team jumped out quickly and ran to get the outside hose.

Little John came up beside me. He was a man of conscience as well as heart.

"That wasn't right, Jo. Wilmer was set up."

"Sure looked like it. But Nancy said he was a real pain. He doesn't do his own work and makes up stuff to snitch on the guys. He doesn't clean up after himself either. Guess now he'll be forced to. I know what you mean though."

Dave caught up to us. He was still laughing.

"What *do* you mean, Jo?"

"Oh nothing. Quite a way to end our last night here though."

"I'm going to the shower block. See you guys tomorrow." Little John gave me a side wink and picked up his pace. I was left with Dave.

He touched my arm to stop me. "Hey, want to see the vampire bats cave? We still have an hour or so before dark. I know where it is. One of the local guys showed me."

I was curious about these bats. Dave was an enthusiastic researcher as well as someone who liked to enjoy himself wherever he was.

"Alright, but we better head out now. We can slip away before anyone notices."

"This way." Dave indicated a path starting behind the ablution block.

We stepped carefully into the jungle. There were snakes, biting insects, monkeys, coatimundis, wild turkeys, exotic birds, various sizes and species of lizards and … jaguars. We both carried knives in our pockets.

Dave stepped ahead to clear the path as we approached what looked like a large mound. There was a strange acrid smell as we advanced toward an opening.

We spoke in hushed tones to each other.

"Is this it?" I asked.

"Yes, but we have to go down into the cave. Careful you don't slip."

Dave went first and extended his hand to help me drop down. The cave was in semi darkness, but as my eyes adjusted, I could see what looked like large piles of earth scattered throughout the cave. Up above us it seemed like there were a sort of stalactites.

"See these?" Dave pointed to one of the piles near us. I crept closer.

"Oh God!" I gasped. It was a pile of feces dripping with dried blood.

"Look up," Dave directed

"Oh no. Now I know what I smelled. Blood." There was blood everywhere. What I thought were stalactites were actually hundreds of vampire bats with their wings folded tightly, hanging upside down to sleep. They were nocturnal creatures.

We heard a fluttering sound and felt the air move around us. Singular bats were flying in and about the cave, finding a place to perch upside down and congregate with their cauldron. Yes, that's the name for a group of bats. Many cauldrons make up a colony. The atmosphere in that cave provoked fear.

Vampire bats did attack mammals, including humans. Most often they attacked those who were already weak from illness or age. We later found out a number of children in the area contracted rabies from their bites. They didn't realize they were bitten because vampire bats have an anesthetic in their saliva. They pursue their prey when the animal or human is sleeping. They secrete a chemical which keeps blood from clotting so they can suck or lick it in easily. They have sharp slicing incisor teeth which make tiny cuts.

Once the prey is weakened after their "meal," the bats can sense this prey night after night. If the bat or bats are not stopped, they will suck the blood out of their prey until they die.

These bats have sonar "echo location." They are technically blind but use sound and a keen sense of smell to find their way. They spread disease without being affected themselves. They are truly dark creatures. In the natural order of life, they are there to thin out other populations. They prey on the weak.

"We should be getting back," I muttered. I was scared but didn't want to admit it. The humidity accentuated the smell and gave a sheen to the blood. It was a spine-chilling scene. It was like the aftermath of a crime, with psychopathic vampire bats blissfully sleeping it off in their habitat. It was disturbing. Every part of me wanted to flee.

"Two more minutes, Jo. I want to explore the back of this cave."

"You go ahead, Dave. I'll wait here." I wished at that moment, that I had worn a hat. Drops of fluid were dripping from the walls and top of the cave. I couldn't be sure if they were water, blood or both. I tried not to inhale too deeply.

"Far out," Dave hissed from the back. He bent down to inspect something, then rose quickly. He inched his way back to where I was standing.

"Bones. Not sure from what animal but they've been here for some time."

"Okay, let's vamoose out of here." I started toward the entrance.

"Here, let me." Dave went in front so he could help me up out of the cave. We both took deep breaths when we reached the outside. The sun was setting.

"What did you think?" he asked me as we brushed off our clothes.
"Creepy. Fascinating but creepy."

Most of our fellow students were still up working on their notes until total darkness chased them back to their cabins. I took off my boots and flopped onto my cot. It wasn't worth changing out of my clothes. I was exhausted and unnerved after being in the vampire bat cave. I just took off my socks, secured the mosquito net, and drifted into slumber.

At about four o'clock in the morning I woke out of a nightmare. I sat on the edge of the cot and felt like I should take a little walk outside to shake the dream off. Without thinking and without putting my socks on first, I plunged one foot and then the other into my hiking boots. Immediately my right foot, ankle, then leg felt like it was shot with fire. The pain was wickedly sharp. I screamed.

My cabin mates woke and rushed toward me.

"What happened are you alright Jo?"

They told me when I came to, that I had simply pointed to my boot then promptly fell unconscious. When they took off my boots to place me on my cot, they discovered the scorpion. They waited until it ceased movement then placed my boot outside on the step. One of the girls, Kathy, wanted to keep the scorpion. She went to the kitchen to look for an onion and an empty jar.

Kathy sliced the onion in half, searched my foot for the pincher marks and placed the onion over them to draw out the toxin. Nancy had Benadryl in her first aid kit. When I came to, she was ready with her canteen and Benadryl for me to swallow. Antihistamines reduce the swelling and speed healing from toxic bites. Benadryl contains diphenhydramine, a strong antihistamine. Kathy used the small glass jar to preserve the scorpion for all to see. She closed the lid tightly.

By 5:00 a.m., my right foot, ankle and leg were swollen and had taken on an angry, red color. I couldn't fit into my boot and I could only hobble. I felt weak and dizzy.

Doc Pippin was called over and he clucked over me, assuring me I would be fine in a day or two. I was to keep drinking clean water and keep taking the Benadryl. He called Jude and another Belizean guy to carry me and my gear over to the back of the only truck in our expedition transport.

An army blanket was laid on the open bed of the truck, and I was placed on top with my gear behind me. I felt woozy and the muscles in my leg and foot kept contracting uncontrollably. Little John and Dave came over to me.

"Bit by a scorpion. Wild Jo. Guess that's their way of saying, "Welcome to the jungle." Little John could always cheer me up.

David handed me a thin metal flask and gave me a half smile and a nod. He had saved some of the rum. I didn't need to be alert and if it made me drowsy, I could sleep easier on the bumpy ride ahead. Once we were all on the road, I took a few sips.

Our next outpost was a few kilometers outside Tikal. These were larger wooden cabins with an open walled eating area, wooden tables and an outside industrial sink. There were two ablution blocks. Once again, I asked for us girls to be near one of them. I was obliged.

For the next three days I sat with my right leg and foot elevated as I watched my teammates do butterfly sweeps, collect soil samples and toil in the miserable heat. Slowly, the swelling went down, and my skin returned to a patchy version of its natural color.

By the fourth day I was able to put weight on my foot and gingerly walk. My mates came to me with their nets. I carefully extracted their catch for them. By the sixth day I could walk normally and put on my boots. I was ready for the next mission of our expedition.

Doc Pippin divided us into groups of four. This time we could choose our colleagues. Our group consisted of Little John, Nancy, Dave and me. We were tasked with following Spider monkeys. Another group followed Howler monkeys who were larger, ornery but more lethargic. They also had a horrific howl ... hence their name.

The other groups were assigned different animals and two groups were assigned to chart the flora in the area where Agent Orange was sprayed. I was pleased with our study. It meant having to hike fast through the brush with machetes to clear our way. Dave volunteered to be the front man. He liked wielding the short machete.

Nancy and I collaborated on hand signals to code the behaviors we observed. We avoided speaking, if at all possible, since we would disturb the monkeys and alert other animals. We used hand signals for activities such as grooming, eating, resting, gathering, playing, territory disputes and nurturing. Little John volunteered to be the scribe and timer. We would need to record the time spent on each of these activities. Dave would be the scout and map our way in and most importantly, our way back.

We carried binoculars, flashlights, compasses and Swiss Army knives (no GPS, no cell phones or internet—we didn't even have printed maps of the area). We needed to keep track of our band of spider monkeys for twelve hours each day for four days. We brought food and water and ponchos in case it rained; we could spread the ponchos if we wanted to rest.

We needed to be fully covered because of the insects and poisonous plants. It was actually cooler to have loose-fitting, long-sleeved cotton shirts, long pants, long socks and a hat with a broad brim. It was recommended to tie a bandana around our necks which all of us did except Nancy. She said it chafed her and preferred to put her collar up for sun and creature protection. We packed plastic bags because this was a "pack in/pack out" expedition. No trash was to be left in the jungle.

Of necessity, each of us brought extra clothes, soap, cloths and tissues. Little John carried the medical kit. We were given salt tablets and beef jerky. Nancy packed clothesline rope, I brought mosquito netting. We wore waterproof watches. We made checklists and checked with each other. Once out in the jungle we were on our own for half the day.

We practiced our hand gestures and signaling to each other. We had lots of laughs trying to communicate correctly. Dave was a natural at imitating the spider monkeys' calls before we trekked out. By the end of the week, we were all "calling" to each other in spider monkey lingo.

The second day out in Tikal we decided to hike up the overgrown stone steps to view the jungle canopy from above the treetops. We would have an easier time tracking our spider monkey group, which had moved on the night before.

I was first since I wanted to scout with my prized binoculars. The steps were far apart and steep. Slowly, I approached the flat upper platform which served as the Mayan's altar centuries ago.

As I poked my head over the final step, I spotted a creature which made me freeze in fright. A Fer-de-Lance snake was semi-coiled just ahead of me on the large flat stone. I silently gasped and froze. The large triangular shapes alerted me. We were warned about these pit vipers in a lecture just days before. We were told to stop and walk back slowly since their line of sight will catch you moving in any other direction, but you have a chance stepping back in a straight line. Only my head was above the flat stone. I prayed silently and slowly back stepped down giving a "stop/halt" hand gesture to my companions.

When I was a few steps down, with no chase from the Fer-de-Lance, I turned around and quickly scampered down the steps.

"Fer-de-Lance! Turn around! Pit viper!" I hissed loudly to my mates.

We all climbed down as fast as we could.

Collectively, catching our breath, Little John proposed an alternate tall structure.

"Over there, that one is straight up and there is no alcove or altar. We could try that for a viewpoint."

He wasn't giving up on securing a vantage point. We hadn't seen or heard our spider monkey "family" yet. I was hesitant after my near encounter. Pit vipers are dangerous, poisonous and their bite is deadly if you can't get to specialized emergency aid right away.

We tramped over to a high pyramid at the back of the reserve. All of us were scanning the ground and surroundings with extra caution. There were steps to a flat, vertical stone about 180 feet high. The base was overgrown with ferns, tall grasses and brush plants. Dave took out his machete and started cutting a path. Little John volunteered to be the first to climb up. This time we all arrived without incident at the small space to stand near the top. The view was resplendent. We took out our binoculars before we sat down. Each of us took a different direction to cover more area. Nancy spotted the spider monkeys first. We all pointed our binoculars where she indicated. They were in the process of grooming. I fished in my backpack for my notebook and pencil. We started timing, noting and following from a place the Mayans used to worship and become closer to their gods.

In 1974, the Guatemalan government hadn't created a national park yet. The ruins were untended. No one else was there except our group. It felt like a sacred, secluded site. We hardly spoke for the many hours we spent there. We looked forward to our week of research with our distinctive monkey family. We are all related after all.

Figure 4. Tikal at sunset, Guatemala

On our final day in the jungle, before packing up transport jeeps, we had a full expedition team meeting. Doc Pippin and two other professors briefed us on our next movements. We would be traveling overland to the Stann Creek District. From there we would hop aboard a boat to Glovers Reef Atoll for our month of marine biology and ecological research.

We were each handed plexiglass boards with a yellow, wax pencil attached by a thickly waxed string. We would use these to communicate and take notes underwater. We were to separate our gear into land and marine sections. Our individual diving masks, snorkel and fins needed to be near the top of our packs along with our personal medical kits.

We would be staying in thatched huts on stilts on the island. Each hut would house two people and have a thatched wall partition where we could hang our portable camp showers. There was no plumbing on the island. They constructed large rainwater tanks and used deeply dug outhouses. There was no electricity on Glovers. They used battery run tools and radios. We were also notified the food would be nutritious but could get monotonous. The staples were freshly caught Caribbean Sea fish, coconuts, coconut milk, seaweed soups and conch.

"You'll be eating lots of conch, guys. Conch burgers, conch fries, conch salad. One benefit is the protein and the other is that conch is known to be an aphrodisiac ... so be careful how much you choose to ingest. Alright, be ready to go first thing tomorrow at sunrise. Make sure your cabins are spic and span clean, too."

One of the Belizean guys emitted a howler monkey howl of approval.

Dave let out a spider monkey expression of pleasure. Nancy, Little John and I automatically responded in spider monkey hoots.

Our next month would be spent swimming and diving for hours every day. We would be underwater and silent. We could wash away the jungle. We lived in simple grass thatched huts on stilts. Nancy and I shared a hut at the far end of the island, away from everyone else.

We each chose projects to research in addition to our collective studies in marine life. I chose to try to grow two seaweeds which contained carrageenan, Eucheuma isoforme and Gracillaria verrucosa, out of their natural environment. Carrageenan is used as a binder in foods and a substitute. MacDonald's corporation used it instead of real ice cream in its milkshakes. I swam among the seaweeds and over the barrier reef marveling at the sea creatures who seemed unafraid of us.

The Belizean divers could hold their breath for up to three minutes. They dove for the rare black coral. This species fetched a high price in Belize City.

On one of the last nights on the island, a boat load of rum was unloaded. The island staff made coconut/rum drinks for the group. Nancy and I realized our American team were completely inebriated and passing out, while the local island men were holding back and watching them ... and us. We made our way quietly back to the hut, climbed the ladder and locked our thatched door with the wooden latch. We sensed there might be trouble.

About midnight we heard a group of men approaching our end of the island. We threw open the back thatch opening, which was our only window. They were almost upon us. We pulled up the ladder and refastened the door. They were singing and calling out to us now.

"What should we do?" Nancy was frightened. She took out her diving knife.

"That won't do much good with all those guys. It just gives them a weapon if they don't have one."

"We've got to do something ... quickly!" Nancy started searching her bag for another weapon. I was thinking fast. I saw the kerosene lantern. It was full of fuel. We had matches, too.

"Alright, I have an idea," I whispered.

The guys stopped right beneath our window. They egged on one of the strongest divers to climb up to us. "Give us a kiss, give us a kiss," they chanted. They moved as a pack closer to the hut. They boosted the diver and he climbed up.

"Wait," I shouted. I put my head out the window.

"What?" he said still climbing.

"I'll give you a kiss. A nice juicy kiss, but I'm shy."

The pack laughed and chanted again. "Kiss, kiss, kiss."

Nancy was behind me; she still clutched her diving knife. I had the kerosene fuel in one of my hands behind the thatched wall.

"Come closer …" I tempted. He kept climbing and stopped at the window opening. "Okay now, close your eyes."

As he tried to lean in, I threw the kerosene on him and he fell back.

His mates laughed out loud. He was trying to wipe it off and he was fuming. We had embarrassed him. His manhood was on display. He started climbing up again. This time the pack sounded ferocious as they cheered him on. Nancy was breathing heavily behind me.

"Stop!" I yelled at him, but he kept climbing. I could smell the kerosene.

I felt I had no choice. I showed him the box of matches, took one out and threatened.

"You come any closer and I will light you up. Understand?"

He paused for a second. The pack quieted down and waited.

"I mean it. You all need to go back to your own huts now!"

I lit the match and held it near me. The diver leapt off our hut and gestured for everyone to follow him back to the other end of the island where they bunked.

Nancy and I stayed at the window taking turns on watch until sunrise.

By breakfast time, our group was roused with terrible hangovers. The local staff men were unusually quiet. Nancy and I put our ladder out and descended. We walked the sand path to the open area dining corner. She concealed her diving knife. I washed my hands and face in the large utility sink. No one mentioned anything about the night before.

Little John sauntered over to us.

"Morning. Hey, how come you smell of kerosene?"

"We'll tell you another time, ok? Let's not eat any more conch though. I'll stick with coconut and fish."

Figure 5. Map of Belize and islands

Years later, when I was living in New York City, Little John came to visit me. By then he had earned his PhD and was doing specialized research on liver diseases and glaucoma. He told me he followed up on most of our expedition companions because he had a theory about our Agent Orange exposure. I had just recovered from the Hepatitis A, I thought I had contracted by eating oysters while traveling to do shows in Edinburgh, Scotland at the Fringe Festival in 1983. Ordinarily, I never ate shellfish.

Little John asked me about my symptoms and how I recovered. I recounted my first experience with Chinese medicine and acupuncture. I lived on the border between Little Italy and Chinatown in the Village downtown. He said it might not be from the food. It might be a residual effect from our exposure in Central America. He showed me some of his research and buried news reports about the effects of dioxins.

In 1979, a class action lawsuit was filed on behalf of 2.4 million veterans who were exposed to Agent Orange during their service in Vietnam. Five years later, in 1984, in an out-of-court-settlement, seven chemical companies manufacturing the herbicide agreed to pay $180 million in compensation to the veterans or their next of kin.

Challenges to the settlement followed, including lawsuits filed by over three hundred living Vietnam veterans. In 1988, the US Supreme Court finally confirmed the settlement.

In 1991, President Bush signed the Agent Orange Act, which mandated that some diseases associated with Agent Orange and other herbicides (including non-Hodgkin's lymphoma, soft tissue sarcomas and chloracne) be treated as the result of wartime service. This helped codify the Veteran's Affairs (VA) response to veterans with conditions related to their exposure to Agent Orange. Finally, they were eligible for disability payments, though thousands had already died by that time.

Vietnam reported that some 400,000 people were killed or maimed as a result of exposure to herbicides like Agent Orange. Vietnam stated that half a million children have been born with serious birth defects, while as many as 2 million people are suffering from cancer or other illnesses caused by Agent Orange. The environmental damage, defor-estation and defoliation in Vietnam as a consequence of *Operation Ranch Hand* continues.

Little John confided in me. He didn't think he had long to live. He had liver cancer and glaucoma. In fact, in Traditional Chinese Medicine, they are related. He said that sadly many of our expedi-tion members who had gone into the fields to do soil samples in that sweltering heat, had contracted some form of serious illness later. I seemed to be one of the only ones who didn't, although I had a liver sickness—hepatitis. But I had recovered fully.

Little John moved back with his mother outside of New York City and planned to work on his research until the very end of his life. He experimented with alternative treatments for glaucoma back in the early 1980s, including using marijuana. He tried to get the results of his research published, but incredibly, the case against Dupont still hadn't been to the Supreme Court.

Dupont leveraged scientific and medical journals to stall published research unless it was supplied by their own research and development departments. They wanted to put their interpretation of data forward.

Little John and many of our expedition partners died before they turned forty years old. We heard our Belizean friends died too.

Before he passed away, Little John and I discussed the possible reasons for me not being as adversely affected. I was not in the fields for as long as everyone else. I was not as diligent a researcher or student as most of the others doing those butterfly sweeps.

That scorpion may have saved me. Being stung kept me out of direct contact longer than all of my colleagues. While I suffered for a few days, the scorpion died immediately.

Yes, we are all related.

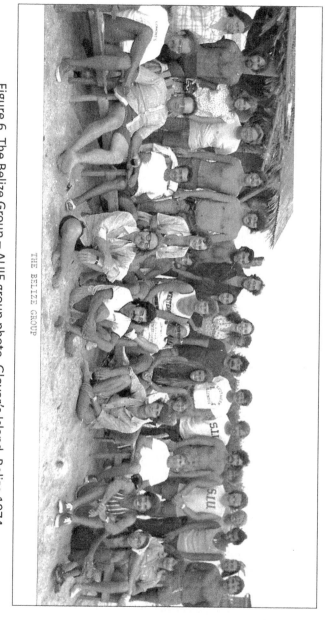

Figure 6. The Belize Group – AUIE group photo, Glover's Island, Belize 1974

3. ON THE MARRAKESH EXPRESS – MOROCCO

The year 1975 was designated as the first International Holy Year. We travelled in places where pilgrims flocked to shrines of their faith in Vatican City, Spain, Greece and now Morocco. We came by boat through the straits of Gibraltar to a place with rows of brightly whitewashed walls, homes with doors painted mystical shades of blue. The world-renowned town of Chefchaouen.

As I wandered up the hills and through the medinas with my *bon ami* (my good friend), we were often stopped by curious children. My companion had brilliant copper-colored, long hair. He was kind and patient with them and let some of the younger ones touch his hair, but this made the day longer since with all the pauses, it took more time to get to the places we needed to visit.

We were warned to be on alert for petty thieves, especially young boys trained to lift any wallet, watch or purse, and yet we had only friendly encounters. They wanted to hold our hands, try out various languages and be our *gides* (guides) in their hometown. Their Arabic and Berber sounded harsh and guttural to me, but our English probably sounded worse to their ears. We tried a common tongue with French. These street urchins had a melee language all their own, with words from Berber, French, Arabic, Spanish and a smatter of German and English. I was very impressed at how quick they were. We all laughed at our attempts to communicate, then stopped to eat at a local family restaurant. We were encouraged to try their specialty: golden couscous and lamb tagine.

"One more bite and I won't be able to get up from this table." Christopher patted his stomach to illustrate.

"Mint tea? *Café?*" The waitress ambled over gracefully with a silver tray. The people here, especially the woman, had beautiful complexions and their skin seemed to exude health and strength. She smiled at me and displayed her very white, full set of teeth. Christopher was entranced.

"*Akdar chai, min fadlik*" (green tea, please). I tried a few words of Arabic.

"*Shugar?*" the waitress placed a small bowl on the table.

"*Shweeya,*" I replied. The waitress looked surprised. I answered with Maghreb Arabic specific to countries in Northern Africa (Morocco, Algeria, Tunisia, Libya) and not the standard Arabic or Egyptian dialect.

Christopher gazed out at the sky as we relaxed on the patio. I reminded him we needed to catch a train to Casablanca and should think about making our way to the train station soon.

"It feels as if we can stretch time here." Christopher groaned and took out his wallet. He left enough money for a good-sized tip and hoisted his backpack on his shoulders. I asked where I could find a "*toilette*" which meant a squat, but at least it would be more private than at the train station.

"Ready?" He appeared eager. "Oh yes," I replied. "*Yellah habibi*" I enjoyed interspersing my conversation with some local language.

We were fairly crushed into the ticket booth and fortunately between my French, and Christopher's hand signals, we were able to purchase the tickets we needed and hurried out to the platform to board the train.

We were in third class carriages, which meant slatted wooden seats next to open windows, but at least there was a breeze. We were also the only different looking foreigners in that carriage. People openly stared at us. I felt uneasy, but it was only a seven-hour ride, we could manage.

The man across from me unpacked a pipe to smoke *sheesha*.

"English?" he asked between inhaling.

"No, American," Christopher answered politely.

"American, good!" This was a time when Americans were still welcomed abroad.

"Where do you go? Casa ... Casablanca?"

We were hesitant to answer this man right away. Silently we consulted with each other and then both of us nodded.

"You should miss Casa and come with us to Marrakesh and then Villa Bens. Special time to go. You can see Casa, later. You will fly from Casa, no?"

"What's happening in Villa Bens?" Christopher asked earnestly.

"*La Marche Verte!* The Green March, march of peace. We go support our brothers and sisters and stand against the Spanish who try to take our land. No guns, no weapons; we will just sit and sleep and pray for peace. You can join us ... why not?"

"Where is Villa Bens?" I was curious now and took out my fold up map of Northern Africa.

The man looked at my map upside down and placed his long finger in the southernmost part of Morocco.

"There. Also called Tarafaya. Not so far by train from Agadir. We change in Casa and take the Marrakesh express? You know the song ..." He started humming the Crosby, Still and Nash, popular American song: "Marrakesh Express."

"How do you know that song?" Christopher and I were DJs at our university radio station. This man just found a common reference. We were intrigued.

"I work at radio station in Casa. I love American music. Excuse me, my name is Ahmed." He extended his hand to us and returned with a handshake.

"Far out!" Christopher continued, "We are trying to find Jajouka music to record and report on back in America. Do you know about the Jajouka festival? Have you ever been?"

"Oh, you are going wrong way. Jajouka is north but we can go after Tarafaya if you like. You want to hear music like 'Dancing in Your Head' ah?"

"You know your music! Yes, what kind of music can we hear and maybe even record in Villa Bens?"

We continued our conversation about music and *Maroc* (Morocco) for hours. I could see from the windows it was already nighttime when we pulled into the Casablanca station.

"Come, I go with you to change tickets. No problem *mashi moskil*."

By now we had decided to join Ahmed and venture down to the Green March. We hauled our backpacks and followed him to the main ticket booth where hundreds of people were standing in lines. They carried woven, plaid, hard plastic bags, cardboard boxes, their children, their food and their temper. While we couldn't understand what they were saying, we heard raised voices and hands slapping the counter. Ahmed read the schedule above us.

"Marrakesh Express train leaves in two hours. We make it. Give me *dirhams* and I buy for us." Christopher hesitated, as did I. Maybe he was going to take our money and run. We heard about worse thefts from expats in Africa. We had worked two and three jobs for over the last year to save for this trip. Reluctantly, I handed Ahmed a few large bills reckoning train tickets all the way to Marrakesh to be expensive. Ahmed returned two of them.

"This enough. Wait here please."

There were no seats, so we sat as well as we could on our gear and scanned the crowd for Ahmed's route. Other travelers scanned us with their eyes.

"Think he'll come back?" I voiced my trepidation to my partner.

"Counting on it, but I really don't know. Very hard to read him. I want to believe he is just excited to be with Americans and we like the same music but ..."

I spotted Ahmed bargaining with some people in line and soon he was at the counter, holding his hand over his heart and handing the man the bills.

"Watch my things, Christopher, will you? I need to find a restroom."

I looked for a door with the outline of a woman and saw the word *"Femmes,"* The cleaning woman sat by the entrance and took a few *dirhams* in exchange for some grainy toilet paper, but I also brought some small packets of tissues since most places we travelled did not have western style facilities. The water coming out of the taps was a rusty brown and I wondered if I chanced getting more germs from washing, than not.

Once back in the main hall I bought a bottle of sparkling water, opened it and used the first drops to wash my hands. One woman near me openly stared. It was, to her, a waste of expensive water. I hurried back to Christopher.

"Good timing. Ahmed is about finished. Let's see if he returns."

"Ok, ok ... no problem, here are your tickets and your change. We go to the platform outside. You hungry?"

We both were but we hadn't wanted to tell Ahmed for fear it would put him in the position as host to buy us a meal. The culture of hospitality in Morocco and many other countries bordering the Mediterranean Sea dictated that guests, especially from other countries, do not pay for food while you are with them.

Bundled with flatbread, bottled water, hummus, olives, some sort of goat cheese and dried apricots, we set off as a trio to the platform and found a bench. It was still dark, and we had another hour to wait.

Figure 7. The Marrakesh Express – Marrakesh train, Morocco 1970s

Onboard the train were men carrying cages with chickens and tea services. Men were selling newspapers, sandals, prayer rugs, flashlights and batteries. Children of all sizes and ages tagged along and hauled bags for their families, the women wore long, colorful *djellabas*; some had painted henna on their hands, their feet and even parts of their faces. We were in exotic company.

The Marrakesh Express was anything but a fast train. We crawled through the night stopping at points in the desert where there was no station or even a platform, and yet somehow people got on and people got off, walking out into the darkness. Christopher and I took turns staying up. We still had trust issues with Ahmed.

When we arrived in the early morning to Agadir, we saw banners painted with green stripes proclaiming *"La Marche Verte"*-The Green March, written in Arabic, French and a few signs were in English. Crowds of people were chanting this phrase and musicians supported by drumming in time with their cries. There was palpable excitement in the air. Ahmed clapped his hands in rhythm and kept nudging us forward to the exit doors. We were pressed tightly to other passengers. I could smell their breath.

"We stop here for the market and rest, then take a share taxi to Tarafaya, Villa Bens."

"Taxi, Ahmed? Won't that be expensive? Why not take a bus or another train?" I asked.

"No, no, non Joowan, don't worry. Taxi here is very cheap and we share with other people. Much faster than a bus. I know where to find. Relax."

"Yeah, relax," Christopher teased me. This was a phrase he often counseled me with back in the States.

We trudged over to the "Taxi" stand. All sorts of men started hounding us, but Ahmed fended them off. After a few minutes he flagged one down. A driver pulled up beside us, and I saw two women sitting in the back and they were not wearing *djellabas* but long, embroidered skirts and colorful long-sleeved blouses. They had ribbons and decorations in their long hair and bands of necklaces, large silver dangling earrings and many silver bracelets.

Ahmed sat in the front chatting to the driver while I moved in beside the women in the back seat with Christopher sitting next to the back door. It was a squeeze, but the women wore scents of myrrh and sandalwood. The car smelled fragrant. This surpassed taking the train.

The journey took a little over three hours. We arrived just before the afternoon prayer call. The driver let us off at the huge gathering of people and tents right by the border.

A *muezzin* mounted the tower by the border gate and put a megaphone to his mouth. First, he cleared his throat, then fairly weeping his call to prayer, he visited his cries on the motley congregation beneath him.

Rugs were unrolled from under garments and unburdened from camels. A multitude knelt and chanted in unison with the leader of prayer.

In respect, we bowed our heads while the prayers continued plaintive and wailing. Then it was finished. The man started climbing down from the tower and within minutes the carpets were packed, and crowds started milling around a large well in the center of the camp.

Ahmed and Christopher unloaded our belongings and set up two tents while I was sent to look for dry grass to help start a small fire. We would use this for cooking and for light since the sun would set soon. People were exchanging greetings to each other all around us. *"Salaam"* (peace) could be heard like a round in a song or an echo, at intervals and with varying pitches. *"Salaam ... salaam ... salaam."*

Figure 8. Green March camp, Morocco 1975

In the shimmering shadows of twilight, we fashioned a campfire site. As we sat, late into the night smoking earth ground *sheesha* and singing songs from an unfathomable language, Ahmed, seeing my joy in such an atmosphere, hugged me and kissed me on the cheek with happiness. I was taken aback but felt his genuine emotion. Christopher nudged me and raised his eyebrows, but then broke into a grin.

Ahmed looked at us and told us seriously, "This is the last time we have a peaceful march. We can do it one time, but next time we don't have chances. Nobody will believe we win. We will win without guns. Tonight is history. I am with my people and you are with my people. We won't die for many years to come. They won't catch me; see I can fly. I am so happy!"

Ahmed leapt into the air and twirled before landing. A boy in a nearby camp took out his wooden flute and blew a lively tune to celebrate. We began clapping our hands in rhythm, rocking with the music. We kept up this motion for another few hours; then the border guards placed their guns by their sides and watched us all in lonely amazement.

By dawn the fires were smoldering. News passed around the camp that the Spanish had conceded ... without a fight. After a two-week sit-in, the Moroccans had succeeded. Everywhere green and red banners of *"La Marche Verte"* flew in the desert winds.

Before settling in the tent Christopher had set up for us, I remember being handed a glass of mint tea. I imbibed it slowly and heard Ahmed whispering to Christopher.

"King Hassan is no friend to our people. He will take credit, but he is a feared king. He works with your CIA and they teach him more ways to keep power. One of our comedians on the radio make a joke about King Hassan's boat and call him, "his maj jet ski." He was tortured and had to run to France. The king here is not a man of peace. I have to be careful. You have to be careful."

When I awoke the next day, Ahmed was gone. He left a note and two *djellabas* for us. His message said: "Go to Essaouira. Tell my cousin, Fatima I send you. Give her this note. She will give you place. I will not see you again. Have good life. We are the peace marchers. Allah is great." He had another paper with writing in Arabic for us to give his cousin.

"He's right," Christopher read the note aloud and commented: "We won't see him again, but I sure am glad we took a chance. This trip is amazing. This trip is trippy. But we need to pack up."

"It won't be easy getting a taxi ride back to the train station or getting tickets to Essaouira without Ahmed helping us."

"Relax, people are in pleasant moods right now. I think we'll make it out, ok."

"Ok, *y'ella then, habibi.*"

We packed up all our gear together, heaved it up on our shoulders and made footprints in the sands. Wearing our *djellabas* was partly our personal tribute to Ahmed, and to the remarkable and unique event we were fortunate enough to be part of, "La Marche Verte." We needed to return to Marrakesh and ride once more on Moroccan trains back to Casablanca.

As the songwriter Graham Nash described:

Looking at the world through the sunset in your eyes
Travelling the train through clear Moroccan skies
Ducks, and pigs, and chickens call
Animal carpet wall-to-wall
American ladies five-foot tall in blue

Sweeping cobwebs from the edges of my mind
Had to get away to see what we could find
Hope the days that lie ahead
Bring us back to where they've led
Listen not to what's been said to you

Wouldn't you know we're riding on the Marrakesh Express
Wouldn't you know we're riding on the Marrakesh Express
They're taking me to Marrakesh
All aboard the train, all aboard the train

4. TIME TRAVEL – ISRAEL

Fortunately, I've been able to make a number of trips to the hotly contested Holy Land. After Morocco, we made our way back across the Mediterranean to the island of Samos and parted in Athens. Christopher had to get back to the States for work in December 1975. I continued to Israel on my own from Greece.

In a homey hostel in Jerusalem, I met up with an Australian girl named Jackie. She wanted to travel down to the Sinai, stay in *kibbutzim* for a few months living and working as volunteers. (meetnatdevit-as it's phonetically pronounced in Hebrew). She told me about their system of "equality in work," collective children's houses and security for Israel's borders. She was passionate about building "this new nation." Jackie grew up on a sheep station outside of Perth, so desert-like landscape was familiar to her.

We decided to go by bus down to the Negev Desert and from there further to Eilat. Jackie had the phone number of the *kibbutz* office. We would call from the Negev to let them know we were coming to Kibbutz Elot. Kibbutz Elot was situated between Kibbutz Yotvata and the town of Eilat on the Arabian or Arava highway in southern Israel. When we arrived with our backpacks at the shack, which served as a checkpoint entrance to Kibbutz Elot, the two guards were expecting us.

Up on the sandy hill before the paved road into the *kibbutz*, other guards with Uzis stopped us. They radioed in to announce our arrival. These men were young, about our age (early twenties), but their faces were already hardened having grown up in war. They gave Jackie and me a bit of a hard time before they let us in. They inspected our hands and said we were "too soft." They spoke quickly in Hebrew knowing we wouldn't understand. They were gruff but also teasing us to see how we reacted. It was an inauspicious beginning, but we ventured forth.

All the adult members were under forty years old, and most were in their twenties and early thirties. They were just starting families, children's houses, a transmitter parts factory, agricultural fields and the various workstations. They needed volunteers.

Many of the young men had been in the tank division during the Six-Day War in 1967. My kibbutznik work captain was in a tank unit in that war. He survived but suffered from insomnia and what we know now as post-traumatic stress reactions. He had slept outside his tank the night his unit was hit. By sleeping outside away from his team he was spared, but everyone in the tank was burned alive. He could "sleep no more" with his memories. His haunted young eyes and restless walking, monotone voice and bowed head were a daily reminder of his pain.

I remember his name was Yotan. He was patient with me trying to learn Hebrew and the tasks I was assigned in the transmitter parts factory, then as part of the irrigation team and worker in the dining hall. In those days we often sat around small fires in the desert night. We would exchange stories in English. English was the bridge language. The volunteers, like me, came from many parts of the world, diverse backgrounds and religious beliefs. We were keen to "help the new nation."

To the south of the *kibbutz* was the road to the town of Eilat and the Gulf of Eilat or the Gulf of Aqaba* (depending upon which side of the border you approached from). This gulf was an arm to the Red Sea, east of the Sinai Desert and west of the Arabian Desert. It was also on the border with Jordan.

You could see the red Edom mountains in the distance to the east from the *kibbutz*. This was a secular *kibbutz* created in the biblical land of the Levantine Semites with ancient history, grudges, prophetic warnings and majestic, harsh beauty.

One of the Friday adventures on Kibbutz Elot was to cross over the border into Jordanian territory at night and bring back "souvenirs." During that time every work team had members carrying guns, mostly Uzis. However, after a 'recon adventure' by some of the younger men, other types of weapons would be casually displayed in the dining hall or in the security/checkpoint office. It was a "don't ask and we won't tell" escapade.

Kibbutz Elot in those days had only very basic living conditions for the full-time members and very rough accommodations for the volunteers. No air conditioning, corrugated iron roofs, particle board walls and floor, no screens on the windows and basic metal framed twin beds. The shower and toilet blocks were a short hike up toward the main body of the *kibbutz*. The volunteer quarters were right across from the cow sheds. The smell was almost overpowering when the wind blew our way. See Figure 9.

Figure 9. Volunteer quarters Kibbutz Elot, Israel 1975

There were delicious medjool date orchards and agricultural fields the size of American football fields created with a combination of sand, earth, compost and sewage water, bordered by tall cypress trees planted in single straight rows as wind breaks. They used drip line irrigation with the sewage water and covered the furrows with clear plastic to form a miniature greenhouse effect keeping needed moisture in the parched desert terrain.

Eventually, I was voted as a work captain with the responsibility of delegating work assignments for all the international volunteers on kibbutz Elot. I learned enough Hebrew to communicate and even to joke. When the *kibbutz* committee learned I had already done graduate field work in marine and terrestrial biology in Central America, and knew how to dive in coral reefs, they sent me to night classes at the H. Steinitz Marine Biology Laboratory established by the Hebrew University of Jerusalem (HUJ) in 1968, on the Eilat coast. The researchers and lecturers at the institute spoke English quite well and helped with my Hebrew.

Additionally, they asked me to be part of a team to grow experimental crops on the *kibbutz* and chart the results. I was in charge of the mangoes, a fruit I was and am, very fond of. I tended them with loving care.

I felt at home on that land. Decades later I would learn my genetic ancestry indicated I had a significant percentage (16%) from the Levant region and Sephardic Jewish 'genes' as well.

We wore the same dark blue uniforms we were issued for use during work hours six days a week. Bunkers were shallowly—built under the ground. They were easy to access. Sirens hardly sounded in the south during those years. Bunkers were places where we played cards and escaped the heat.

As did many volunteers during that era, I went on *tiyul* (hikes) with *kibbutzniks* (members of the kibbutz), learned more card games, read voraciously and had an Israeli *haver* (friend/boyfriend). He taught me more about work ethics, forthright speaking, debate in three languages (French, Hebrew and English) and how to go to sleep for 10–20 minutes for a "power nap." This was before the term 'power nap' was in common use. *Gil* was a *sabra,* born in Israel. He had been an officer in the Israeli Defense Force and was still in the reserves. Our common fluent language was French. His native language was Hebrew. He didn't speak many words of English, but we found our own ways to communicate.

There was only one television in the communal lounge room on Kibbutz Elot. Radio was the main source of information and media entertainment. Radio Shalom would play rock music and had DJs who spoke English. It was the favorite station at our posts. When we went camping it was with very basic gear. We prided ourselves on traveling light and always staying off any possible "X." We were all constantly on alert. We didn't rely on surveillance equipment. We didn't have any except binoculars.

Figure 10. Sinai camping with Kibbutz volunteers, Israel 1976

Figure 11. Camel riding Eilat, Israel 1976

After six months in the desert *kibbutz*, I was sent to study Hebrew and Israeli culture in the *ulpan*, a special school usually for immigrants to Israel. This was on Kibbutz Sdot Yam on the east coast near Caesarea. My work hours were less than on Kibbutz Elot. I was assigned to the banana orchards. It was strenuous work in the mats (clumps of banana plants). I didn't realize banana plants were herbs and not trees.

The 1976 Olympic sailing team from Israel came from Kibbutz Sdot Yam on the Mediterranean Sea coast. Everyone was tense during those Olympic games after the Munich massacre of the Israeli team in the 1972 Olympics in Germany. During the opening parade of the Montreal 1976 Olympics, a special mourning ceremony was conducted in the stadium. A black ribbon was unfurled on the Israeli flag in memory of the Israeli athletes and coaches who were killed at the previous Olympic games.

My roommates were from Finland. Lena's brother, Antii Kalliomaki, was representing Finland in the pole vault. She was nervous for him although this time the Olympics were held in Canada. We listened to the radio every spare minute and at night joined the other *kibbutz* members to watch the games on the communal TV. Kibbutz Sdot Yam had their sailing team qualify. The energy of support was electric across the waves.

The Olympic games were boycotted by twenty-nine countries on account of New Zealand in 1976. New Zealand's national rugby team had played in South Africa earlier that year. The Olympic committee refused pressure to ban New Zealand and as a result twenty-two African countries, and a few other nations withdrew their teams in protest. The Olympic games became more of a political tool in the 1970s, and thereafter.

My Finnish roommates told me about farming work in the mountains of Norway. They informed me Norwegians paid very well, had comfortable accommodations and you only worked five days a week. After completing my study and work, I left Israel in September to do farming work in the Hardanger mountain district of Norway. I needed a change.

Time speeds by. Although I had been to Israel a few times since my first visit, it wasn't until 2009 that I was able to return to the far north of this extraordinary country. On my own, I boarded a bus in Tel Aviv, met my friends in Rosh Pina, then drove with them up to Metullah and beyond.

Delicate fragrances carried by the winds wafted over me as I stood outside their home. It is a quixotic thought to consider that in the Golan, I am unable to discern if these scents begin in Lebanon, on my right, Syria on my left, or just down the path by the fences in Israel.

Hyenas pay no heed to the three parallel rows of fencing. Steel and barbed wire cannot prevent them from creeping across either side's borders whenever they laugh the 'all clear' in their barking communiques. Deftly they stalk stray dogs and dawdling birds to their resting places negotiating the newest human constructions and borders in their strides. A soaring cedar tree is guardian, sheltering creatures from all sides. Somehow this lone tree is permitted to grow in the midst of gates, security checkpoints and three rows of barbed wire barriers.

On the highest hill a young couple strolls arm in arm with a thermos of water, a picnic backpack and their M-16s. Young soldiers lounge anywhere they can find a free spot at makeshift bus stops everywhere. They are dressed in all hues of green and beige decorated with plasticized insignias of martial symbols, swords, fire and planes on their shoulders, sleeves, or front pockets. Some plug-in earphones, using music to transport them to another place and time until they reach their posting. Others punch in texts or cradle their cell phones in pretty pink shades contradicting the black of the weapons on their laps. Older citizens move aside in silent respect as they watch the young ones tromp about with their kit packs, adopting a staunch deportment to appear as if they know what they are doing.

There are many uniforms here. Headscarves are tied in a particular fashion, skirts are worn at specified lengths, *tefillin* hang or are hidden, *kippahs* are specific colors, as are coats, *chadors,* hats, wigs and shirts.

The religious garb of the Chabad bear insignias from their own sects. Each community of believers keep their members corralled not by snarling orders but with reproaching glances, whispered gossip or nods of silent approval. The pale and often flaccid bodies of their young concealed in loose fitting clothing contrast sharply with the bronzed, hard muscled youth of both genders in all branches of the military trees of Israel.

Martial trees thrive in all directions here with roots deep in the history and growth of these lands. Whether cultivated from native shoots or grafts from other parts of the Earth, they form a feature of this landscape on the move wherever the breeze of policy directs them.

This land has many places for healing—from the heights in the Golan to the River Jordan.

Figure 12. Eli Cohen Memorial, Golan Heights,
Israel 2009, photo by author

The medical expertise and facilities in Israel are respected worldwide—even by their enemies.

Reliable, air-conditioned buses carry tourists and patients from a myriad of countries into the desert and the Dead Sea in hopes of improving the quality of their lives. Piped out music and filtered water are sprayed on them at the various resorts bordering the Dead Sea. Languages and gestures at differing pitches mix with the drone of cooling machines.

People with a congress of ailments walk or are pushed in wheelchairs to the troughs of buffets, pools, and private beaches. After soaking in prescribed areas for prescribed durations, many of the guests walk with greater ease holding onto the handrails built for ushering hundreds into the super salty sea. Surprisingly some tiny fish survive in these conditions.

Youngish blonde and red-haired women usher older men with long, terry cloth robes out to the crystallized beaches. Open barrels of deep gray mud and nearby shower banks offer opportunities for complete tactile, texture experiences for whatever parts of the body one may wish to expose. Here the sun, fresh air and water are package deals for medical clinics and eco-tourism firms. Russian, Scandinavian, and Eastern Europeans flock here during their winter.

Nearby is a *kibbutz* which houses guest tourists for extra income. There are guided trails into natural springs, walkways above the fields worked by kibbutzniks and volunteers. I had been here before, decades ago, but much had changed.

Figure 13. Kibbutz Ein Gedi, Israel 2005

I am reminded of the time when I worked in the fields of Kibbutz Elot, on the southern desert border of Israel in 1975-1976.

In 1975, the Sinai was part of Israel since the 1973 war known as the Yom Kippur War. The governments of Egypt and Syria launched a two-pronged attack against Israel on the holiest day in the Jewish religion—Yom Kippur. Israel fought back fiercely after the initial surprise and asked for support from the USA. Unfortunately, under President Nixon and his adviser and Secretary of State, Henry Kissinger—who was a Jewish refugee to the USA in 1938, and one of the special School of Foreign Service Dean's seminar leaders at Georgetown University during my time there—deliberately delayed humanitarian and military aid to Israel in favor of Egypt. People are either ignorant or forget this fact. Israel suffered heavy losses but did succeed in winning that war and gaining territory for a few years thereafter. The borders were re-drawn ... again.

Thirty years on almost every natural paradise in this Holy Land is quantified and measured. Fencing and gates secure comfortable encampments. Sectarian and agrarian settlements are veritable prisons since no one can enter or leave without being checked and granted permission to enter or leave.

Now, security lights blast the area. We must sacrifice a view of the stunning starry nights. Yet, this is viewed as a necessary trade-off since well-lit boardwalks are accessible at any hour under the guard of mechanically operated, swiveling, surveillance cameras. There is less chance of surprise attacks. A trade-off for security and protection.

Everyone has adjusted, tolerated, and now accepted these cage conditions. Camels and domestic animals are tagged. Soon to follow all Bedouin and children will be chipped, ensuring implants with data bearing and data gathering devices are to be part of the requirements for the privilege of citizenship. All will be biometrically monitored and subject to tracking and inspection at any time. Spy phones will make the government's job easy.

Even the hyenas, ibex, rodents, foxes, and birds have re-directed their routes to avoid electrocution. Creatures scavenge where the most delicious scraps can easily be found at predictable times. They discover this after only a few seasons of hunting.

I suppose, we will be able to predict where the hyenas and other creatures will go and where the night fragrance of jasmine comes from. Soon, there will be no place to run, no place to hide. We will be able to locate, catalogue and name all their secret places.

But as my wise uncle once said years ago, "Naming is not knowing."

Figure 14. Jo Patti Munisteri – Caesarea beach Kibbutz Sdot Yam, photo by Maria-Elena Villacorta-Cortez, Israel 2009

5. CLUBBING IN THE CAPITAL – USA

This capital city has been an international hub since the beginning of the 20th century. Tourists come from all over the globe to view the "seats of power." While the John F. Kennedy Center for the Performing Arts presents politically influenced, carefully chosen works for the public at exorbitant prices, this city is not known for its theater, music and art as much as New York City or even Chicago or San Francisco.

But in the late 1970s, the capital of the United States benefited from a number of grants for the arts and became known as a place to experiment and "audition" new works in front of a paying public.

When I returned from my initial travel to Europe, North Africa and Israel, I came back to Washington, D.C. I decided not to pursue a career in Foreign Service or work with other government departments or agencies. I felt it was time to try doing what I was passionate about while I was still young and without family responsibilities.

My plan was to re-train my body toward dance, improve my singing and acting skills from amateur to professional levels, and expand my musical knowledge. I had already passed my Third-Class Radio Engineering exams and hosted a radio show at the Georgetown University radio station, WGTB FM in my senior year. They partnered with Pacifica Radio and needed more volunteer staff. I signed on.

A few of my friends formed an independent theatre group they called Georgetown Classical Theatre. I helped them write the first grant they received for a full summer season of plays, music and readings in an under resourced part of the city. We did everything including rebuilding the inside of an old theatre, building sets, acting, directing, doing the maintenance, being the front of house staff and assisting the designers. The next step we planned was going to New York City. Two of us prepared our auditions for the prestigious Circle-in-the-Square Theatre School in New York. Washington D.C. was the place for us to make mistakes and learn from them.

In the little spare time we had, we hung out in the newest clubs to support the emerging local music scene in D.C. bands with edgy names like the "Urban Verbs" and the "Slickee Boys." They were garnering local and national attention. Media called it "The New Wave."

There was one club that was all the rage at the time. Residents of D.C. and tourists patronized the place. It wasn't as diverse a crowd as clubs I had seen in Belize or in Texas, but it was a place that welcomed new talent, sold alcohol and turned a blind eye to other activities. It was called the Atlantis Club.

The bar was a nightmare. The band members were only given one free drink. If they wanted more, they had to pay for it. The stage was only two feet off the floor. The crowd was dangerously close. There was no real security making it easy for thieves to slip in from the main street and slip out with patrons' wallets, purses, cash, and drugs. I wanted to be supportive of my musician mates, but I loathed hanging out in the Atlantis Club. Everyone was competing to be as punk as possible. To me, it was inauthentic. I recall one particular night in detail.

Teman, the lead singer thrust his head into the bass drum for the last time. The final song of the final set was about finished. He dulled himself for the assault. The soft covered sticks pounded against the skins into his semi-circular canals. Ear drums pounded by bass drums. He knew it was a crowd pleaser. He had done it for the crowd.

The Atlantis management deliberately limited seating and placed only a few tables in the main room. They wanted people to be up and dancing all night long. The lighting pulsed frenetically in the windowless, cave-like club. This place was its own small world within the capital city. My eyes strained to see the stage.

"Chipping away. They're chipping me away."

Screaming into his microphone, Teman ripped out the last note. Guitarists, percussion players and Teman bowed their heads irreverently. The show was over. None too soon for Teman. None too soon for me.

Teman was shaking from thirst and fear. He hadn't been able to score anything of substance to quench his outrage. He almost struck a young girl during the second set because she got too close to his personal "space." He leaned against the back wall of the platform and sucked in his cheeks.

"What the fuck do they care?" he spat. I tried to console him.

"You smashed it tonight, Teman."

Figure 15. New Wave band at the Atlantis Club, Washington, D.C. 1977

"Fickle, fickle," Genji teased, mocking me under his breath. For a drummer, he was very vocal at times. Teman watched as we dismantled the equipment.

He spied three safety pinned girls making their way to the stage. One of them he recognized. She was a blonde, punk groupie.

Teman slid over to the amplifiers stacked at the back of the stage. He pretended to be occupied with packing up cables.

"Hey, T-man … too blasted to come over and talk to a couple of your fans?"

"Fans?" He pivoted away from them. "Parasites," he hissed. Teman continued wrapping the cables around his arms like great eels.

"What a mouth on ya! Can't even say 'fuck you bitch,' You swear with filthy biological terms. Love you anyway, T-man. The harder you reject us, the more it turns us on!"

The shorter girl stood with her leather legs shoulder length apart. Her jacket fell open revealing her beer gut and a thin t-shirt sheathed her breasts. She wore a necklace of multi-colored safety pins dangling down her chest. Teman tried to focus his eyes on an iridescent button she had in her hair. The effort cost him his concentration. In his attempt to appear busy he was careless. He forgot to wind the cords from right to left.

"Taking a good look 'round T-man? Was wondering when you'd recognize a soul mate. Stop for a drink with me?" She nudged the two girls beside her with her elbow. They shoved off to a darker corner.

"How come I'm the fly paper for you buzzing little brats? Try your tricks on that bouncer over there."

Teman pointed to an enormous one-legged man standing by the outside door. The man had shoulders that seemed to be bolstered by football pads. His head pivoted on his thick neck. He balanced on a metal crutch. In his capable hands it served as a menacing sword, skillfully fending off any intruders. He kept the club "clean" for the Arab bosses. He was blonde with chiseled features. It was rumored he was a Vietnam veteran, but the girls all brushed him off as their buddy, their friend, their "brother" … and nothing more.

I watched Teman as he hung his head trying to find the tails of the cable. In his confusion the cords were twisted into medusa knots. Genji, the drummer, came over to hurry him up.

"Teman, you've lost the umbilical cord. Make yourself useful. Cart the drum cases out to the van. Wave bye-bye to that little girl."

Genji inhaled on his cigarette while concurrently heaving the amp onto a dolly. His forearms shook with exertion. Teman picked up a beaten, black, cardboard drum case and handed it to me.

"I could help you with that you know." The blonde-haired girl wise cracked a smile to Teman who tried to put on a poker face and ignore her.

"Want something to pick *you* up? A little snow for a summer evening, mister?" she tempted.

Teman swallowed with resolve. He did want the numbness to return, but he resisted. I sensed his struggle from across the room.

Teman checked to see where his cohorts were. Genji was loading the van with Roscoe and Tim. They were out of eye reach. I was still in the club.

"You always bribe to get your way?" Teman asked ungratefully.

"Why not? My folks got good results by doin it. Look, don't think you are doing me any favors. Do you want a line or not?" She had a strident voice.

Teman undid the straps on the drum case and parted the

compartments. Licking his lips, he lifted a snare drum into place and closed the case again.

"What's your name?" he asked routinely.

"Nina Ninja. You know me. I write to you at least once a week even though you never answer. Gonna be sweet now or what?" Nina took two steps toward him. "How did you get a name like T-man? It means something special?"

I backed up to make myself less visible. I didn't want to be in the middle of this scene.

Genji came back inside and started shooting sidelong glances toward Teman. Teman continued his conversation, paying no heed to Genji or me.

"My father gave me the name. Teman was an ancient place and the men there were known to be wise. Hard to live up to. Anyway, tell me what you have in mind."

She showed him a pocket mirror. Teman followed her to a back table. Sitting down, he managed to scrape some powder into two wispy lines. The girl handed him a rolled twenty as a straw.

"Sip it first. I'll tell you where I want to go after. Don't worry T-man, I won't be any trouble for you. I swear."

In the light we could see her face more clearly. Her complexion was pasty, indoor, pale, yet made more grotesque by her insistence on wearing globs of jet-black eye make-up. Teman nodded and dove down to the glass tray. With one long snort he inhaled a line. He surfaced still inhaling.

"Whoa, "she laughed. "They don't call you hoover nose for nothing. My turn."

Teman handed her the mirror.

"Umm, all gone. Damn. Getting high always reminds me I have to piss. Be right back, T-man." The girl fumbled to her feet and tittered to the ladies' room.

Teman focused his sights on the stage. The lights were still on, but the platform was empty. From the rear, the stage seemed miniature, not at all what we had imagined or felt when performing. From where we sat now, it all appeared unspectacular. It was humbling.

We heard a horn honking. Repeatedly. Teman blinked to attention. He dragged himself to the door. We ran outside, banging on the van to get our mates to slide the door open for us. Teman pushed me inside, then hopped in beside Roscoe who maneuvered out of the parking lot. There were still fans lurking around out front.

"We get cash from that bastard?" Tim whined. "Don't need another of his bad checks. I don't care if we do have to get our next gigs out of town. I'm done with Abdullah what's his name!" Tim hung over the front seat. Genji nudged him in the ribs.

"Lead guitarists always whine," he announced. "We got cash. Here's yours. Now, go cut your fingernails."

Roscoe laughed and sped through a yellow traffic light. Teman was rushing with the car's motion. His place was the first stop.

"Teman, you really let loose on the last set. Got to get those lyrics down for the first song though. Dry run tomorrow afternoon. Rehearsal okay with you guys?"

Roscoe was the unofficial group leader. His suggestions were understood commands. Lately he did most of the 'suggesting' to Teman. The others in the band had developed their own effective form of non-verbal communications. Teman was instrument less and impotent. He probably wished he could pluck strings every night instead of his psyche. His procaine mouth was wired shut, forcing him to listen. I felt him shiver.

"Four o'clock in the basement. That way we can warm up before the show. Gonna be opening for that band, Splayed. If we're hot, we'll wipe them. There's supposed to be an agent in the audience. He's looking for opening acts at CBGBs in New York City."

Genji and Tim acknowledged their approval. Teman was silent. The van crawled to the curb. Teman clicked his tongue behind his teeth. His eyes flashed a warning to Roscoe.

"Let's not play Queen for a Day, Teman. Is 4:00 alright, or not? If not, we can make it later."

Three of the other band members brandished their jaws and immutable profiles. They wanted an answer.

Peer pressure had never worried Teman. In all his years at boarding school, he hadn't succumbed to the group norms. He was an outlier. All the whispers behind his back, scowling faces or shaken heads and fingers amused him rather than shamed him. He was beyond those conventional forms. His parents and teachers had been at a loss when he would wander from their control. He meandered back to them on his own terms.

Now, with a sudden distaste for the company he was keeping and the music he was whoring, he felt his insides pushing out and his ego roaring. He had had enough. Only his inner discipline kept him from shouting into the night. His face remained neutral, but I heard his breathing change.

Teman sat on the vinyl seat gripping his belt. The engine was running.

"Teman!" Roscoe snarled. "You zonked out or pausing for effect?"

Teman took one more deep breath while Genji curled a strand of hair from the back of his neck. I bit my thumb.

"Teman, I don't want to have to come down hard on you, but we need a fucking affirmation."

Roscoe tapped out a cigarette. Genji ran his hands through what was left of his Mohawk style haircut. Teman longed for a cigarette but sensed it was not an appropriate time to bum. He shifted his gaze to the windscreen but couldn't see beyond the shatterproof glass.

He had performed with these musicians for almost two years. This was a last-ditch effort to keep the band together. He had thrashed about with other groups over the past six years hoping for a 'big break.' But it wasn't happening. Teman was the eldest in our troupe.

Roscoe turned off the ignition. It began to drizzle. Tim decided to speak.

"Hey, what happened here? Two hours ago, we were tight. I mean easy, ya know? So, Roscoe asks for a little discipline and you pull in tight, Teman? Why has this gotten so complicated, man. I mean something set this all off that I don't know about?" Tim searched the others faces for a clue, then retreated after a silent shrug from Genji.

Genji tapped his foot with impatience. He knew to leave the prodding to Roscoe. He beat out cadences with his fingertips as they waited.

Teman opened his mouth to speak.

"You pull me right out of my night dreams with your after-gig notes Roscoe. Give me time for a little high, huh? We sure aren't getting any fuckin financial satisfaction."

Teman pressed his hand against the front seat.

"It's bleeding me, the mundane rigor of it all." Teman couldn't even look at them anymore.

"Yeah, ok—I'll be there at 4:00."

Teman opened the van door and motioned for me to join him,

before turning to say "Night" over his breath. He didn't bother to gauge their reactions. I waved as they drove off.

Teman was in the mood for a fight. He shadow-boxed the air in frustration. He kicked at the night as we walked down the deserted city street.

In mid thrust he remembered something which whipped him with secret joy. He had a stash of firecrackers in his mailbox.

"Hey Jo. Come with me. I've got something to show you."

We started running to his apartment almost giddy with anticipation.

Teman grabbed a key from his back pocket and ran to the foyer of his building. Inside were rows of mailboxes. He slapped his to open it and reached into the tiny tunnel, groping its recesses. There, at the far end were three strings of thumb sized sidewalk firecrackers. He pulled them out swiftly.

"Sometimes ..." Teman said to himself defiantly. He slammed the mailbox shut. Behind his row of apartment buildings was an empty lot. This time in the morning, not even night stalkers or drunks were lurking about. Teman ambled over to the center of the lot and knelt down. He needed to set up his blasting site. He told me to stand back.

There was a dumpster a few paces away. Teman foraged around and retrieved some tin cans and a hubcap. He turned the hubcap over forming a metal bowl, then spread the strings of firecrackers around the circumference. Next, he twisted off five or six extra firecrackers and put them under cans he placed in a semi-circle. He stretched out the fuses.

"X marks the spot." Teman surveyed his handiwork.

For a brief moment he panicked. He couldn't locate a pack of matches. From inside an inner sleeve pocket, he felt for his lighter. The flame would serve his purposes absolutely. Then he unzipped his leather jacket.

The fuses would be long enough. The noise would be eye opening. This would be risky in a paranoid city continually on edge because of all the factions and international power players who resided there. Undoubtedly someone would immediately notify the police ... maybe even the bomb squad. We decided it was worth it.

Teman lit the strings. He ran by me and grabbed my hand to pull me behind the outer gate. Even from the distance we had been able to run, our ears split with the sound. The beer cans exploded, the hubcap reverberated, spun, cracked, and thundered metallically. The blasts were celebratory. We were gasping with pleasure. Teman held his stomach in an effort to stem the hysterical laughter which swirled up inside his gut. His inner explosions were a match for his outer ones.

Lights flicked on in the surrounding buildings. It was all over as soon as it began. Ignition to take off to landing. Teman looked confident and happy for the first time in months. Maybe in years.

We marched away from the site as we heard police sirens shrieking down a side street. We leapt up the back steps and closed his door quickly. Teman didn't need to turn on the light. Opening the freezer, he felt for—then rejected—a pack of cigarettes.

"You're not going to smoke?" I whispered.

"No, I've decided to quit," he announced.

I flipped on a light and went to wash my face in his bathroom.

Teman stumbled into his bedroom and switched on the fan. He needed cool air to speak to him … gently. He fell back onto his mattress and beckoned me to him with his eyes and his hands.

"I can't stay long, Teman."

"Just lie down next to me for a little while, will you Jo?"

Teman was content to simply lie in the dark, to melt into sleep with me beside him.

Drifting off, I remembered hearing the police sirens warning us as they screamed down the alley. It didn't matter; no one would know of Teman's performance tonight. His actual explosion. This was his solo. His own ideas in his own time.

He was authentic.

He had not done it for the crowd.

Figure 16. Headshot of author, New York, USA 1980

6. GUMBAYNGGIRR
DREAMING – AUSTRALIA

Since I was ten, I dreamt of a landscape I thought was on another planet. It was a recurring dream of a golden red mountain surrounded by desert. Inside one of the mountain caves, women sat chanting in the dark around a fire. In my dream I am outside their circle observing until they motion me to come toward them. Just as I am about to join in the chanting I wake up.

I never considered that the place in my dream might actually exist until one evening I was invited to a reception hosted by the Australian ambassador. At that time, I was living in the Village in downtown Manhattan. The party was on the Upper East Side and would be full of the posh social set. Because I was the first female to win the Circumnavigator's fellowship, back in 1973, I was often invited to events hosted by some member of the Circumnavigator's Club. Usually, I politely refused, but the thought of meeting some Aussies roused me to RSVP "yes."

It was not my scene. I would have to dress for the occasion. New York City has shops for all budgets and styles, and I found a second-hand store in the East Village which carried vintage clothes. One of my friends who was a costume designer for Creation Productions, the downtown theatre company I was working with at the time, joined me to choose an appropriate evening dress. She altered it for a perfect fit. I would be one of the younger invites, I reckoned. I'd need to use my theatrical skills to summon the courage to mingle.

When I arrived at the spacious home, I signed the guest book, checked my coat and found my way to their expansive living room. Chairs were set up facing a large white screen. Waiters walked around tempting us with trays of hor d'oeuvres and alcoholic drinks. No one looked familiar until I spied a tall, older man in the hallway. He smiled at me. It was Ray Dinsmore, one of my mentors and former president of the Circumnavigators Club. I felt relieved to know someone and to see him again. We shook hands grinning at each other; then he introduced me to a number of guests including the Deputy Head of Mission for the Australian Embassy. The lights flickered indicating it was time for the film to begin. Mr. Dinsmore and the Australian directed me to our seats. I sat between them as the lights dimmed to complete darkness.

Figure 17. The Olgas, Northern Territory, Australia-author in 1986

The first few minutes showed famous tourist spots, Australian animals, birds and sea creatures with narration and music. However, in the next few minutes images of the Northern Territory desert appeared. Then, a landmark I recognized from my dream spun across the screen. My body responded automatically. Tears started to form and run down my face. I couldn't explain why, but I started trembling. I tried to calm myself and stop my silent crying, but it was difficult for me to remain still. I kept wiping my eyes hoping no one would notice.

Figure 18. Headshot of author, New York, USA 1983

After another twenty minutes the film ended. Lights came on and the Australian ambassador gave a short speech in front of the screen. I couldn't listen properly and worked on regaining my composure. Eventually, everyone started rising and returning to the open reception area. Mr. Dinsmore pointed the way and I followed. As the Australian Deputy paused at the buffet table, I mustered my courage and spoke to him directly.

"Excuse me, sir. Do you know that part of the film where they showed a large red/orange desert mountain? Is that an actual place people could visit?"

"Why yes." He smiled. "That's called Ayers Rock although the Aboriginals there call it Uluru. It's their sacred place, but I believe you can go there. I've not been yet, myself."

"Oh, thank you," I responded in an almost hushed tone. I felt lighter knowing my dream showed me an actual place on Earth.

Mr. Dinsmore turned to me. "Will that be your next trip, Joanne?"

"I don't know yet, sir. Possibly. I hope so."

The rest of the evening was uneventful as I recall. I rode home in a cab with a couple who lived near me and who insisted they pay for the taxi.

It would still be a few years before I travelled to Australia, but when I arrived in 1986, it was to do a healing workshop in New South Wales, not the Northern Territory. Little did I know that would be the first step toward Uluru and a life-long relationship with my new Gumbaynggirr family, as well as the birthplace of my son.

My first time in New South Wales I spent with a group of women in what was then a small town called Nambucca Heads. The beach wrapped around the east coast endowed with fine grain sand and clear blue waters.

It was in Nambucca that I first met a few of the Gumbaynggirr women who would prove to be pivotal in the rest of my life.

They asked me to come over to Bowraville one day and see "the mish," short for the mission, a place similar to reservations in North America but much smaller. One of my Australian contacts drove me over to Bowraville one afternoon. There I was introduced to the families, their children and their homes. I could tell the Aboriginal families were not comfortable with my Australian contact. She was not Aboriginal, she was a *gubba* (a white, "Anglo" person). They didn't speak much, avoided her questions and dutifully offered us tea, biscuits and a "lookaround." As we were leaving, one of the women called out to me. I went over to her.

"You're welcome here Joann ... a. Come back." I nodded to her in thanks.

The next day I was driven north to another part of New South Wales. We meandered on the narrow roads through the farming area of Bellingen and over into the Thora Valley's only transport passage called "Darkwood Road." On one of the hills were various shaped buildings of wood and stone. At the entrance to the driveway was the sign, "Chrysalis Steiner School." We drove up the hill to the area paved for a parking lot. A polygon-shaped building, with large wooden inlay on its front windows, was the first place we spotted. It was Sunday, but one man and his family were outside working. They were planting flowers around the building.

"G'day," he greeted us. "What can I do for you?"

"We've come to look about if that's alright?" The three children stopped their digging and looked over at us.

"My name is Yvonne, and this is my friend from America, Jo."

"Glad to meet you. I'm Matt. No worries. As you can see, we're still in the building stages. This will be the kindergarten. Down to the right is the class one, further down to the left is class two. We have a small office building. We plan to build all the way to high school going down the hill. Parents are building this school. We're using river rocks and timber from around here. We want to be part of the landscape as much as possible. Most of our students come from the Valley and Bellingen."

Figure 19. Chrysalis Steiner school, Thora, New South Wales, Australia 1986

"Fantastic." Yvonne commented. I loved the way the building

blended with the surroundings. We ambled over to the other buildings and down the hill. Little did I know then, that not only would I be teaching at the school later, but that both my children would start their education here.

While the workshop turned out to be disappointing, it did include a trip to the center of Australia and a walk about on the red rock monolith of my dreams. In 1986, it was permitted to climb Uluru (then it was still called Ayers Rock). I climbed with a sense of reverence, holding the chain as I ascended and marveling at the massive Mars-like formations.

It was late afternoon when I arrived at the top; I sat to pause, then lay down to take a rest. Promptly, I started spiraling into a trance-like sleep. I dreamt vividly about my future and about my death in a 'previous life' on this same rock.

My companions had to shake me awake since I didn't hear them calling to me. I rose, shaking inside from what I had seen in what seemed to be an altered state. The energies were strong on Uluru.

One of the park rangers stood near me as I went to climb down. He was a Pitjantjara man. He didn't say anything, but I looked directly at him for a few seconds. I was still somewhat dazed. When I turned to grasp the metal chain which served as the guideline to descend, images of a program I was in at Georgetown years before surfaced and flashed in my mind.

After I graduated from Georgetown University and returned from travels and study in Central America, Europe, Africa and the Middle East, I contacted Dr. Arnold Mysior. He was one of my mentors and the head of the Psychology Department. He had invited me to be in his first course on Psych cybernetics in 1973-1974. He, General Alexander Haig, Dr. Alexander Christakis and Dr. Jack Shuman were the seminar professors. They had pushed me forward during my senior year to meet people in various organizations and participate in a battery of tests.

I started private counselling sessions with Dr. Mysior, which included hypnosis. He tried this to help me uncover memories and increase my capacity for compartmentalization. We also did extensive dream analysis, which continued for a few years. Dr. Mysior instructed me how to insert ideas just before bedtime and "recall" them during a nightmare to wake myself up. I was also to keep a notebook or journal by my bed to write down the strongest impressions from the nightmare or dream. When I woke up for the day, that was the best time to ana-lyze dreams on my own, initially. Then I brought my journal to the two to three sessions I had with Dr. Mysior every week. We unraveled their meaning together.

Once I established a routine of recording my dreams, he introduced me to the concept of inserting conscious directions into my nightmares or dreams. For instance, if I had a nightmare where people were chas-ing me, I could say in the dream to myself, "I can fly away from them … now." I could redirect my unconscious with a conscious inception. This was/is an effective method of rewiring and changing patterns in your conscious and unconscious behavior.

One step further involved experiments with inserting suggestions over distance and time. We used remote viewing to locate and then concentrated meditation to "send" a message or idea across to a spe-cific person or "target."

Before I was hypnotized, I imagined someone had to hold a shiny object like a watch at the end of a gold chain and swing it in a pendu-lar motion with suggestions such as, "You are getting sleepy … very sleepy." These ideas probably came from old movies. In actuality, I was taught to sit in an upright, relaxed position with my hands on my knees and my feet solidly on the ground. Then I did deep breathing, and a sort of guided meditation with my eyes closed following Dr. Mysior's voice.

Right before each deep session, he would "guide me" to imagine going down a long corridor, opening the door slowly and then walking down some steps. He would count the steps and when I got to twelve, I would imagine opening another door and there, whatever landscape appeared I would enter and truly begin the trance. The end of the hyp-nosis session would be the similar ritual of walking back to the door, ascending the twelve steps, opening another door walking down the corridor and hearing, "When you open your eyes you will remember everything and be back in my office at Georgetown. One, two, three … open your eyes." Over the years I wondered how many sessions I might have been directed to, "Forget everything you have just seen and experienced."

Dr. Mysior also taught me how to do self-hypnosis sitting in the same position, grounding myself and "traveling" to other spaces. I had been tested in "remote viewing" abilities in my senior year although I knew I had these abilities since I was a child. Dr. Mysior and later Dr. Charles Socarides explained that children who have endured extreme trauma learn to excarnate from their bodies to cope with the pain. Sometimes, while excarnated they can 'see' themselves, other people, places and even transcend time while in this state. As a child, I didn't have control over when I would start 'traveling,' but as an adult I was learning to navigate step by step.

"It's like you have electricity coursing through you without a ground," Dr. Mysior told me once. "You need to be able to ground this energy, or it could harm you." I found myself counting down the last twelve 'steps' on Uluru.

Scenes from my past (and as it turned out, my future) flickered in my mind before I touched the red earth at the base of Ayers rock. "Come back here." I *heard* in my consciousness as I walked to rejoin our group. I pondered what the land was saying. I was between thresholds for a while, as had sometimes happened after a hypnosis session with Dr. Mysior. Strange.

It was difficult to leave Australia, but after two months in the Southern Hemisphere winter, I had obligations with San Jose Theatre company at the end of the Northern Hemisphere summer. I did two successful shows on short contracts from New York with San Jose Rep. They invited me to join their company full time for the following season.

This was a major decision-to leave New York—to give up my tiny rent-controlled apartment in the Village. I'd been based in Manhattan for over six years, the longest I had lived in one place. I'd be leaving my family and good friends with little chance to visit them. Yet, my life was changing. My trip to Australia restored much of my confidence to try the next steps. To move to the West Coast was akin to going to another country in some respects, but I knew it was time to take the risk. I signed the contract with San Jose Repertory Theatre. California dreaming was soon to become my reality.

Figure 20. Onstage at La MaMa E.T.C. as "The Assassin" in The American Mysteries by Matthew Maguire, New York, USA 1984

7. SANTA CRUZ – USA

In the 1900s The Valley of Heart's Delight was the name given to the area outside of San Francisco which was blooming with fruit orchards and luscious agricultural products. By the 1970s it became known as Silicon Valley. Industries manufacturing and innovating using silicon chips moved in and took over the fertile valley covering much of it with concrete. The area was growing, and the city of San Jose sprawled in all directions. In 1980, James Reber founded the first resident theatre company in San Jose, California. He contributed to the artistic evolution of that city. The theatre grew to be a fixture of the San Jose and San Francisco Performing Arts community. It was a stimulating experience to be part of their new resident company. I arrived full of enthusiasm in 1986.

The theatre suggested I share a rental house to save money. There were two possibilities: one in San Jose near the theatre, but in the city, and another farther away and over a hill nicknamed "Death Highway." The house was on the beach in Santa Cruz. I decided to buy a used truck and commute. My drive time would be easier over the treacherous hill highway since I'd have a different schedule than most urban commuters.

Tuesday through Saturday we had evening performances, and matinees on Saturday and Sunday. We had to perform in eight shows a week. Rehearsals for the next show were during the day since this was a Repertory Theatre Company. Only Mondays were off. I was thoroughly occupied, but I thought about Australia at some point every day.

The San Jose Rep Theatre Artistic Director was good friends with a colleague of mine. Ken and I had known each other since we were twenty. We graduated from Georgetown and Circle-in-the-Square Performing Arts School. He recommended me for the new Len Jenkin's play, *OO7 Crossfire* to be directed by Ed Hastings from San Francisco. I performed well at my audition. This was before I went to Australia.

Ed Hastings had cross cast against stereotypes. My role in *007*

Crossfire was that of a Korean mother who had lost her son in the Lockerbie bombing of Pan Am Flight 103 in Scotland. My character roved up and down the theatre aisles searching for her son, asking various people if they had seen him. She couldn't find his body. I played an Asian character while two of my Chinese American actor friends played the pilot and air hostess. It was an intense time for all of us.

The new 'core company' consisted of a handful of Actors Equity Union (AEA) members (of which I was one) a few directors and technical staff. What we didn't know when we signed our contracts was that David Lemos, the Artistic Director, had AIDs. He was dying.

The house I shared had two levels. I lived upstairs with three other people. We each had our own room and shared the kitchen, living room and two bathrooms. Two military guys who were transitioning out of the US Airforce lived downstairs. One of their friends, who was a USAF pararescue man (PJ) came to visit them. He came over a few times and apparently asked about me. One Sunday night, after I finished my week of performing in the musical *Godspell*, they convinced me to go out with a group. That's when I met Marty. His full name was Martin Walter Schmidt.

I don't want to write much more about our time together in California, but I will say it was a whirlwind. I was introduced to a world I knew little about. He was introduced to mine which was just as foreign to him. Santa Cruz is a very romantic spot on the California coast. We took long walks on Black's Beach out to Black Point, ran in 5K charity races, did meditation retreats at Green Gulch Zen center in Muir, skied near his family cabin in the Sierras, snow camped in Yosemite Valley and swam in the ocean. Outside of work hours, we spent almost all our time together. We fell in love.

I was wary of several character traits which concerned me about Marty. In my mind, he was a unique and capable man, but seething beneath his California smile. He had a huge ego, took unnecessary risks, and he was moody. I didn't see flashes of his raging temper until later. He was good company as a change from the sort of men I knew and worked with, but he was definitely not someone to get into a serious relationship with. Besides, he was younger than I.

Figure 21. Onstage at San Jose Rep as "Peggy" in Godspell by John Michael Tebelak and Steven Schwartz, San Jose, California, USA 1986

But Marty was undeterred by the difference in our age and our lifestyles.

He told me later, "You were my mission. I wasn't going to fail. I wanted you to be my wife and the mother of my children. I dreamed about a smart, beautiful, hard-headed woman (he used to play that Cat Stevens song all the time) and you were it!"

He achieved his goal. David, the artistic director was fading from life fast. A new artistic director was chosen for the following year. She wanted her own 'company.' The writing was on the wall that we would not be offered another contract. There were options to join another company in San Francisco and I had worked for San Jose Cleveland ballet in their new outreach program for schools. They were expanding. I needed to make a decision.

I was considering these possibilities when I received a phone call from Australia asking if I would like to return to work on an international conference and interview for a teaching job at the Macksville TAFE (Technical and Further Education Community College) for the next year. The conference was to be held in 1988, in Nambucca Heads, Australia.

Marty decided to form his own mountain guiding business. He wouldn't re-enlist in the US Airforce. He had a number of ideas which we discussed. His first contract would be as an assistant guide on Aconcagua in South America. This was a big break for him into the international climbing scene. I told him to go; it would work out well for him. He felt he needed to prepare by returning to Alaska where he was a PJ. There, he had climbing contacts and could train in the Alaskan range. In my mind this was the chance to "break it off" naturally.

We made plans to go to Mt. Shasta to climb and participate in "The Harmonic Convergence" meditation on that mountain. I invited my good friend from New York, Jo Anderson, to come along. She was visiting from Los Angeles. Two weeks before the climb, I started having nightly dreams about Australia again. I also worried I might be pregnant, but it was too soon to be certain. We both always used birth control, but it was possible.

I could confide in Jo. In addition to being involved in the New Theatre Movement in New York City, we had both been part of initiation ceremonies conducted by Katherine Leonard, a Tsalagi (Cherokee) elder woman. These were part of preparations to become 'warrior women' and face our fears. As Jo put it, New York City was 'bootcamp for life.' We had both been victims of violent crime our first few years there. Many of our close friends in the performing arts had been attacked at some time in New York. Some were held up at gunpoint; others I knew were stabbed; a few were shot but survived; some were beaten and robbed. It was a dangerous place in many parts of the city before Rudi Giuliani was elected mayor.

After Jo returned to LA, Marty decided we should try Mt. Whitney. It would be on my upcoming ten-day vacation. We left the car at the starting point, hiked in with our full packs and after hiking out, we hitchhiked back to Marty's car. After this short adventure together, I confirmed my pregnancy when we returned to Santa Cruz.

There was no question in my mind about continuing on with my pregnancy. I would not go for an abortion, as some of my friends counselled. But I knew as much as I loved Marty, he was not someone I could envision living with as a husband. He was ambitious for his new company and centered on his own pursuits. He had a roving eye, was terrible with budgeting and I doubted he would be much of a father. I called my contacts in Australia and explained the "complication." Fortunately, they were keen to support me. I knew my own family would not.

When we each left for different destinations, it was not in my mind to accept his offer of marriage. Marty proposed on two occasions, but I wasn't ready to commit to him. My uncle Arthur, an attorney in New York whom I told of my situation, sent me paternity legal papers and coached me how to file this uncontested lawsuit. He said regardless of where I lived, for my child's sake and for later on, I needed legal proof.

It was important Marty accepted responsibility. He agreed and signed the papers. He left first for Alaska.

A few weeks later my theatre company buddies helped me pack, sell my truck and take me to the airport. It would be the end of my life in the USA for many years to come.

Fast forward, after working on the conference, teaching part time at the TAFE and finding my own little house in Nambucca; Marty decided he would come to Australia to be there for our child's birth. Marty arrived from Argentina and settled in with me. We decided about a month before Denali's due date that we would get married.

We had our legal marriage in a Macksville courthouse in March 1988. My Aboriginal 'family' and a few work colleagues came to our house afterwards to celebrate.

Figure 22. Marty Schmidt and author Mt. Shasta, California, USA 1987, photo by Jo Anderson

My new friend—a strong Aboriginal woman named Tracy—gave birth to her son Jerara, in the same small Macksville hospital a few hours before I gave birth to Denali. We were there together to share our joy for a few days, and the hospital was generous about letting a lot of visitors come to our rooms. It was a small, eight-bed maternity ward in rural Australia.

Less than a week after Denali's birth on April 27, 1988, Marty left again for his second assistant guiding job in Alaska. He wouldn't be returning for at least three months. I was recovering from an emergency C-section birth as well as coping with being a new mother on my own. But I was lucky and blessed. In a sense, I was in better hands and had more support in the Gumbaynggirr community than I would have had in the States. We could talk together ('have a yarn') about everything, including fears, doubts, challenges, and we could have a good laugh at ourselves.

There were no cell phones or internet then. Without my asking or messaging them, often when I needed help, within an hour someone or a few Gumbaynggirr would arrive outside my door. Sometimes they stayed the night, sleeping on cushions on the floor. They cuddled Denali, kept me cheerful and made sure I ate enough since I was 'feedin' him. Children as well as adults came by, so I was never really alone. Uncle Ken Walker, one of the elders, came by, too. He and his wife, Auntie Ruth, would say Denali was "a little Gumbaynggirr boy." He was quiet in their arms.

As soon as I recovered enough, I placed Denali in a front carry sling and walked to the beach. Very few people walked in Hyland Park in those days. We mostly had the beach to ourselves. There was no way to communicate with Marty. No SAT phones and mail took weeks to arrive.

Figure 23. Hyland Park, Nambucca Heads, NSW, Australia 1988

Denali was a delight although he had colic for a few months which taxed my energy walking him up and down. I could bring him to work with me and my Gumbaynggirr 'family' would be near me and take Denali for walks if he woke whilst I was teaching. It was a bonding, happy time for us.

When Marty returned to Nambucca, he was restless. He had plans to expand his guiding business, but he had nowhere to train or guide in Australia.

He wanted to go to New Zealand. He had met some Kiwi climbers who told him about the Southern Alps in the South Island. He started making plans.

I was enjoying my routines and my students. Denali was able to be with me and the pace was relaxed. The landscape and beach around Nambucca and Macksville were soothing to me. My own work was also expanding. Tracy told me about her sister and many other Gumbaynggirr children who were taken by 'the authorities.' They were kidnapped on their way to school or from the mission and never heard from again. Her mother believed she was still alive somewhere and "calling out" to her.

A certain group of former 'Stolen Children' were helping reconnect families. They called themselves, Link-Up NSW. Tracy put them in touch with me.

Figure 24.

Until the 1970s, other Gumbaynggirr women had their babies taken from them at the hospital right after they were born. They were told their babies had died, but never saw their bodies. Then, they were told to go home. They had no rights in those days and no recourse. They didn't know how to go about proving they had children or finding where they were either taken or buried. They naturally were inconsolable. They had to find out exactly what happened to their babies and where they were. They needed help.

Whenever my Aboriginal colleagues tried calling government or church offices, they would be diverted and given the runaround. They weren't sure what questions needed to be asked.

One of my jobs back in Washington DC after Georgetown, and before I went to New York, was working for the investigative reporters Jack Anderson and Les Whitten. They had a number of independent projects going along with their daily columns in the *Washington Post* and a slot on the *Good Morning America* TV show.

In an unassuming block of row houses, they launched the Assassination Investigation researching the Kennedys and Dr. Martin Luther King assassinations, and the National Suggestion Box which solicited ideas for investigations and improvements the government should be involved in. I started as a researcher and moved up to be the head of a small team of investigators for the National Suggestion Box. These skills I learned would be of benefit to my Aboriginal family and colleagues. I agreed to make some calls. I started with the Catholic diocese offices. They kept meticulous records, mostly handwritten. They were also more forthcoming hearing my American accent and the fact that I was a graduate of a Jesuit run university. I was making progress by the end of September 1988.

A PhD researcher from UCLA came over to do a study on rural Aboriginal communities. He brought his young son with him and needed someone to take notes and assist with his surveys on the mission. Somehow, through connections with the Macksville TAFE, I was recommended to assist him. His grant provided for paying me for the month he would be in our community.

I met the doctor and his son at the TAFE where we arranged our times and places to interview. He had some simple tests and questions to ask children aged 7-12, but he needed their mother's or parent's permission. I enlisted Auntie Jessie, one of the respected Gumbaynggirr elders whom I knew, to help us. She would be the first approach out of respect to the families before we asked them to participate. She approved the questions we formulated. This arrangement proved fruitful. Once again, I could bring Denali with me. He especially enjoyed being with children. He was still "nursing" which made it easy to feed him no matter where we were.

We interviewed families in Bowraville and Macksville and the small former mission area in Nambucca where the Ballangarry family started a Gumbaynggirr language and culture center. I was learning first-hand the extent of the Gumbaynggirr and Dungutti tribal relationships, but I knew I had heaps more to learn. The more I knew, the less I knew I knew.

Meanwhile, Marty made plans for New Zealand and for guiding on his own over the next season on Aconcagua in Argentina. He wanted to break into the European guiding scene after guiding in Alaska. Our goal was to move to New Zealand, if possible, after Denali was a little older.

Unbeknownst to me, Marty had asked his parents if I could live with them while he was gone. He wanted to save money. I could foresee trouble ahead. His parents grew up in Nazi Germany. They were both part of the Hitler Youth Movement in different sectors. His father served as an officer in the German army. He was awarded an Iron Cross for his service. Marty's mother worked for Nazi officers outside of Bergen-Belsen concentration camp during the war. Her family was prominent in the Bremen local government in Germany. Marty's parents didn't meet until they had immigrated to the USA. I didn't know about his parents' background *until after* we were married.

Figure 25. Leo Schmidt (Opa) Denali and author in Castro Valley, California, USA 1989, photo by Marty Schmidt

Marty encouraged me to find a way for us to stay in New Zealand. He was self-employed and not in what was categorized as an 'essential business' nor did he possess what the New Zealand government considered an essential skill. We wouldn't get more than a tourist visa based on his work.

I decided to apply to become a Waldorf/Steiner teacher. An Austrian/American man, Carl Hoffman, was the Director of teacher training at Taruna College in Havelock North, New Zealand. Coincidentally, he had been a class teacher at the Washington, DC Waldorf school years before. He encouraged me to join the following year's class intake in January 1990. We could see the campus and meet him when we came over at the end of 1988. It seemed my life was pointing in another new direction, in another country.

Once again, I was sorry to be leaving Australia and my Gumbaynggirr family. I did promise to continue helping them with finding their stolen children, no matter where I was. They told me they would "sing me back."

As it turned out, it would be a number of years before we returned with our two children to Gumbaynggirr country, but we did return.

Denali was crawling about by October. He was alert and making all sorts of sounds, including imitating the kookaburra birds which perched on our back porch every morning. Marty was busy selling household items we wouldn't need and finding someone to buy our van.

Every morning I put Denali in a backpack Marty made and walked through the bush to the tranquil beach in Hyland Park. I would take Denali out to let him crawl around in the smooth, warm sand and hold him up to wade in the ocean waters. I wanted to make sure my little Gumbaynggirr boy remembered his homeland.

When we went to the train station with our luggage, our Aboriginal family came to see us off. I noticed we received some hostile looks as we hugged farewell. Prejudice was strongly against the Gumbaynggirr in rural Australia back in the 1980s. Australia had only recently granted Aboriginal people their full rights in 1984, under the 1983 Commonwealth Electoral Amendment Act. It wasn't until 1984 that all Aboriginals in Australia were given their right to vote in all elections.

Like some other cultures, Gumbaynggirr didn't really say 'goodbye,' they said "See yas." We would be back, but not for a while.

That night in Sydney we stayed with friends I'd made the first time I was there in 1986. She was an artist and puppet maker. She had worked with Tony B., a cousin of mine. They both worked with Jim Henson. Tony worked the puppet "Robin" (Kermit's nephew), and she was a puppet designer as well as a puppeteer. Her partner was a professional photographer. They were both Kiwis-originally from New Zealand. They had a three-year-old boy and lived in Bondi, a very different environment than rural Australia.

Denali was tired after the stimulation of his first train ride and new people. I was excited to see these friends and the city beach. Marty was in his element talking to everyone he met. We all knew we might not see each other again. All three of us, Marty, Denali and I, fell asleep easily on a large mattress.

My dreams of being in caves at Uluru started again. I woke up before sunrise, curious. The city lights made it difficult to see the night sky or the stars. I wondered if the dream was letting me know I hadn't finished my work in Australia. Maybe my Gumbaynggirr family was already starting to "sing me back."

We had the whole morning in Bondi before we had to leave for the airport. Traveling was less stressful in 1988. There were no checkpoints, no personal or bag screenings. You and your family and friends could go right up to the gate to greet or send off your loved ones.

It was a less complicated time.

Figure 26. Tracy holding Jerara, author holding Denali and Paul Knox Jr. in Bowraville, NSW Australia, photo by Marty Schmidt 1988

8. KAHURANGI – NEW ZEALAND

L and of the long white cloud is the formal translation of the Maori name *Aotearoa*, for the north island of New Zealand. We had been here briefly at the end of 1988, when Marty had summited Mt. Cook or *Aoraki*, for the first time. We returned for my studies at the end of 1989. The year between was spent travelling in the States and Europe together while Marty climbed. The first place we landed was Auckland. We were invited to stay up north for our first week in a place by the beach. My friends from Sydney had arranged for his mother to meet us and take us to her home in Kerikeri. It was a peaceful entrance to *Aotearoa*. From there we headed south to Hastings.

By now our son, Denali, was walking and starting to talk. We were waiting to move into a small cottage on the hilly grounds of the Taruna Teacher Training College in Havelock North. It was off the main road up to Te Mata Peak. This peak is where one goes to see a panoramic view of the Heretaunga plains, and on a clear day the volcano Ruapehu. There is a fantastical story about Te Mata, who was believed to be a giant and the leader of the Waimarama Maori tribes. We felt privileged to live there.

I was to start my studies in a little more than a month. In the meantime, we were staying with a Waldorf teacher and her family in Hastings, New Zealand. Hastings is a flat, inland town with a concentration of Maori from the Ngati Kahungunu *iwi* (tribe).

Unlike the indigenous populations of North America, Malaysia and Australia, Maori were a significant proportion of the entire population. Maori had defeated the British, who sailed to try and conquer, acquire and colonize their islands. The Maori language was still a living language. Maori were represented at all levels of power and in all professions.

While Denali and I were getting to know the center of the town, I saw posters plastered on door fronts and in shop windows advertising, "A Night of Maori Cultural Dance and Music." Reading the bylines, I learned this particular performance group was named *Kahurangi*. What piqued my interest even more was that they were listed as performing overseas including in the USA and Canada. There was a performance that evening, and it was in Hastings.

Figure 27. Ms. Strewe, Denali and author in Kerikeri,
New Zealand 1989, photo by Marty Schmidt

As soon as we returned to our home base, I asked Marty if he could watch Denali for a couple of hours while I went to the Kahurangi performance. It was December—summer in New Zealand. The weather was mild, and the days were long. We made a picnic for supper in Cornwall Park. I slipped away while Denali was happily playing. Marty told me he'd come by in about two hours to pick me up.

When I found my way to the building where the performance was to be held, I saw two young Maori in traditional dress right inside the doorway. The woman had flowers in her hair, a beautifully embroidered bodice in black, red and white. She wore a long flax skirt and was barefoot. The young man was bare chested with a Samoan-type skirt that went to his calves. He had an engaging smile and welcomed me by using both Maori and English phrases. They asked me to sign the guest book and showed me upstairs to a large hall with a slightly raised stage. I was one of only a few non-Maori in the space. I sat near the front. I enjoyed seeing dance close up.

While I waited for the performance to begin, I perused the program.

It described the history of Kahurangi and included the names of all the performers, composers, choreographers and *kaumatua* (elders). As I was reading, an elder Maori woman came over to me and sat in the empty seat beside me. She looked at me and nodded. Then she spoke.

"You aren't from here are you?"

"No, we just moved here. I'm from America."

"Ah, good. But you won't know what they're saying if you don't speak Maori. I'll translate for you. You can call me Ybel."

"Thank you. My name is Joanne."

"Why did you come to this show? We don't get many *pakehas* non-Maori) here."

"I was a choreographer and a dancer professionally in America. I worked mostly in theatres in New York and California. I'm keenly interested in different cultures' dances and music. I read Kahurangi toured in North America and performed at the Apollo Theatre in New York City. I'm very curious to see this group."

"You say you worked professionally in theatres in America? Well, then tell me what you think of this lot. I want to know what we could improve. We have an important celebration coming up next year called Waitangi. The Queen of England will be there. This group with be performing. Aie."

"Well ma'am, if you ask me I *will* tell you. You don't know me yet, but I say what I see straight out."

"That's good. That's what we want to know. Are you here by yourself then?"

"No, actually this is the first time in over a year I am out by myself. I have a young son and my husband is walking him in the park till after the show."

"Ah, lovely; then I can meet them after, too. I'll introduce you to some of our *whanau (*family) at the interval. It's about to start now." The lights were dimming.

After each scene, Ybel would ask me what I thought. A few dances were based on modern steps and show tunes, and more which were what I thought must be traditional Maori songs and dances. Maori sing and dance at the same time. This requires different breathing and concentration than just singing or just dancing.

The most impressive scene for me was their use of *poi*. Ybel explained that originally these balls on string were made with flax, but now they used plastic and yarn. The girls twirled, slapped and wrapped these props expertly and effortlessly as they sang and moved in concert.

It was the first time I'd seen a performance like this one. I clapped enthusiastically after the show and spoke with Ybel for a few minutes before seeing my husband come into the theatre. My son started crying a little. Ybel turned around and waved them over.

"Ybel, this is my husband, Marty, and our son, Denali Schmidt."

I reached my arms out to hold Denali. I had missed him these few hours. He stopped crying and smiled at Ybel. She smiled back at him and then said, *Kia Ora* to both Marty and our son. She said some other words in Maori to Denali. At that point in time, I didn't understand what she said to him.

Ybel brought us over to another section where her husband and other family members were sitting. She introduced our family in English and again said more in Maori. Her husband was an Anglican minister and a Maori elder. Later, I learned he had served as chaplain for the 28th Maori Battalion during World War II. He served in North Africa, Sicily and Italy. He was introduced as Canon Wi. His full name was Wiremu Te Tau Huata. Ybel's full name was Ringahora Heni Ngakai Ybel Tomoana.

The Canon asked me if I would meet the director of the show I just watched. He said he could arrange for me to go up to where they rehearsed. He and Ybel said it would be good to have a professional from America talk with them. I looked at Marty and he agreed. This was the start of a life-long relationship with the Huata *whanau*, Kahurangi and the Ngati Kahungunu.

On the day and time arranged, I stood outside the building Canon Wi had indicated was the rehearsal space and office for Kahurangi. A number of rough looking guys were milling around the entrance. I hesitated a moment and one of them said, "Kia Ora, you the American coming to see Tama Huata? I'll take you up. He's waiting for you."

"Huata. Is he related to the Canon Wi Huata?" I asked as we ascended the stairs. The old building smelled musty.

"Yeah, he's the Canon's son. His office's right here." He showed me into an office with a large desk and a couch with a table in front. The table was piled with papers. There were framed photos of performances and playbills from various shows in different parts of the world.

Sitting behind the desk was a man with a stocky build, untamed curly salt and pepper hair and a moon-shaped face. He was looking straight at me. He didn't stand, he simply indicated I was to sit on the couch. I thanked him and sat down. He asked me about my family background, performing arts background and what I knew about Maori. Then he stood up and said, "Let me show you our rehearsal in progress."

We went to a large hall where about thirty performers were standing; others were sitting on the floor in the back, and some elders were sitting on chairs on the sides. The Canon was one of the elders who was seated. The Maori man and woman who greeted me at the performance were in casual clothes and up front conducting the rehearsal. They acknowledged my presence as we walked in.

Tama ambled to the front and said a few words in Maori. Then he motioned for me to stand next to him and he spoke in English.

"This is Joanna from America. She's gonna be observing today and giving you some directions. *Whakarango* (listen up)."

He caught me off guard. I didn't think I would be running any part of a rehearsal for which I didn't know the language or movements. I was on the spot.

"*Kia Ora*," I managed. (From the beginning, please.) Tama counted off in Maori. "*Tahi, rua, toru, wha ...*" (one, two, three, four)

The entire hall filled with sound and motion. I could see some general movements and patterns which needed refining. Some of the performers were holding back while others were showing off. They weren't quite working together yet. They didn't blend one movement into another; they still looked like a "set" of moves added to another set. I noticed this during the performance I'd seen, too. But they were all talented and able and had energy streaming into their bodies and voices. The temperature seemed to rise.

They were a very attractive and strong ensemble. One of the young men stood opposite me in the front row with a face of fury. He stepped forward. I could smell alcohol on his breath. He was holding a long, spear-like prop. He was continually behind the count and disrupting the line.

"Again, please." The troupe commenced singing with the movements I knew now to expect, but this one man was still behind. It seemed like he was doing so deliberately.

"Stop," I shouted over the music. "You need to start together. Make it crisp, clean ... move all as one. Again."

They started their singing and moving once again. The same young performer was more than two steps behind.

"Ok, stop." I knew I was being observed by all the people in that room. I had a choice to make. I could let it slide that this one, strong, alpha male Kahurangi performer was slack, or I could address him right now as it happened. The wrong move and I could alienate everyone. I took a deep breath. I moved closer to him and swiftly lifted the spear from his hand before he knew what I intended. Simultaneously I shouted in a sharp, strong voice right in front of him.

"Again, 1, 2, 3, 4 ..." The music recommenced. The group started together this time. I held onto the *taiaha* (Maori name for the spear). "Stop. Good. Just the beginning ... again."

Now, the young man was angry, but he was able to keep in step. After the third time doing it correctly, I quietly handed his *taiaha* back to him. Out of the corner of my eye, I saw the Canon nod and smile slightly. I exhaled slowly and deeply. After another thirty minutes, Tama paused the rehearsal to give them a break. We went back to his office. This time he pulled up a chair on the other side of the small table. He sat facing me.

"Watching you, even though we come from completely different backgrounds and training, I'm amazed how similarly we rehearse."

Tama paused.

"I had no idea how stupid I looked," he said.

We scrutinized each other's faces for a moment. Tama burst out laughing and I joined him. He had a backhanded sense of humor.

His father, Canon Wi Te Tau Huata was coming down the hall toward Tama's office. He walked slowly with a cane, and he wore thick glasses. He looked up from under them as he entered the office. Tama moved so his father could sit facing me. He went back behind his desk.

"Kai te pai, kai te pai." (It's all right, all good)

"Tell me Joanna, what is your father's full name and where was he born?

I told them my father's full name when he was born was Giuseppe Georgio Patti. Later, his father died and his mother remarried; his legal name in the United States is Joseph George Munisteri. He was born in Rome, Italy although both his parents' families are from Sicily and Sardinia. There is a "Patti" town in both places. My father was made a US citizen after he came over to New York. He lives in Texas with my mother, Theresa Josephine Grasso. Her family is from around Naples, Italy. She was born in the USA in the state of Connecticut."

"*Aie, aie.* Hmm. It seems our *whanau* may have killed some of your *whanau* during the war. I was in the Maori battalion during the Sicily campaign in World War II."

I shifted in my seat and waited. I wasn't sure how to respond to his observation.

"I'll choose a Maori name for you, but I have to think about this one."

Figure 28. Canon/Reverend Wi Te Tau Huata, 28th Maori Battalion, Egypt 1943

He and Tama started speaking in Maori. Then, Tama switched to English.

"What do you think? Think you can work with Kahurangi? You handled yourself well with Pene. He has a bit of a problem with the drink sometimes, but he's a strong performer."

"Yes, sir I think so. I'll have to learn more Maori though."

"*Aie*. You'll learn if you want to. Can you work with us at least until the Waitangi Celebration in February? The year 1990 will be the 150th year anniversary of the Treaty of Waitangi signing with the British. We don't have much time."

It was December 1989. My teacher training course started after Waitangi Day. Marty would be in Argentina all of January and February 1990.

"I would like to very much, but I'll need to find childcare for my son. My husband will be working out of the country in Argentina. He's a mountain guide."

Canon answered first.

"You can bring your boy to rehearsals. There'll be many hands to help here."

I considered the possibilities and potential problems working with Denali by my side and having less time to settle into our little cottage and prepare for my studies. A voice deep inside urged me to go ahead.

"Alright, yes. I'd be honored to help you get ready for Waitangi."

"Good. I'll take your word on this and you can take ours. We'll draw up formal papers next week. We would want you to sign a Confidentiality Agreement, eh? You would be the only *pakeha* choreographer and tutor. The *kaumatua* (elders) would need your word that what you see and do with us is kept private. Is that clear to you?"

"*Aie*. I will honor your code of silence. It's not so different with Sicilians."

We laughed together. The Canon rose first.

"Now, we need to formally introduce you. One of the *whanau* will walk you on and do the *karanga* (the traditional call). She'll tell you what to do and what not to do. Just follow her."

And so, I did.

Figure 29. Waka launching Waipukarau, New Zealand 1990, photo by author

9. THE INFERNO CLUB – ASCENSION ISLAND

"You will be going through Brize Norton-RAF Royal Air Force base in Oxfordshire. This is not a country, it's a military base. UK, US and some other military members, mostly from South Africa and local nationals from St. Helena. They call themselves, "Saints." They have their own way of speaking English. A Creole English, really. You'll catch on quickly working with their children."

"Which passport should I use?" I didn't realize there were still parts of the world which were not part of any recognized country.

"The Commander is from the US Air force, so it's best if you use your American passport. They will photograph you for an ID at Brize Norton and you will get your briefing there for the first three days. You cannot leave Brize Norton once you've checked in and you will be assigned a room in the transient barracks. You will be given your flight schedule once you're there and are permitted two pieces of luggage, no more than 30 kilos each. Do you have any questions?"

"Not at this time, sir."

Inwardly I had hundreds of questions, but I knew this was not the person, time or place to start asking. I grasped the handle of my large suitcase and wheeled it to the waiting shuttle bus. Once up the steps near the driver, I saw a couple of women who were in civilian clothes. They looked at me curiously. *They must be "Saints"* I thought and smiled at them. I know it is not protocol to smile in military situations or on bases but I figured I had nothing to lose. One of them shyly smiled back.

They had very attractive faces which had hints of features from the East and maybe from Africa. They both had long, straight, black glossy hair. I read that the "Saints" were a mix from the sailors and women who were left or drifted off somehow to St. Helena from boats and ships travelling between South America and Africa, or down the coast from Spain to Southern Africa. Sailors had come from

Brazil, Great Britain, China, the Philippines, Spain, the Netherlands, Germany, France, Portugal, India and various African nations. No one really knew their origins I was told, since there had been a mix over hundreds of years, but the result was a beautiful people with almost every racial ancestry. Supposedly, Ascension Island was uninhabited before the British East India company started using it as a stopover, as they used St. Helena Island for hundreds of years, too. In a way, just like their ancestors, we are all still indentured workers who may only enter and exit with permission from our "bosses."

My last few jobs were in the Gulf states and Northern Africa. I had a year contract in Casablanca—yes, back in Morocco—during the bombings just blocks from my apartment across the courtyard from the Yeshiva and around the corner from the Jewish Quarter and Synagogue.

Figure 30. Marrakesh with colleagues in Morocco 2007, photo by Ahmed

This was my first kinesthetic exposure to suicide bombers. Two brothers had blown themselves up in front of the American Council

School and the American Consulate. They were recruited from the *bidonvilles* (slums) around Casablanca. There were four other bombings within a six-week time period. The whole atmosphere in Morocco changed for the worse.

The Gulf countries were more peaceful. I took a short-term contract in Manama, Bahrain followed by being recruited as the team leader for the United Arab Emirates (UAE) for an ambitious project they named, *Madares Al Ghad* (Schools of Tomorrow).

Figure 31. Manama with Lebanese colleague
in Bahrain 2007, photo by Amina

When a new *sheikh* (leader) came into power in the UAE, he determined South African and Canadian educators should replace Americans. My contract was pulled. I had to find another job.

In those countries, I had to cover my hair and most of my body most of the time, as part of the "uniform for women" no matter what the weather. These countries had no labor laws and no rights for non-citizens. At least with the US and UK contracts there was some recourse if they didn't honor their agreements.

My room has four beds, but I am the only one in the room when I check in. After locking the door, I take out my contract and read all the fine print again. I am a "relief" teacher and may leave for family emergencies and approved holidays but only with permission. The following information is also in my contract papers.

"There is no cell phone service on the island. BFBS (British Forces Broadcasting Services) for "Her Majesty's Armed Forces" is the only television and radio on the island. No civilian programming and no personal USBs, flash drives, CDs are permitted in Ascension Island government offices or workplaces."

Segments from the old TV program with Patrick McGoohan called, "The Prisoner" came to mind. Isolation on an island mid-way between Brazil and the Horn of Africa in the middle of the South Atlantic Ocean with only one restricted airfield run by two of the most powerful militaries in the world. Wild what I signed up for this time. Still, apparently there are children, a school and a clinic where I will be working. It is only for five months. It's a challenge I can rise to, I reckon.

The whole island is only 34 square miles. The highest elevation is only 860 meters, which is not even 3,000 feet. You could bicycle almost everywhere there is a path although I understand most of the island is lava, igneous rock and difficult to navigate if you want to climb or bike. Ascension Island is one of the most unusual places on the planet with unique animals and microclimates. I might also get to see the famous green sea turtles who lay their clutch of eggs every three to four years after a six-week swimming journey from Brazil to Ascension. Exotic and determined creatures who only exist in three locations: Brazil, the South Atlantic Ocean and Ascension Island.

I need to case this terrain for the next few days. I wander down to the main building. The RAF provides free phone calls for military members and there are a few men in uniform talking with their backs to the public. I overhear one telling how he "just got back from the Afghan." He appears nervous, thin and he is coughing. I pass them by to find the mess hall, a strange name for a place to have your food, but more accurate than the 'dining facility' Ascension Island (DFAC) since most people there scoff their food down and don't have the luxury of 'dining.'

There are sentries in front of most buildings here and some of them are women. They are sturdy looking, carry weapons and most of them happen to be pale and blond, paired with a male sentry who is usually taller and sturdier. I show them my badge and they pass me through. I am one of the few civilians on this part of the base.

The day we are scheduled to fly out we are required to be at the departure building five hours before the flight. This is not a commercial airport. There are no shops, no anaesthetizing music piped in and few places to sit.

The Saints women motion me over to sit by them. I gratefully lug my large suitcase and drop into a serviceable deep blue seat. We chat about "the Island" as we watch the flight schedule panel. We are already delayed from the original departure time by three hours. It is going to be a long day.

On one large screen is BBC News and on the other is BFBS (British Forces Broadcasting System) news. One screen is speaking about a "draw down of troops" in Afghanistan and the flight schedule screen is full of flights to various bases in Afghanistan. It is almost humorous.

It is dark by the time the huge pot-bellied plane takes off. There are many more rows of seats across than on commercial airlines and most of them are filled with soldiers going on to the Falkland Islands. There are women who are air hostesses (no men) on this Omni flight. They go around giving out blankets, ear plugs (not headsets) and saying, "Thank you for your service." There is no provided entertainment, but there is lots of processed food. I try to get comfortable, place the earplugs in both ears and close my eyes.

As we approach Wideawake airfield I am wide awake looking out the nearest window.

It is pitch black all around the small island and lights illuminate only one side of the island. We bump to a landing and I follow the Saints to a section of the airfield where we have to wait in a literal cage until the military escort arrives. It's warm and windy and the ground crew is efficient and quick. Our bags and the plane's pallets are unloaded; the plane is checked and takes off again as we wait to be escorted inside.

Figure 32. NASA base Ascension Island, South
Atlantic 2008, photo by author

As the plane climbs back into the night sky I suddenly feel very far away from everything and everyone I know. I check my cell phone. No signal.

British military open the cage and we are released to retrieve our bags from a trolley just outside the only airport building. I see a young, fit looking Saint's man holding a placard with my name. We nod at each other.

"You must be te Yank teacher? I'm Colin, teacher at the Two Boats School. Welcome to Ascension. Here let me help you with your tings."

"Thank you, glad to meet you."

I had heard the Saints had their own way of speaking English which included dropping the "th" in many words.

"Got your kit? My truck is over here. Nothing is very far. Be at te barracks in a tic."

Colin pointed out the British and the American military sections, the Commanders Hill, the main street of Georgetown; then he drove up to the civilian barracks which were small apartments joined in a row facing the range, a night club and down to a beach. He parked the truck in the alley behind the fourth apartment. This was to be my new home.

"Here's your key. All should be in order. You have your linens, towels in te hall closet. Put some food in te fridge for you and te stove goes off gas in te bottle under te sink. Do you know how to turn on te gas for cooking? Yes? Good. Bottled water is delivered every week. You should have enough tere for a bit. Don't drink te tap water. I'll be by at 7:00 a.m. to pick you up and take you to te mess for breakfast and ten te Ministry office. You have a landline phone tat goes through te main island switchboard. All calls off te island are charged to your account, but all calls on te island are free. Goodnight."

"Goodnight, Colin. See you in the morning."

I latched the door after he left. My brain is spiraling with all the information Colin delivered. I sit on the lumpy couch and catch my breath.

I realize I didn't know what time it was on the island, but it must be late because most of the other apartment lights were off. It would be Tuesday and probably around 10 p.m. I set my alarm for eight hours hence and open a window so I will hear when people are stirring. It is pleasantly warm, and the breeze makes it easy to fall asleep.

Dreams came easily. I had different scenes of my children when they were younger and of hearing strange sounds in my closet and seeing a large rat circle around my bed, then climb up and start biting my big toe. It seemed so real I felt pain as the rat took his first bite. I sprung up out of my dream, fully awake to see a real rat actually biting my big toe. The rat and I locked eyes for a nanosecond before he/she scuttled back into my closet.

Startled, I hobbled to the bathroom to clean the wound, then hunted for my purse to find bandages. The rat didn't scare me as much as the thought of rabies or some other vile germs entering through the broken skin. It was still early, so nothing would be open to civilians.

When Colin drove up to my door he saw me limping and hopped out to lend me his arm. Quite a way to start my first day.

"What happened to you? You right?"

"Well, really strange but I was fast asleep dreaming of a rat biting my toe and woke up seeing an actual rat biting my toe. Hope he or she didn't have any nasty diseases. Are there many rats on this island?"

"Didn't used to be when we had cats, but te cats were killing te birds so tey exterminated all of tem. Now we have a rat problem, see? Tere is a rat catcher on te island. He should be at breakfast. He's a former Special Forces fella. I'll find him for you."

We walked in together to the mess hall. It was more like a dining room with small round tables with tablecloths. I sat down while Colin went to get breakfast for both of us.

"You Yanks like coffee, right?"

"I like both tea and coffee, but if they have strong coffee I'll take that this morning." Colin returned with two trays and a big, brawny, red-haired Scotsman.

"This is Angus. He used to be a 'Black Rat' and now he's a rat catcher."

Angus laughed and shook my hand.

"Can be coming round 16:00 this avo, if that's alright?"

"That's great, I really appreciate this."

"My pleasure." Angus grinned, patted Colin on the back, then went back to his table of mates.

"What do you mean when you said he used to be a 'Black Rat'?"

"Member of te 4th Armoured Brigade, was in Iraq, catches some big tuna fishing here, too."

I ate my breakfast and looked around as discreetly as I could. There were only adults in the British mess and almost all were men.

"Where are the children and the mothers on the island, Colin?"

"Children live with teir parents in housing near where you live. Everyone but children must have a job here to stay here. Once children reach sixteen, they have to go back to St. Helen's or te UK or wherever teir family come from."

"Why can't they stay till they are eighteen and finish school?"

"Don't know. It's always been tat way since tey started te school here about fifty years ago, I tink. You about ready to go see it?"

Colin was kind enough to take my tray so I wouldn't have to walk any further than necessary. We got back in his car and drove up to Green Mountain. The throbbing pain in my toe was much less.

The Two Boats School was on top of a hill overlooking some of the island. Children walked to school with or without their parents and were able to play in the outdoor playgrounds, sit by the fishpond or just see their friends until the bell rang, a real bell not an electronic buzzer. At the first bell, all the students from kindergarten through high school lined up by class outside before being dismissed by the head teacher to start their day.

My first impression of the children was they were polite, relaxed and orderly. They knew and followed established routines and were easy with one another. They were a mix of Saints and British children; however, the Saints form of English seemed to dominate on the school grounds. Most teachers were Saints, but the head was a stern, pale, tired looking woman, most probably in her late forties. She seemed out of her element. Colin brought me over to meet her.

"Good morning M'em. Tis is te new teacher just arrived from America."

"How do you do. Ms. Joanne is it?"

"Yes, thank you. I'm very pleased to be here."

"Well, you have your work cut out for you. The teacher for the high school humanities had a bit of a breakdown and didn't prepare them at all for their exams. You will only have about three months to get them ready when they should have had all year."

"I'm up for the challenge. Is it possible to observe today?"

"That's what I prepared for you. You will shadow Ms. Yon, and Colin here, will show you around before his first class. You are the first American teacher they've ever had here. This is a small island; please remember that Ms. Joanne. This is an Ascension Island government school, but we are run like a British school. I read your CV. You do have some experience with the British system and exams, eh? It won't all be new. We have a faculty meeting after school today. We'll catch up with you again later. Welcome."

She turned on her heels and walked back toward the school office. Colin blew a whistle, and the students began to recite a school motto and the teachers took attendance. Then the entire school community sang, "God Save the Queen." There was a moment of silence and then each class filed out with their teacher. It was impressive how respectful the children were to their teachers and each other. This reminded me of the way it used to be in the USA, many years ago.

Colin found me and started the tour.

"Over tere is te old NASA facility. It's on te Devil's Ash Pit. From up here you can also see 'Te Inferno' Club. It's supposed to be off limits for our students, but sometimes you'll see te high schoolers over tere. You can see te airfield and communications center from here."

He pointed to a far set of buildings. "Tat's te clinic. We don't have a proper hospital. Over on te other side is te Devil's Riding School also supposed to be off limits to children. Up tere past te airfield is Commanders Hill. Tere are two residences for te different brass. Te

Brits and te Yanks. Tere are sections of tis island tat are technically off limits to us, but I'll show you later, eh? Now the easy part, we'll go have a look at te classrooms and te rest of te school. You can meet the oter teachers, too."

"Beautiful up here. I'm grateful to you, Colin, for showing me the ropes. There's a lot to learn."

Colin looked at me seriously. "Yes, more tan you realize."

He motioned for me to follow him and then turned back to me. "One more ting. Rules here are from te military, not te island government or the UK or USA. Lots goes on here tat doesn't really concern us, see? Best to keep to your work here and at ta clinic ... if you know what I'm saying."

"Think I do, Colin." We looked at each other intensely for a second and then continued on to view the school.

At lunch break, one of the assistant teachers, who was also the mother of two boys in high school, came over to sit with me. She was friendly, very pretty and warm hearted and had a different accent. She explained she was from the Seychelles islands but came here with the visiting UK dentist and stayed with her boys. She was concerned her eldest son had not been prepared for exams. She was keen for him to gain one of the scholarships to finish high school in England. The dentist was not their father but her second husband. She called her sons over from where they were sitting with their classmates.

"John, James ... this is Ms. Joanne. I want you boys to mind her and learn all you can. You help her out, too. Hear me?"

"Yes, mum. Nice to meet you, Ms. Joanne."

I smiled and shook their hands before they ran back to be with their mates.

"Fine looking sons you have. Don't worry I'll make extra efforts for all the Year 2 students who are sitting exams this summer. That's my main reason for coming to this island."

The first few weeks I was introduced to anyone "of consequence" on the island: the Commander, the British officers, the American civilian contractors, the Bosnian contractors, the chaplain and the clinical staff. The communications sectors staff, Special Operations rehabilitation unit and the missile silos crew mostly kept to themselves. They were on for only six weeks at a time, so there was a high turnover. They spent their off-work hours at the pub down near the airfield.

Hell's Kitchen and The Inferno Club were their haunts. Satanic names were the standard on this God-forsaken Island.

There were only a few kilometers separating where the children were and these dens of depravity. The Inferno Club was less than a kilometer's walk for most of the residents on Traveler's Hill, where the Brit military bunked and the civilian quarters where I lived. We could hear the bass music pounding until three in the morning most nights. The patrons stumbled out, some vocalizing their rowdy emotions, other vomiting, spitting, or guzzling more alcohol outside on their way back to their rooms.

For some, the mission on their last night on the island was to get as drunk and debauched as possible before getting on the plane out. Going for an early morning swim was one way to fix a hangover. The sea water and strong current smacked you awake.

One of my new colleagues from the UK was originally from Nigeria and had never learned to swim. I agreed to teach her, giving us both motivation to 'hit the beach' every afternoon for at least an hour. I love swimming and diving, especially in warm water. This was the paradisiacal aspect of the island. She also had a car which was a real luxury on Ascension. I usually walked or biked everywhere but some of the best views and most spectacular hikes were miles away, and it was already hot, sticky weather in April.

On Saturdays and in the late afternoons, I worked in the clinic or administered acupuncture treatments privately for those who requested my services. There were active servicemen and a few veteran women from the British teams who had some serious pain management issues and wanted to wean off pharmaceutical drugs. Insomnia was a common complaint. A number of the military men who had lost limbs and were recuperating on the island had residual or phantom pains. A few were in severe pain, pain referred to in Traditional Chinese medicine as 'steaming bone pain.' They would try anything for relief.

Figure 33. Green turtle tracks on Ascension Island beach 2008

One woman, a former soldier, had critical post traumatic reactions. She was in a terrible emotional and physiological quandary because she needed to speak to someone about what she had witnessed and executed during her time on active duty, but she felt bound by secrecy protocols. She was married to a former SAS guy who was re-training as a butcher on the island. They'd had their first child a few months earlier. It was a tricky situation. I treated her to the best of my knowledge. Soon she started to improve. Her baby had a sweet, cheerful disposition and I relished going over to their apartment. She preferred I treat her there rather than at the clinic. Lots of secrets were maintained and buried on Ascension.

My students were responsive. I pushed them in their exam preparations and included them in the choice of the end term school play. Together we chose, *The Tempest* by William Shakespeare, an ambitious and very relevant piece for us to attempt. It was also one of the plays they would be queried on for their exams. This part of my job was the most enjoyable and rewarding. I was also assigned to teach music and decided to have them learn theory through singing in parts, harmony, and movement.

To raise the stakes and the standard, I chose music in four languages: Xhosa, Latin, Maori and English. There was some resistance from the head who didn't believe our students were capable of such a demanding repertoire. She suggested I was, "Setting them up for failure," but I respectfully disagreed and pointed out my aim was, "Setting them up for success in a public forum." The songs were from South Africa, New Zealand and England. The Latin hymn was the famous, "Panis Angelicus," translated as: bread of the angels, from the *Sacred Solemniis,* written by Saint Thomas Aquinas. They were to perform the challenging two-part round in concert. I felt we all needed as much divine assistance as possible to balance the demonic influences swirling around life on the island.

The high school students were keen. Some students preferred the Maori action song, others the plaintive South African song about the children's march massacre during the Soweto uprising. Others preferred the hymns. I made it clear from the beginning everyone could sing and we, together, would create beautiful music and stirring rhythm. I believed in their potential and was a rigorous taskmaster, but we also had a lot of fun in those rehearsals.

Social life on the island was more active than I imagined. There was a fiercely competitive chess club started by the two doctors at the clinic, a diving club, fishing, biking, a hash/hiking group which had as their motto: "Drinkers with a running problem." If you wanted you could participate in cooking for potluck dinners, Pictionary once a week, fitness and training, island golf on sandy not grassy 'greens,' environmental tours, turtle watching, gardening, a library, church service once a week, and one of the new teachers opened a small café. All these diversions were in addition to the clubs, which were open every night hosting dancing, drinking, darts and fights.

In 2008, there were no large screens in the clubs, no cellphones, only SAT phones, landlines and portable radio communications. The night sky and dawns were spectacular on Ascension. I walked up to the school at night when no one was about to use the internet. There was no way to connect in our accommodations, but the connection in my classroom was reliable. This was the only way to consistently be in contact with my children. I would nap between 7-10 pm, then stride up the road under the stars and work until one or two in the morning. At that hour, almost no one was out, and the Inferno club was closing down.

Those quiet periods on the island and the occasions when I was able to go to the uninhabited side of Ascension to hike and explore, were times I treasured. I often felt the unique energies and the pristine, extraordinary majesty of the island.

Yet there was always an edgy, troubled undercurrent pulsing through, producing what many called, "A Beautiful Hell."

There was a company store on the island for civilians which featured every sort of spirits (alcohol), tinned food, junk food, frozen meats, packaged breads and root vegetables brought in by plane. Locals sold fresh tuna and other fish, privately grown vegetables and crafts. If you wanted more variety, you had to be invited to the DFAC (short for dining facility) on the US military side or the British "mess" for meals. Fortunately, I was invited fairly often and that saved time on cooking and cleaning as well.

Daily routines and working in two different sectors filled my days. The first two months passed quickly. Rumor had it that a new American Commander and his family were due on the island quite soon. My means of inside news was through the conservation manager who was like a park ranger. He had been on the island for over fifteen years. We became friends when he and I spoke about experiments using different types of algae/seaweeds while I was on Glovers Barrier Reef in the Caribbean. He knew so much about the flora, fauna, microclimates and sea life of the area. I was fascinated. He was permitted access to parts of the island most people were not. Often, he was able to take me along.

"Te turtles be coming soon," he told me. His name was Michael, but most called him "Mick."

"Tere was a fella here to study tem do some proper research, but he was one of tem fey men, see? Te don't like tat sort here, you know. He looked pretty bad beat up when he got on tat plane ta next day." Mick kept walking up the trail we were on, hardly missing a step.

"Whoa, this is fantastic up here. Why is it so much greener, almost like a jungle?" I caught up with Mick as we neared the plateau area on the hill above the British barracks.

"Tey created this, see? Brought up lots of water, changed the climate just here. Twas one of teir experiments. Your NASA used to do lots of tem all te time. Tey still have one station on te oter side of te island. We can go tere anoter day if you like?"

"What other types of experiments did they do here, Mick? Do you know?"

Mick looked concerned for a moment.

"Can you keep quiet. Not really supposed to say, see ... but someone should know."

"Know what exactly?" I asked carefully.

"Sometimes tey bring people here. Tere are underground places. Holding cells. I seen tem taken down tere but don't see tem brought up, see? Tat Colonel, you know ta one you play the games wit? He's been here a long time. He goes down to tose places. Wouldn't be goin diving wit him, Jo."

"Why not? He seems pretty harmless, just a little absent minded. He does like his drink, though, doesn't he?"

"More. He likes te women, but he seems to have bad luck wit tem. Five of his oter girlfriends here went diving but te all got te bends or had some sort of accident. Most of tem were Saints' girls, too ... see."

"Were?" I probed. "Did they die?"

"Yup. Te colonel said one, just blew off his boat in a storm. Te oters had 'accidents.' Faulty gear. Strange, eh?"

"Yes," I agreed. "I'll stick to swimming and snorkeling in the coves."

"And see all tem towers and electric lines in a grid down tere?"

Mick pointed to an unusual configuration of tall posts, cables, electrical lines and bubble domes.

"Aren't they communications equipment for the BBC or something?"

"Well, tey say tat see, but do you know about Nikola Tesla and te HAARP?"

"What's HAARP?" I asked, curious.

"Stands for High Altitude Auroral Research Program. Weater weapons. Deadly powerful, too."

Mick's new information spiked my interest although I knew I had to tread gingerly and not appear too inquisitive. Yet, he clearly wanted to confide in someone. Everyone knew I was only there for five months. I was also from the outside, not military and not British, or from St. Helena Island. I could fly out in a few months, and no one would ever see me nor I see them again, in all likelihood.

We rambled around the 'jungle' area, took some photos, then began our downward trek. It started to drizzle just inside the area where we were hiking, and not around us or down below. Mick and I looked at each other and he nodded. Colin was right on my first day. This was a place where what you thought you knew, you didn't. You had to learn all over again.

We could see a new plane load of men disembarking on the landing field below us. They carried bags of gear and most were in uniform.

"New lads are in."

Mick quickened his pace. Luckily I always was a fast down climber. I enjoyed the slide, crunch of the switchback downhill.

"Are you coming to see the high school play and concert next weekend?"

"Might do." Mick paused to look out to the Atlantic all around us.

"Please do. It would mean so much to the students. They look up to you."

"Might do." Mick resumed his pace again. I was tracking as best I could.

We went our separate ways when we got to the sand golf course. No one was around, so no tongues would be wagging about us spending time together.

Next morning was Saturday, my day at the clinic. My colleague needed acupuncture and the nurse there asked to see a treatment. She was from Scotland and married to one of the radio communications engineers.

"Morning," she said brightly. "Mind if I have a wee look?"

"No, not at all. Here are the needles I'll be using."

The nurse looked them over with a puzzled expression on her face.

"They're so thin! How do you grip them?" she asked.

"Takes lots of practice, actually. You have to hold them like this." (I demonstrated with some of the longer needles.) "And there are various techniques for insertion depending on the body type, skin type, depth of your needling, whether you are going into the muscle or near the bone and so on. It takes years of perfect practice and placement to really become adept at it."

"Right." The nurse surveyed my colleague when all the needles were placed.

"Does it hurt?" the nurse asked my colleague.

"Not at all. Feels like little rivers really."

"Oh, how curious." The nurse bent forward to have a closer look.

"Alright, just relax here for thirty minutes and I'll be back to check on you. Go ahead and close your eyes." I drew the partition curtain closed.

"Thank you!" My colleague was on her way to sleep. The nurse and I crept out of the room.

"Can acupuncture help with migraine headaches?"

"Yes, however I would have to know how long the patient has had them and other particulars of the type and duration of pain. I don't have herbs here, but I can help with pain and even lessen the frequency of most headaches. It's a condition I've treated heaps of times."

"Would you mind ..." the nurse said slowly,"if I brought someone to you confidentially, who suffers from migraines? She wouldn't want anyone else to know."

"Confidentiality is very important to me," I assured her. "She could come in tomorrow afternoon. Very few people are at the clinic on Sunday."

"Cheers, Ta. What about two o'clock? Most people will be at the beach."

"Fine by me," I whispered.

While I was waiting, I did some research online about migraines and what Chinese traditional medical texts called: 'wind evils' and 'damp conditions'. They are called 'agues' here, as Shakespeare noted in his plays, producing aches, pains, fevers and chills. The weather was fickle and forceful. People coming in from the cities or the military bases in various deserts were caught off guard by the warm, salt winds at high velocity and the chill of being damp at night and in the early mornings.

Figure 34. Command Hill, Ascension Island,
South Atlantic 2008, photo by Mick

I was very busy with work at school and with patients after hours; yet I was quite happy being occupied. The high school students were progressing well and had finished their exams. My own daughter had just finished her last exams and would graduate with honors from high school in Texas. I was given leave for a week to attend and celebrate with my own family in Houston and then return.

While we waited for exam results from the UK, we refined our rehearsals for the performances on the island, the next weekend. I was excited for these students. They had visibly improved and improvised on my original directions. Their parents were sewing fine-looking costumes; the younger students helped with the sets and the chaplain loaned us his portable keyboards and percussion instruments. There was cooperation within the Saints community and many of the Saints teachers and workers came up to ask me "how tings going?" or to let me know they had heard positive comments about our show.

A few of the Saints parents worked in the pubs on the island. One young and very attractive mother was the bartender for The Inferno Club. Her thirteen-year-old daughter inherited her beauty and was at the club most nights helping at the bar. Her mother was quite strict, she told me, about her daughter not drinking or 'fraternizing' with soldiers or any of the contractors. She kept her eyes on her daughter and in a genial way let the patrons know she was 'out of bounds' for rude comments or fighting.

Her daughter had a curfew of eleven at night and one of the other Saints men, who was part of their extended family, walked her daughter home and made sure the door was locked. This had gone well for three years.

The night after the successful performances of *The Tempest* and "Music from Across the World" at the high school, the Inferno Club had a huge bash and 21st birthday party for one of the Brit military men on base. The carousing was noisier and wilder than usual. I could hear the celebrations most of the night into the early morning since my windows were open.

About four in the morning, I heard several men shouting and a few women shouting back. I didn't want to go outside since these matters were usually settled by the parties involved and there was nothing I could do. The fire officer was at the pub anyway and there was no law enforcement, just military police on the island. Most of them were at the Inferno Club most nights.

Then I heard crying. This was a sound seldom heard, even in the elementary school during the daytime. I heard harsh whispers and some man commanding them to "Be quiet." I assumed whatever the trouble was, it was taken care of and not my business.

The next morning was Monday. I had less than two weeks to go on the island before I would fly back to the States, see my own grown children and prepare for my new position at the State Medical University in Yerevan, Armenia a landlocked country in the Caucasus.

As I was about to leave my unit and walk up the hill, the only lawyer on the island, a woman from Edinburgh whose children were in the school, was at my front door, knocking.

"May I have a private word with you, Joanne. Before you go to the high school?"

"Certainly, come in."

"You may have heard there was an incident last night that involved two of your students at the Inferno Club."

"No. I heard commotion but didn't know."

I was shocked and alarmed but tried to listen as carefully as possible.

"The two girls won't be at school today and maybe not the rest of the week while we sort this out. Fortunately, they have finished their exams, haven't they? At the moment, there are no real legal protections for children on the island. I'm working on it, but this would be a first if we try and bring it to trial. Their parents are also considering their options."

"May I ask what happened?"

"Sexual assault of a minor." It happened in the ladies' toilet at the club. We know the soldiers involved. They are being flown off the island today."

I was a bit stunned. If they were being flown off, how could there be any complete investigation or meting out of justice? I felt it wasn't the time or my 'place' to inquire further about that part of the story at this point.

"Was it Marie's daughter?"

I pressed, saddened when I realized it must be her.

"Yes. Her best friend, Chelsea walked in and went to get help for her, but it's all rather a hot mess, I'm afraid. Shouldn't really say anymore at this time. I'm sure you understand. It's best if it's not spoken about in class or at school by the adults. We want to remain professional and not distress the other children."

"Yes, of course," I responded, as if on automatic pilot. My inner self was gradually absorbing this terrible news.

"We appreciate your discretion, Joanne."

The solicitor pursed her lips, but I could tell she was doing so to remain stalwart, herself. We all knew these girls. We knew the victim's mother as well. The work at the club was her only income as a single parent. Most likely they would be forced to leave the island now, too. Most likely there would be no punishment for the men involved.

Ascension was/is a military base essentially, not a country. It has its own set of rules both written and unwritten. Many of these rules are fair but some have simply evolved as traditions and are designed for military aged personnel, not children. Children have no rank on the island. They are part of the "resources" according to some. They were considered exploitable and exploited, most often with impunity.

The solicitor was an assertive, bright, and capable lawyer with excellent credentials. She would be going up against decades of silence, stubbornness, skullduggeries, and closed ranks. I prayed for her success, even on the grounds of the Devil's Riding School.

The first bell rang. I collected my materials and my thoughts, then walked steadily up the hill to the Two Boats School.

I realized how fortunate I was. Soon I could leave the island and had another contract in another place. These Saints were not so lucky.

The second bell rang as I approached the entrance. The winds carried its tones over the island and out to the vast South Atlantic Ocean.

Figure 35. Closing night The Tempest Two
Boats School, Ascension Island 2008

10. HAYASTAN – ARMENIA

You can taste the air in the city this afternoon. It is moist, ashen, gritty and chilled. No snow yet around the towering Christmas tree erected opposite the National Museum, but people are dancing to blaring, electrified Armenian folk music. An announcer is shouting encouragement and at awkward intervals instructing them to stop while technicians adjust cables and microphones.

The wind picks up and the music is carried further over Yerevan streets and buildings. I shiver since I neglected to wear a hat believing the milder winter weather would persist into evening.

Looking for shelter, I spot the National Post Office not far from where I am. Outwardly it seems quiet, so I march over to the hefty wooden doors and push my way into the heated building. The guard in a glass cubicle at the entrance is discussing 'women' with two gray-uniformed police officers. He scarcely nods in my direction.

I enter a large vestibule with hanging chandeliers. There is only dim light no matter what time of day, but I can discern a long, oval, onyx table looking as if the Last Supper could be set there. A beatific stained glass angel hovers, watching from the back center wall. She is clothed in a long, draping, velvet, green gown with her hands out-stretched toward two doves facing each other. One dove in profile has an added contemporary envelope in her mouth implying the posts here will be delivered by heavenly messengers.

I stride forward to the high marble counter and find a place in the line designated for "regular mail." This is such a homogenous society that any outsider can easily be spotted. A tall, blonde Russian woman tries to cut into line raising her voice to the postal worker sorting through piles of white envelopes on the floor. I wonder if my few letters will ever make it to the airport let alone onto the correct plane for their destinations.

Everything appears to be in disarray. Fraying plastic woven bags, dirty dry sponges for sealing envelopes, low lighting so workers and customers must squint constantly. Handwritten signs designate which lines are for particular services. Most of the time the signs are in fact, incorrect. They use scales which must be tapped or banged to coax a digital weight. Sheets of stamps overflow cluttered drawers. The ubiquitous "stamping" sound indicates any receipt is made official with the smell of cigarettes, alcohol and human sweat. There is constant construction noise in the background.

The women serving postal customers peer up over their glasses and gracefully respond in Russian to the rude foreigner. She receives three answers from three different women and with a harrumph stands at the back of the line to wait her turn.

It is a long, orderly line by Armenian standards. People barely speak to one another yet almost breathe together. A few chat over their cell phones while others pretend not to listen.

At times like these I am grateful for only understanding some of the language. I can drift off until it is my turn and concentrate on observing.

It is almost twilight outside. The last daytime rays attempt to illuminate the stained-glass portal just in back of the main counter. The angel with flowing hair, eyes gazing heavenward in a forest green background, is soothing to me in such a discordant environment.

Was this once a chapel? I wonder. There is a subdued echo in this building giving it a strange reverential quality. Now, instead of sending messages on bended knees to the divine, we are here standing, paying money for someone else to deliver our messages on paper. My sense is I should still pray for my messages to get through. I take these minutes to inwardly ask for guidance and favors. Certain places, even entire countries, merit more contemplation than others.

Hayastan motivates me to remember God more often whether it be a plea for safety, or a reminder of ethereal beauty. Here I pray for courage, deliverance or gratitude, or—in a nanosecond—all of the above whenever I attempt to cross a street in any Armenian city. They still don't have reliable, working traffic lights in this former Soviet country.

However, the doctors and medical students I teach stand up when I enter my classroom. They maintain a respect for professors and teachers that we used to have in western countries. My students are earnest, conscientious and spark me to create new materials for them and find fresh ways to teach.

Figure 36. YSMU medical students in seminar, Yerevan, Armenia 2008

There aren't enough textbooks but there are copy businesses in Iran. Once they can obtain a book, they can copy it and send it back to Armenia and out to Iraq, Syria and Lebanon. Often the quality is poor, and all are printed in paperback. But at least the information for medical and technical texts is disseminated. Knowledge is shared.

Here books are almost sacred and hard back copies are lovingly displayed in beautiful wooden bookcases with glass doors. Here, children are able to walk, skip or run about freely since there is virtually no crime against children. Here I miss my children terribly no matter what their ages.

My son, Denali, was able to visit me here for two weeks in the Golden Autumn months of October into November. We were able to travel to the ancient stones of Karahenj and Tatev, walk on the Silk Road, peruse the paintings of the outdoor Vernissage market, sample delicious Armenian and Georgian food. Most importantly, Denali was able to meet artists who inspired him and encouraged him. He went to their studios, spoke with them in English and witnessed their craft. Arman Hambardzumyan and Vrej Kassouny were the most influential. These men showed him by their actions, passion and skill that you don't need a lot of money to be an artist and to live fully.

Figure 37. Karahunj, Syunik, Armenia 2008, photo by Denali Schmidt

It was in Armenia that Denali made a vow to pursue his passion, his calling to art. We drew up plans together for his next steps to gain entrance to an excellent university in America. Denali left Hayastan strong in his resolve.

I gaze at this angel in the post office once more and strive to recall the phrase for purchasing stamps. I don't have much time because there aren't many days left before Christmas.

My letters include an invitation to my daughter Sequoia, who is about to turn 18. Sequoia graduated from high school the previous June. She had just started studying business at the University of Houston. I want to show her around Armenia, for her to see another culture from the East. My students and colleagues would like to meet her, too. Maybe meeting in a neutral place will ease her fury. She is still angry with me about the divorce. I am hoping we can restore the love we used to share when she was younger. Her attitude and coldness grieve me deeply, but I cannot force her to make an effort. I honor her request to "give her space." My father counsels to "give her time."

It is almost my turn. Hayastan is a country abandoned by its allies, yet strong in its resolve to cherish its culture, language, and religion. A country of rugged beauty and vibrant spirit. A people who have known deep melancholy and passionate love. A country I have come to love, too.

Once again, I pray silently. I pray my expressions of love are delivered intact. "Dear God, please let my letters arrive safely at their destinations."

I send my thoughts upward and trust this angel in Armenia understands.

Figure 38. YSMU students with author, Armenia 2009

Figure 39. Denali Schmidt and author, Armenia 2008

11. FESTIVALS OF WATER – ARMENIA

It is after midnight, so in anticipation of a shower I kneel by the bathtub and turn the faucet on full. Gurgles, grudging drips and swishing sounds come but no pressure and not enough water for a cleansing spray.

I am told this is usual in the summer months since a combination of maintaining the city fountains and the new amusement park have diverted this most precious resource for more than half of each day. I plan accordingly, but it is after midnight and still no water in my apartment since seven o'clock the previous morning.

Tomorrow is the "Festival of Water." In Armenia this is a festival of transfiguration celebrated with water, by water, about water once being turned into precious wine. However, to me tonight, it is water and not wine, which is most precious, most needed, most desired.

Returning to bed steaming hot and sweating, I drift into a semi-sleep until birds and neighboring infants awaken me with their cries.

The sun is already burning the rooftops by 8:00 a.m. I hear glee in the little one's voices as they rush out after breakfast to their play in the courtyard under the grapevines and slender ash trees. They whisper and shout, waiting together until the first unsuspecting adult walks by the back steps pretending to be shocked as the children pour a full jug of water onto his back, soaking his blue cotton shirt. He waves his hands at the water bearers, and they all laugh. Their target continues past them to the street while the children quickly refill their containers, waiting to ambush the next person to venture by the back steps.

In the courtyard I hear children collecting water in every container they can find: plastic liter bottles, ceramic jugs, empty tin cans. I am amazed and curious. Where do they find this water?

On the sixth floor I am privy to the movements below. I fantasize about having all the containers of water lovingly thrown on me but settle for retrieving my "emergency" stash of 5-liter plastic bottles to wash my face and clean my teeth.

Everywhere in Yerevan children, teenagers and lovers of mischief are pouring, spraying and throwing water over each other, but I, as a conspicuous foreigner, am not included in the revelry.

Perspiration streams down my back and through my scalp. My hair is stuck together so I decide to go to a place where there will probably be water aplenty, the beauty salon.

On the way I must walk through an urban arch where a young lad is squirting everyone with a hose. He catches my ankles as I pass. I smile at him, forgetting for a moment the unwritten law of grim which is strictly adhered to in Hayastan. He looks at me as if I am a fool and maintains a somber stare as I cross the street. He has cooled me down and I am grateful.

The salon is not busy today. I am able to be ushered in right away and in halting English am asked if I would like a shampoo first before a trim. Ah yes, I nod vigorously and am escorted to the sink area where I savor the sound of running water and active spray nozzles.

The hairdresser grins, clicking his tongue behind his teeth. Bending down behind me he tucks a towel gently under my collar and curling stray wisps of my hair with his index finger. Gently he tips my head back into the sink, where for a moment I feel suspended in air. He turns on a tap testing the water temperature with his palm until he is satisfied the sensation will not burn or chill me.

He caresses my hair as he drenches long strands and then massages oils into my scalp cradling my head and causing me to smile again with his quips about life with his new baby, about his failure to lure fish with the phlegmatic worms his cousin gave him. Then he tempts me with vivid descriptions of Middle Eastern delicacies which his mother makes for him every Friday. Rinsing with a sensual steady stream of warm water, he whistles a melody from Lebanon and with a skill few women possess, twists my soaking hair into a circle atop my head as he carefully wraps a soft towel around me to keep my neck and face dry. I feel cared for and cleansed by this fellow who washes and trims my hair. I am transfigured by his acts. I do not need wine.

He leads me to a comfortable, high back, vinyl covered chair in front of a full-length mirror. Unraveling the towel, damp strands of my shoulder-length hair fall easily while I watch like a spectator as he flicks on a mini-wind machine and curls each section over a hairbrush; simultaneously drying and styling. Soon my face is framed with clean, tamed, colored hair.

I am grinning at his work but only for a moment since my cell phone unexpectedly begins emitting electronic pulses prodding me to push in a key and hear the deep throated voice of a colleague who is in need of a sympathetic ear. We agree to meet by the fountains in Republic Square as soon as I am finished.

I must decline an offer of fresh mint tea or watermelon juice since I am now pressed for time.

It is about midday when I arrive at the fountains. I hide behind one of the large pillars by the national museum so I will not be saturated before my meeting. There I catch sight of my colleague lumbering toward me and am about to warn her as a young lad rushes by and drenches her with cold water. She shivers in surprise and stands upright, indignant.

I stifle my laughter before cautiously approaching her. For the first time in public, I see her beaming. Indeed, she is transformed by her grin. This is an event I could not have foreseen ... a celebration for the "Festival of Water." I feel truly revived.

Figure 40. Republic Square, Yerevan, Armenia 2010

There is little time for revelry; however, I am obliged to attend a reception at the US Embassy. My second year of working with the medical university, named after Heratsi, is almost over. My colleagues urge me to stay another year. They desperately need funds for continuing a conference we initiated at the Center for Medical Genetics. It is a worthy cause, but I must make my plea to the ambassador.

We have met before, madame ambassador and me. She started her post the same year I did, 2008 and she will continue into 2011. While she has complimented me on the programs I implemented, she has consistently turned down any of my requests for more funds or more time. In addition, she is an outspoken Obama supporter. I keep my political views to myself, but I don't agree with policies or points of view I believe are contrary to my beliefs and principles. At this point in my life, I am not the best at presenting a poker face, which is one reason I eschew embassy parties.

Nonetheless, I am in a better position to press our request forward if I go in person and hobnob at the outdoor reception this evening.

My colleague walks me back to my apartment, dripping as she goes. We agree to meet after the reception at the Artbridge Bookstore Café in the central district of Yerevan. Artbridge is one of my favorite places to relax, drink and chat in the city. My son enjoyed it, too when he visited during my first year working in Armenia. As often as possible I try to sit at the same back table where we shared meals, discussed the merits of original artworks displayed throughout the store, and his next steps in life. Denali was inspired by the art he saw in Armenia.

People dress up for most occasions in Yerevan. An embassy reception requires one of my best outfits, make up, and fashionable shoes. I will have to avoid any areas where children are tossing vessels of water. I hail a taxi on the main street and roll up the back window, hoping my hair won't be windblown before I arrive. The new embassy buildings are over the bridge out of town and built like a fortress.

Figure 41. Denali Schmidt at Vernissage, Yerevan,
Armenia 2008, photo by author

Quietly I prepare myself for the real possibility that the ambassador will turn down both my requests and those of my supervisor at the university. In that case, I will have to leave Armenia at the end of the summer and apply right away for another position.

After passing through the checkpoints and presenting my US passport, I am joined by my local national contacts working in the embassy. They are smartly dressed and heavily made up. The reception is well attended, but it is easy to spot the ambassador. She has a clearly identifiable way of speaking and she is a redhead. There are very few red headed Armenians.

I spy two of my medical doctor colleagues hovering around the lavish buffet. In Armenia, as in many countries, doctors do not earn a high salary working for public hospitals or clinics. They work long hours in poor conditions and rely on tips and favors to meet their expenses, especially if they have a family. They don't have enough supplies or up-to-date equipment and keep hoping to gain funding from US and NGO programs.

I pushed a few of my medical resident students to apply for internships and further study in the US and the UK, if their English was proficient. My high rate of success in preparing them for the applications, medical boards and interviews was noticed by the embassy. There is a large Armenian diaspora in America. They wield considerable influence for such a relatively small voting population. One of the doctors waves me over.

"Oh Joanne—Jan. Good to see you here. We spoke to the ambassador about keeping you with us next year, but I'm afraid she said it's not possible. As it is, most from your program only stay one year and this is your second."

"I will be sad to leave here, you know. Excuse me for a minute. I see she is free, and I need to talk to her about the conference."

"Go, go … the conference was a big success, *che*? It should happen every year."

I edged my way in to be right near Marie. She smiled automatically hearing an American voice and turned to speak to me.

"Good to see you here. I've been hearing glowing reports about your work at the medical university."

"Thank you, Ambassador. If I may, we do need funds to continue the Center for Medical Genetics International Conference. It's incredibly important to have the network of doctors from other countries and expand on the research discussed at these conferences. This is a growing field."

"Well, send me an email with the specifics and the public affairs officer can get back to you."

"Actually, ma'am, I did send two emails over the last few weeks since the funding deadline is next month. May I call you to follow up next week, after you have time to read them? I can also resend the emails if you like."

The ambassador shifted her weight and gave me a cold stare for a second. I knew that look. She thought I had overstepped my "place."

"Give me a call next week."

A tall, stocky Russian-speaking man made his way to catch the ambassador's attention. It was my cue to leave.

"Thank you, Ambassador. I will. Enjoy your weekend."

As twilight faded to night, the lights of Yerevan brightened. I left the embassy in a car with some of my colleagues who dropped me off at the main square fountains. The fountains were illuminated with multicolored lights—iridescent blue, red, green and white. I stood listening to the whoosh of cascading water and hundreds of Armenians conversing, laughing, teasing, cursing and playing in the center.

It was a short walk to Artbridge under a clear, dark blue sky. In all likelihood, this would be the last *Festival of Water* I would be part of in Armenia. I might as well enjoy it. I called my friend and explained that I escaped the embassy party early. Providentially, she had her plans changed and was free. I assured her she wouldn't be ambushed again, but she was hesitant to meet me near the fountains.

"No worries," I laughed. "We can meet indoors and sit at the back table."

One advantage of leaving Yerevan sooner would be I'd have more time to spend with each of my children back in the States. Armenians have strong family bonds even though many have to endure their men going off to other countries to find work. Armenia relies heavily on remittance payments. Three generations often live in one dwelling. They know each other's personalities, idiosyncrasies and insecurities. Sharing love, time and money is part of their identity. They have survived for thousands of years despite numerous attempts to wipe them out. The Romans, Mongolians, Persians, Ottoman Turks and Azeris, their hostile neighbors, have all attacked and devoured Armenians and Armenian/Hayastan lands. Armenians call themselves "Hay." Hay is pronounced Hai. "Duk Hay?" asks, "Are you Hay/Armenian?" Hayastan means "*land* (stan) of the Hay (Armenians)." However, more Armenians live outside Armenian borders than inside. The rate of emigration has been constant since the genocide of 1915-1917 by the Turks.

Armenia keeps losing land to international treaties and agreements. The war in Ngoro Karabakh continues on the border with Azerbaijan. Armenia has no oil, natural gas or diamonds, but in the mountains, there are deposits of iron, silver, copper, zinc and gold. Armenia is consistently the world leader in chess. Their champions continually beat the larger nation's players from Russia and China. They also are known for being astute businesspeople. Armenian women are world renowned for their beauty, grace, and humility.

My colleague approaches with an Armenian friend. I invite them to sit with me. There are still free seats since it's early. Yerevan night life starts after 10:00 p.m. in the warm weather. A waitress comes to our table with a tray and three glasses. She places one glass in front of each of us and takes out her notepad to write our order. ArtBridge café is one of the few places where English is written and spoken in addition to Armenian and Russian. We all simultaneously realize we don't have menus.

"Oh, sorry." She is about to fetch them when she turns and asks us.

"Would you like something to drink first?"

Spontaneously, we answer in unison.

"Water, please."

Figure 42. Lusine, Jo, Denali and Hasmik, Artbridge, Yerevan, Armenia

12. CLOSE CALLS IN
KARACHI – PAKISTAN

When I arrive at dawn to the mustard-colored customs control, the airport is already swarming with porters, dusty taxi drivers, male family members and flies. I am so grateful my bags have arrived. A tall awake man comes forward to greet me wearing a crescent smile and navy blue *shalwar kameez*. He opens the door to the back seat of a shabby car. I slide in greeting the grim-faced driver with the accepted "Salam Alaikum."

The car windows are all half open, so breezes freshen my face as we speed into the vortex of the city of Karachi in the land of the "pure" Pakistan.

I glimpse trees with hanging swamp moss and scores of kites circling in the gray, pink haze of dawn. Still, I am so sleepy; this time I do not see the flocks of people crouching, walking, sprawling on platforms meant to display food later in the day. I just see swirls of color.

This is only my first hour in Karachi, my first visit to this part of Asia. My nostrils flare with concurrent smells—cigarette smoke in the car, beetle juice, exhaust fumes, decaying food, fish, the breath of a city where twenty million people breathe in confined space. My skin feels soaked from my own acrid sweat and the brash stares, disapproving or curious, from those we pass in the early morning, at the end of Ramadan.

But I am still wearing my western clothes. This initial day is a blur of being welcomed, given suitable attire for meeting, greeting new people, hearing folk music at a benefit concert for flood relief, sitting at a table full of assorted textures of food which they insist I try. My mouth is on fire, my eyes are watering and now I am fully alert.

Colleague drivers drive me to the beach after sunset where thousands flock to walk, to picnic with their relatives, ride camels, listen to car radios, wave plastic neon lighted wands, run kites with tiny lights up, up into the night sky, spiraling and diving above the Arabian Sea.

I collapse into a soft bed that night and fall asleep to the whir of a ceiling fan. There is no air conditioning because there is not enough power. This is a fact in Clifton and many other parts of the city. Generators are a way of life here.

Arising earlier than the other family members, I tip toe outside so my feet can feel the warm grass and sense the earth below. Now I have landed. Yet where am I? I place my feet shoulder width apart and begin a slow series of qigong exercises to ground myself in this strange location. I breathe in synchronization with my movements, and I relax.

My host family are Sunni Muslims. Three generations of women abide here. The grandfather was a doctor, but he died many years ago; the husband of the mother left her years ago and her daughter is about fifteen years old and eager to go to America. She comes out to greet me speaking English with a sing song cadence, a toss of her head and eager, bright brown eyes. She asks me if I like Pakistani style clothes. I tell her truthfully, I love all the colors, designs and textures I have seen, but I don't have anything comparable to wear.

Her grandmother, a grand dame, hears us and comes to the doorway.

"Good morning. How did you sleep?" she asks me, fondling her chin as she speaks. She has a hint of a posh British accent. Before I am able to reply, she chastises her granddaughter in Urdu and the teenager scurries away.

"Quite well, I was tired," I tell her. She smiles and ushers me into their dining room for breakfast.

We sit opposite each other as one of the house maids brings us tea and a variety of sweet biscuits. It is already quite warm and humid. I start sweating just sitting drinking tea.

"I hope you don't mind, a few of my friends will be coming over for a book club discussion later. We all speak in English and they would like to meet you."

"Certainly," I respond, though inwardly I am worried that this is the start for crossing a boundary in terms of my privacy. I will be the "object of curiosity." People will come by to "see the American" a sort of human in a zoo. This does not bode well for security and keeping low key. Yet how am I to refuse, living in their home and just arriving?

"I have some lovely clothes you may borrow. Let's see, what colors do you like?"

Hours pass and I am dressed in *shalwar kirta* (long top and long skirt) which are swimming on me and definitely not my style—a leopard spot pattern. A few women are sitting on the lounge sofas chattering animatedly in melodies of English/Urdu about books, politics, cooking and family.

Eventually the matriarch's daughter, who has lived in the USA and is a journalist, online and in print, walks in and takes me aside.

"If you want, we can go to some shops in Clifton to look for clothes or just material you like and have someone make outfits for you?"

"Oh yes!" I exclaim, eager to see more of this part of Karachi and find colors and styles which will be more comfortable and professional to start work tomorrow.

"Let me call the driver." She calls him and waves to her teenage daughter as we climb into the car.

"I want to come, too." Her daughter rushes over to the car and sits beside me.

"Great," I say, "You can help me choose."

As we climb up the ebony steps to what they call a "mall," there is a checkpoint with three severe looking police officers in gray uniforms. I am evidently a foreigner. They check my bag thoroughly.

There are many small shops under one roof going up three stories. We pause at a textile shop with bolts of multicolored fabric. The textures and designs are dizzying. A tall man dressed in plain black *shalwar kameez* strides over. I don't know what he is saying, but it appears he is trying to be helpful and points out fabric behind us. Mother and daughter are civil to him but shake their heads and indicate to me we should leave.

I'm a little surprised that a man would be selling or even managing a fabric store and say so to the mother.

"That is not just any man. That's why we had to leave so abruptly."

"What do you mean?" I pressed her.

"I can't tell you now. Wait until we get back to the house."

Our shopping trip is successful, and I find three combinations which the teenager assures me are the "modern style" Pakistani dress. The fabric flows and feels smooth, light and cool. They are all in hues of blue, my favorite color.

The Mother hurries her daughter into the house, and I pause to gauge where I am in the neighborhood. There are a number of men milling around the end of the walled driveway. Our driver starts shouting and gesturing for them to leave. Some of them shout back at him and it seems to be in a different language.

"Do you know them?" I ask.

"They are trouble." He answers. "Now they are gone, don't worry Miss"

"What language were they speaking?" I inquire.

"Pashto" he spits. "They are Pashtuns. You see?!"

No, I didn't truly comprehend but I nodded my head before opening the door. I carry my new clothes carefully upstairs and lay them on my bed.

The Mother stops by on her way to our communal bathroom.

"That was a success don't you think? Now you are ready for tomorrow." She smiled at me.

"Do you mind explaining why we had to leave that fabric store so quickly?"

She stepped inside my room and lowered her voice.

"Have you heard of the Taliban? Do you know what they do?"

"Not really." I replied. "I've read about them and seen pictures from Afghanistan, but I don't know much more than that. Please, tell me. Were those men Taliban? How do you know?"

"There are many Taliban in Karachi as well as in the border areas between Pakistan and Afghanistan. There are also many Pashtuns and other Afghan families here in Karachi. Most of them are not Taliban but escaping from the war. I will teach you to recognize Pashtun from their features and clothing. But the Taliban are very clever. They blend in and only sometimes reveal themselves by wearing the black head gear, sometimes black *shalwar kameez*, too. We've lived in this neighborhood for over forty years. People know who is working with these groups. They also know if there is a stranger, especially a foreigner, here in Clifton."

"A little like living in the mafia neighborhoods in Brooklyn."

"Maybe. But these people do it for beliefs not just for money. Sometimes, yes, they also do crimes for money, but it is always legitimized by declaring it is for 'the cause of jihad'. Many are very ignorant but fanatic."

"Can be a deadly combination for an 'infidel' like me." I said.

"Oh, they definitely think a divorced woman journalist like me is just as bad." She laughed and then adeptly changed the subject.

"Do you like the comedian, Jon Stewart? I think he is so funny and so handsome. Do you want to watch his show? We have internet downstairs."

"Not this time, thank you. I'm going to need the time to prepare with your mother for work tomorrow."

"Ok, see you later then."

The Mother went downstairs to her room. I turned on the ceiling fan. I could hear the generator switch on and then off again a few minutes later. The ceiling fan stopped. It was a 'brown out' and apparently everyone was used to the electricity going off for hours at a time.

"It should come back on soon. Why don't you try and rest? Aya will bring you up a nice cold glass of watermelon juice." The Grandmother is in her seventies but alert and solicitous. She is definitely the head of the household, and she will also be my boss for the time I am here.

Early the next morning I crept downstairs and out the back French doors to do some qigong on the grass. The neighbors were already awake and lively but the movements in slow motion grounded me again. When I finished, I noticed the granddaughter watching me. She scurried upstairs as I approached the door. I followed and tried on my new clothes. There was no mirror in my room, so I walked to the bathroom. The granddaughter saw me and giggled.

"What's the matter? Do I look that funny in these?"

"No, but you have the dress part on backwards."

I was embarrassed but better she caught it than the women I would meet at work. I thanked her and returned to my room. The granddaughter was behind me.

"Excuse me, here. We pin our scarves so they don't slip down or so we don't forget them." She handed me a large safety pin. I grinned.

"Thank goodness I have you as my teacher here."

Her mother called for her to eat breakfast and I took this as my reminder.

The maid and grandmother complimented me on my new clothes, and I felt ready to face going out into the city. We dropped the granddaughter off at her school, her mother at a private yoga class and then were driven to another part of Karachi to start work.

"Lock your doors." The grandmother advised me to keep away from the windows and recounted stories of carjacking, hostage taking and thefts while waiting in traffic. The driver seemed alert and wove between rows of cars to get us there faster. Whenever we had to stop, young children would come up to beg. Most often they were little girls, so thin their skin was hanging from their arms and face. They were persistent and brave, but it was too dangerous to open our windows to give them a few rupees.

The door we went in was in the back of the building and across was a large lot filled with empty stalls, wooden carts and covered by a huge canvas.

"Is that a market?" I asked my boss.

"Ah, yes but it's only open Thursday, Saturday and Sunday. It is for local people and not safe for us to go there. You can see it from the office window. We are on the second and third floors."

There was a man sitting on a chair just inside the door. He stood when we entered. He had a long grey beard, navy blue shalwar *kameez* and held a weapon which looked more like a musket from the 1800s than a rifle. I looked for a priming rod and wondered if the gun was even loaded. He being the guard did not inspire confidence or a feeling of security.

Just inside the door to the second floor a younger man with a heavy black beard wearing an all-white *shalwar kameez* and a white embroidered pakool cap on his head. He extended his hand to help the grandmother up and inside and put his hand over his heart and nodded to me.

"Mohammed, this is our new adviser from America to help us with our conference and teacher training. Please make her feel welcome."

"Salaam" I managed with a half crescent smile.

"Alaikum Salaam" he replied in a deep voice which surprised me. "Please let me show you our offices."

Mohammed was evidently respected in these offices. The people there almost seemed afraid of him when he knocked and walked by. He was ever so charming to me. Too charming, I thought to myself. His English was very good, and he had a British accent. As if reading my mind, he added: "I spent some time in London but not in America. What state do you come from?"

"Texas, like my son-in-law." The Grandmother answered for me. "We met there before she came. I've invited her to stay with me and my family while she is in Karachi."

"Tikeh" Mohammed nodded. In my mind I had already nicknamed him Blackbeard.

I was shown to a desk which had stacks of papers, a landline telephone and a standing fan next to it. My boss asked me to review the course outlines, the tentative conference schedule and lesson plans for a new program for high school students. It was stifling hot inside already. I turned on the fan and aimed it so it would not blow the papers around. Everyone there seemed to be absorbed in their own work. There were whiteboards filled with brainstorming diagrams, tasks assigned, dates due and personnel notes.

After about an hour I got up to move around and casually count the number of workers. There were three very beautiful young women, five mature looking women excluding my boss. There was one very young man, probably a student, who wore western style jeans, shoes and shirt. He was the most helpful right from the start. There were three other men in their late 30s, I supposed. One other man in *shalwar kameez*, was a driver and ran errands for the office. He came in and out of the office and sometimes brought in guests or other men who went to the back conference room. They hardly saw or spoke to me. It was better I remained unknown. I was glad I had the "proper clothes for a good woman" in Karachi. People were very judgmental just with their eyes, tone of voice and body posture toward me. I always had to be on alert. It was wearying at times.

After a few weeks of a consistent routine of consultation, observation, teaching, meetings, training, report writing, curriculum evaluation and presentations, my boss came to me with a project outside our usual zone.

"We have been invited to Liyari...or rather *you* have been invited with the head of the Access program. We will have dinner together tonight and she will tell you the plans. This is great progress for us."

But Liyari was one of the 'off limits' areas to me according to my security briefing. I called my embassy contact, the Marine security officer I had to report in with every time I changed location.

"You need to discuss this with the PAO. Can you come in tomorrow morning?"

"I'll arrange it and text you the time. Please put me on the list."

I walked over to a map of Karachi with district lines drawn and the names written in English. I searched for Liyari. The name was familiar, but I couldn't place why.

Figure 43. Wedding in Karachi with colleagues Karachi, Pakistan 2010

Since this was the first time the consulate in Karachi was open in thirteen years, and I was the first person on a Department of State special program who lived outside the compound, in the community; the protocol was I needed to text and/or call every time I moved location and en route.

It usually took much longer than I planned to arrive anywhere. When I was dropped off at the consulate checkpoint, they required me to check my phone in. I sat waiting for an escort to the inner offices of the consulate. A local national embassy employee greeted me and walked me to the RSO office (Regional Security Officer).

"Come in."

The RSO was a Marine and to the point.

"What's the movement?"

"I'm supposed to go with my local national colleague and her driver, to Liyari. We'll be going to an orphanage and school to attend an assembly, prize giveaway and share a meal afterwards with their teachers, and members of the mosque that supports the school. It should take about six hours."

"You realize Liyari is the district where Daniel Pearl was held and killed? I advise you not to go to that sector. Don't let some DC bureaucrat who has never been here dictate your movements. You need to push back on this one."

"Thank you, sir. I didn't know that was where Daniel Pearl was…"

"Look, any sense you will be in any danger, you tell the driver to turn around. Understand?"

"Yes, sir."

"From now on any and every movement, change of plans you make, change of location, means of transport, or change of driver— you text me before it happens."

"Yes, sir. I'll try and change the scheduled visit, sir, but I have to pass it with the PAO (Public Affairs Officer) and my boss here. They may not approve."

"We won't be able to help you in Liyari. Is this job worth your life? This is someone else's pet project."

"I appreciate your advice and taking the time to see me. I'll let you know what they decide."

We shook hands over his desk. I left to find the PAO I reported to at the consulate. She would probably want me to continue as scheduled. She lived in the American consulate compound behind the Marriott hotel in Karachi and hardly ever ventured out. When she did, it was certainly not to Liyari.

My boss wasn't even in Karachi. He lived in a secure compound in Islamabad. This project was for him to look good. A check in the box for expanding American presence and promoting English language programs in Karachi. He was in his early thirties and very ambitious. He put in appearances at events in the past, but never stayed for longer than half an hour. He said he literally couldn't take the heat. Most of the places where I had to work or give presentations were not air conditioned. The cars rode in were not air conditioned either. He and other US State Department officers would come in separate, black, air-conditioned cars with armed security, if they showed up at all.

However, I had to make a difficult choice. Would I be willing to be "terminated" if I refused? Not yet. I would search my soul and ask for guidance on this decision. I would also trust my gut instincts; they had served me well in addition to my other observational skills. The PAO sat in a glass-enclosed office with her computer visible to the main room. I waited outside until she saw I was there.

"Come in. Well, how did it go with the RSO?"

She swiveled her plush desk chair to face me.

"He advised against it. Did you know Liyari was the area where Daniel Pearl was held?"

"Oh, that was years ago. He was a Jewish journalist and very visible. Listen, it's already arranged. There will be over four hundred children, their teachers and community members there. You can fit in dressed in the local costume. They've never met or seen an American in person. It's very important to us this goes well. If there's any hint of trouble, just call. Don't text, just call me."

"The RSO said they couldn't help me if I'm over in that sector. How well do you know my local colleague? She's the one who is arranging our driver and security?"

"Oh, I hear she's very trustworthy and an asset to our programs. We sponsored her for training at a summer institute at Stanford and she is going to be in charge of the Access Program in Pakistan. We intend to reach one million children with English outreach programs. She doesn't want to take a chance that won't happen. You'll be fine. Besides, she gets rent money for hosting you. She needs the income. She's a widow, remember."

My senses alerted me. The PAO wasn't going to budge on this event.

"Text me as soon as you leave the house tomorrow morning. We'll be monitoring you and leaving the line open. Let me know how it all goes."

"What do you mean by monitoring? Do you have over watch or some kind of tracking or surveillance to know where I am, when?" I asked.

"No, not yet." She laughed without mirth. "Just a figure of speech."

Her body language indicated she was finished discussing. She swiveled back to look at her computer screen. Yup, she was done.

I was escorted out by one of her assistants. He was a young, handsome, and overly solicitous. I didn't trust him. He had been a fixture at the consulate before the current US officers rotated in for a year. He also had his hand in HR: who got interviews, which projects were put forward, which people were given visas. He was an excellent linguist and a smooth operator.

"Don't worry, m'em. You will be safe tomorrow. You can call me too, if the PAO is busy. Here is my number."

"Thank you, Asir." I dutifully pressed in the numbers of his cell phone.

The fact that Asir and probably all the local nationals working in that part of the consulate seemed to know where I was going was great cause for concern. Now I was worried.

As soon as I received my phone back from the guard, I called the Mother and asked her to meet me later to consult. She agreed. I valued her opinion and advice. She would be able to give me the more accurate read on the level of danger for me in Liyari.

My driver was waiting outside the checkpoint. It felt like a very long walk to reach the car. When I returned to the office, my colleagues were anxious to know the result of my meeting.

"The security advised against this event, but the PAO approved it. I still have my doubts and I don't have enough insurance!"

They laughed. I didn't.

"I will loan you a beautiful outfit for tomorrow. You can sit in the middle of the backseat, and no one will notice. We'll take the family car, nothing special and two cars from the school will ride by us back to Clifton. No problem."

There was a part of me that hesitated, yet I had a strong sense that going to Liyari, just once, would be alright and would ease the way for better rapport and respect if all went as planned.

They had offered me clothes as if wearing more fashionable garments was a charm against harm. I found this absurdly funny but kept my thoughts to myself.

The rest of the day I was briefed about the organization which sponsored the school, the orphanage, and this event. They told me about the Principal, who devoted his life to these children, all boys, who had no home, no parents. He took in many of those abandoned after their families were stricken by the dreadful floods earlier in 2010. Millions were displaced. He was also a Shiite. I then learned that my colleague who was to be the director of this new Access program was also Shiite. This made it even more dangerous since Shiites were most often targets of violence in Pakistan. Moreover, he had invited girls' schools to attend this competition in English, which I was to be part of at their school. If ever there was a recipe for potential violent reprisals, this was one. Once more into the fray, I thought.

More courage, planning, and luck were needed. As soon as I was dressed, I asked the Daughter for her approval.

"You look good!" She exclaimed and adjusted my dupatta.

"Good luck!" The Grandmother said. "This is a fine thing you are doing for that community. No one will ever believe that you, as an American woman, went to Liyari."

"I'm not back safely, yet." I smiled. "I, myself, don't quite believe I'm doing this. If anything happens there will be no sympathy for any of us and no support, you know."

The Grandmother nodded in agreement.

When the car pulled up, I sat down in the middle back seat sandwiched between two women colleagues. The driver was concentrating intensely as we drove out of Clifton.

"You look lovely. Very beautiful," They complimented me.

"You, too." I focused on controlling my breathing. I was already nervous although often this made me more alert.

There was heavy traffic as always. Cars honking, carts, darting motorbikes, children begging, colorfully designed trucks and buses, beaten up vans of all colors, pushcarts, the crush of morning commuters. The driver navigated through it all expertly and within the hour we were there.

As our car pulled inside the gates, scores of little boys in navy blue shirts and shorts ran toward us. Some of these children were so thin their skin hung from their cheeks. A few had open sores and rashes, but all were curious and animated. They extended their small hands to me and against all common sense of hygiene, I shook or touched their hands in return and smiled genuinely.

A few of the male teaching assistants came out and waved the boys away from us so we could enter the inner courtyard. The outside walls and gates hid a treasure. The buildings were basic but the care, compassion, heart of the people within was strong and noble. I felt a tremendous sense of love inside, it permeated the atmosphere. It was a quiet love but persistent. We were guided through the corridors, shown the large kitchen, dormitory rooms, then taken to the office of the principal. He rose to greet us in his humble workplace.

"Salam, welcome. We are so happy to have you as our guest."

My colleague and the principal exchanged greetings and a short conversation in Urdu. I noticed a few diplomas and verses from the Koran framed and hung on the walls of his office. There was a distinct sense of order on his desk, his shelves, his file cabinets and in the school.

For the sake of privacy and security of my hosts, I will not write more about this day. It was a paradigm shift in my experience of Karachi. It reinforced my decision to follow a plan even though it was notably risky. Once again, I realized my gut instincts were sound.

I have lived to write about it, although others have not lived to tell. Unfortunately, the school may have suffered from hosting me. A week after my visit, two of their teenage boy's heads were found in their rubbish dumpster outside. I wasn't told more, but I am sure all who worked and lived there were terribly grieved. We are not sure there is a connection, but it was the first time their peace was disturbed.

Figure 44. Ghulman Abbas School, Liyari, Karachi, Pakistan 2010

The stakes are very high in these locations. Collaborating in any way with those perceived as the enemy can be met with swift and horrific consequences.

A few months later, after traveling and presenting to teachers and ministers in Lahore, Rawalpindi and Islamabad, one of the teachers from a private Montessori school attended my talk in Rawalpindi. He invited me to meet his wife and family. She was also a teacher. He came over to the Islamabad Marriott hotel where I was staying. Our group was more than a little nervous checking into a place which had three terrorist attacks including a truck bombing in 2008, which targeted foreigners. It was entirely rebuilt by November 2010, and security was tight, but we still made easy targets.

My other US State Department colleague was a young attractive woman with pale green eyes and dark red hair. She had been in Pakistan previously a few years ago, posted to Peshawar. Her stories comparing times in the Swat valley and travelling in Pakistan then compared to now, were cautionary. She still took tuk tuks, wooden carriage taxis around town, although we had been warned not to.

"It's the fastest way to get around in Lahore." She said, "Besides, no matter what we do they still think we are sluts and infidels."

We slept fitfully and the next morning I went on my own to visit the Montessori school and meet the teaching couple. They were eager to enlist my help to support their school. After a hearty breakfast we three were ushered into an SUV by their driver and headed up the hills to Murree.

"You know, my wife attended a Catholic girl's school in Murree years ago. It was a very respected school in all the region. The noble Benazir Bhutto, former Prime Minister of Pakistan also attended this boarding school. Did you know her mother was an Iranian, Kurdish woman? The school was closed in 2007, the same year, sadly our Prime Minister Bhutto was assassinated on December 27th, in Rawalpindi."

"She was a brave and remarkable woman." I added. "Her autobiography, *Daughter of Destiny*, was a stunning insight to her path and her struggle. I specifically remember her recounting meetings with our current Secretary of State, Hillary Clinton and her premonitions of being set up for her own death. Her harrowing description of the torture and death of her family members and herself left a lasting impression."

"Ah, yes." His wife sighed. "How different our part of the world might have been had she not be unjustly treated and killed." We all were silent for a moment. The sound of other cars passing, and honking breached the quiet.

Her husband continued.

"The British built churches up in Murree and it's probably the only place in Pakistan where they are undisturbed, although religious services cannot be conducted due to our laws. We can walk near the grounds if you like?"

"Yes, I would like that and I'm glad you brought a good camera because I'm rather hopeless at taking photos, but I would like a few of this special trip with you all."

"No problem." He assured me. "By the way, we are almost there."

As I glanced out the window, I saw a makeshift food stall with similar painting and design to an American brand. Instead of KFC it was HFC and the words, "Halal Fried Chicks" was painted on the front. Whomever the owner was had a whimsical sense of humor.

Figure 45. HFC food stall in Murree, Pakistan 2010

The driver dropped us off near a market. We wandered around viewing the jewelry, carpets, wood carvings and horses. The three of us walked in the road, which wasn't crowded. The couple pointed out where British soldiers and officials used to reside. In fact, there was a military school and sanitorium built originally in the late 1800s. I was surprised at the co-existence of architectural styles and time periods.

Eventually we came upon a church with the name "Our Lady of Sorrows." The gate was closed, and we could see steps up the hill to the church and crosses painted on the fence as well as on the building. I felt a chill suddenly.

"How strange!" I said aloud.

"You mean that there are two Catholic churches here in Murree?"

"No, well yes, that…too." I answered.

"But it is quite a coincidence since I once attended a Catholic school in New York State named, 'Our Lady of Sorrows'. When President Kennedy was killed, I was in school, and the nuns had us kneel down and pray for the rest of the afternoon before we were released to go home. It was the first time I ever saw any of my teachers cry. Our family had to move to Texas the next year. I was afraid since I remembered President Kennedy was assassinated in Texas and he was Catholic and from the East Coast, as we were. I was only ten years old when that happened. I haven't thought about that day in a very long time."

"Isn't it tragic when the really good leaders are struck down?!" His wife shook her head from side to side as she spoke.

Figure 46. Horses in Murree, Pakistan 2010

"America has not been the same since the Kennedys were killed. All three of them, John, Robert and John Jr. and his wife and sister-in-law." I added.

Figure 47. Fatima Jinnah Medical University, Lahore, Pakistan 2010

We walked around the churches and passed an overlook.
"Oh, how beautiful!" I gasped, looking out to the Kashmir hills.

"Wait, just like that. Stay still a moment please." Her husband had his camera ready and snapped a few photos of me, then of me and his wife and finally his wife took one of me and him. As we paused, we all realized how thirsty we were. We hadn't taken water with us.

"Wouldn't you like a bite to eat now?" His wife asked me. I nodded affirmatively.

"Come, this way." Her husband started back up another hill and retrieved his cell phone. He started speaking fast in Urdu. I assumed it was to their driver. That evening they drove me back to the Marriott hotel.

I returned to Karachi, only to find I had been made too visible and possibly endangered my colleagues and my host families, as well as myself.

I was given about an hour to pack. A different driver took me to the Marriott hotel near the Karachi consulate.

There, for the last time the Mother came to bid me farewell. We had our own adventures together including a bike ride early on Sunday morning through Clifton all the way to the beach. She went out of her way to take me to various sectors of the city at night to find a bicycle "walla" who would rent us working bikes. I rented a red bike. She gathered a number of families together to go with us. It was to be an "eco ride." We decided it was better the embassy didn't know until after we were home safely. It was a martial ride but without incident.

Figure 48. Eco Bike Ride, Karachi, Pakistan 2010

The Mother arranged to get me the papers I needed to leave.

The PAO told me it might take weeks, but it took hours. The

Mother knew who to bribe and this hastened my exit. The Mother and her daughter were looking for a way to leave Karachi soon, as well. The RSO arranged for my transport to the airport. I was not sorry to leave, just sorry not to be able to contact those who supported me and possibly risked their lives to help me.

Because of the way I had to exit Pakistan, I wasn't able or permitted to let people know in advance, nor could I say, "thank you" in person. I hope by writing this story, some of those people may hear or know how grateful I am to this day, for their hospitality, patience, hard work, and sheer perseverance in extremely challenging conditions.

I won't forget the brave and conscientious people I met in Pakistan including my Pashtun driver who shielded me and saved me on more than one occasion. My tasking put him in danger, too.

The teachers in remote areas who invited me to their homes and their schools, guided me to local landmarks and landscapes, served me delicious food and protected me from harm, will always be in my heart and memory. They work in the most difficult conditions imaginable.

Although they will not be known on social media or the internet due to restrictions in their country and the need for anonymity, these are the people who will make a lasting difference in the next generations in Pakistan.

They are the true unsung heroes and secular saints.

13. THE NEW SIBERIA – RUSSIA

"**A**ny chance you haven't filled your 'hard to fill' positions? I'm free to go overseas again, Megan."

"In fact, we do Joanne. We can't find anyone suitable for one slot in Russia."

"Russia. Can you tell me a few more details?"

"It's an advisory position based at Novosibirsk State Technical University (NSTU)with a responsibility for ten of the other universities in the area. I can send you the site description. Your previous RELO (Regional English Language Officer) from State (US State Department) was just posted to Moscow. Can I let him know you're interested? We need to fill it right away."

I paused for a moment to look up NSTU online. It was all in Russian, a language I didn't speak or read.

"Yes, you can let him know. I'll read over the details as soon as they arrive."

"Good. You shouldn't need to fill in another application, we still have all your information from your last two placements. You'll just need a recent physical for the new medical form."

After I hung up, I searched for more information on Novosibirsk. I had been to Russia before but that was years ago. As part of my Circumnavigators Fellowship, I went to Tallinn (it was part of the Soviet Union) Leningrad and Moscow.

The army training program I was in at Leavenworth, Kansas was postponed due to "Sequestration." It would be a few months before they knew if it would reboot.

I accepted the offer for Novosibirsk and went to visit each of my children-my daughter in Texas, and my son in California, while waiting on my visa to come through. The State Department said I could process my visa through the San Francisco consulate. This meant I could see Denali's art exhibit in Oakland before I left.

We talked about how he wanted to set up his exhibit. Denali had a number of new paintings but the one I thought was stunning as well as disquieting, was a painting of a young man in an arctic type of red parka, hood and turquoise gloves. The figure wore googles which are blacked out so no facial features can be seen. He wanted to start the exhibit with his painting having ice on top of plexiglass as if it is buried. During the evening, the ice would melt to reveal the painting of the figure underneath. We drove to different stores until we found one in Oakland which carried dry ice. This would be the best material to use since it melted slowly and emitted a vapor. More dramatic.

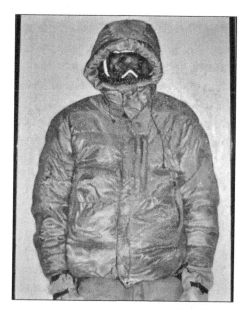

Figure 49. Buried original painting by Denali Schmidt, California, USA

Denali's show included art in different mediums. It was a success. We all celebrated afterwards at a Moroccan restaurant which featured delicious tagine and belly dancers. Oakland is a city replete with family run restaurants offering different national cuisines.

The next day I received a call from the Russian consulate. My visa was ready. As soon as I scanned my visa back to Washington, D.C. they emailed me my ticket to Russia. My flight would leave from San Francisco with two stops before arriving in Moscow. I needed to be there for a week for orientation, briefings, and meetings before boarding another flight to Novosibirsk.

As often is the case with government programs, you hurry up to wait and then must move quickly. I showed Denali my itinerary. As we did whenever I visited, we walked in the nearby cemetery which was the only place with acres of land, rolling hills and few people around in this crowded city. We could walk and talk for hours there undisturbed.

"You know, your great grandfather Waldemar, and his wife, your great grandmother, narrowly escaped being sent to Siberia?"

"No Mum, I didn't. What happened? How were they even in Russia?"

"Well, I'm not certain of their whole history. It's your unique ancestry, but a number of German families emigrated to Russia during the time of Katherine the Great. From what I remember, your *gross Opa* told me his family had been there since that time. They spoke German at home. He went to a small school and had a side business as a teenager weaving baskets.

One night he had a dream which warned him of coming danger. He tried to warn his family and others at school, but no one paid attention except his teacher. She was not much older since she had just started teaching. I think they were about six years apart. They arranged to meet in the forest that night. A short time after they hid there, soldiers arrived on horseback. This was in the early 1900s. Waldemar said they rounded up people in the village and took both his and his wife's family away. They received a photograph years later when they were in America. It showed their loved one's dead bodies lying in open wooden caskets. He kept the photo and showed it to me when we visited his home in Lodi, California."

"How did he escape?"

"He told us (your father and I) about a journey at night with horses and wagons. They actually escaped twice. Once from Russia to the border area of Ukraine and Poland. Then from Poland to Germany. Your grandfather was born in Poland. Moving his family to Germany was a miscalculation he regretted. His sons were forced into Nazi Youth movements and funneled into the army of the Third Reich. Two of them, your great uncles, were prisoners of war for most of the war. They survived by being translators in Russian prison camps. Your grandfather was an officer on the Russian front. I think he started his service in the German army when he was only 17."

"Dad only used to say, 'He served his country'."

"You'll have to ask the Schmidt side of the family for more details.

Your great grandfather Waldemar died a few days before you were born. Marty said one of the last things he asked in the hospital was, "Is Marty's child born yet?" Apparently, he pulled out all the tubes and monitors himself. He died shortly thereafter in the hospital. He had endured so much in his life.

"Are you afraid of going to Siberia, Mum?"

"No, not afraid. It's not a war zone. Pakistan is worse I reckon. You went through the Moscow airport when you flew to Armenia remember? Not that you can know a place just from its airports, but you saw it's quite modern and it's not patrolled by military men. I'll be far away, son, but I hear the internet is reliable. We can speak by phone every week or more often if you want. If there's Skype, we can use that, too. Right now, it's free."

"Listen, Mum…Dad says he wants me to go climb K2 with him… possibly this summer. What do you think?"

I halted. We were in front of a large headstone with the names of multiple family members. I considered my reply carefully.

"Denali, I think it's a terrible idea. It takes years of training, focus and preparation to do those 8,000-meter peaks. You know K2 is the most dangerous mountain and not one to start on. You need to concentrate on your studies these next two years. Priorities, son. Finish your bachelor's degree first and focus on that path."

Denali was looking at the headstone as he started his answer.

"Yeah, you're right. But Dad says he may not be able to climb much longer. He has arthritis in his hips, left over from when he had Ross River fever. He has some other complications, too."

"All the more reason not to go until he sorts himself out, Denali. Look, you're over 21 and a man now. I love you and support you, but I will say this. If you go before you finish your university degree, I will not pay one single penny to help you later. Most people don't finish if they interrupt their studies. I feel very strongly about this, Denali. I want you to live a long life. Going this summer would be ill advised. If you do, you will need to take out a loan to finish. Then you'll have that debt on your shoulders. Understand?"

Denali had as many scholarships as could be granted at CCA to a student who hadn't graduated from high school in the United States. Graduating from a New Zealand high school excluded him from the Pell and other grants even though he was an American citizen.

Figure 50. Denali on Bay Area Rapid Transit (BART),
San Francisco, California photo by Larisa 2012

Denali had his own side business making wooden frames for other artists and art students in addition to manning the front desk at a gallery. He worked extremely hard for extra money and to keep his 4.0 average. He knew he didn't want to have to be burdened by a loan. Denali looked out over the hills of headstones as the sun was going down.

"You're right, Mum. I wouldn't be ready and I'm learning heaps at CCA. I want to finish."

"Glad to hear it, love. Alright then, that's settled."

Denali drove me to the San Francisco airport early on a Sunday morning. We had tried to connect with Sequoia on Saturday night, but her phone kept going to voicemail. I was sorry to miss speaking with her but spoke to my father instead. She felt close to her grandfather. He was in Houston and assured me Sequoia was doing well in college.

"Don't worry, dear. Everything's under control here." I did worry, but I boarded the plane satisfied I was prepared as I could be for my time in Siberia. I wouldn't be given my return ticket until I finished my projects there.

Upon arrival at Moscow airport customs, I noticed there were no lines. People just pushed ahead in a mob and filtered to the various stalls for their stamp to enter. It did not pay to be polite. I mustered my New York City attitude.

A Russian woman from the US embassy staff was there to meet me. She directed the taxi driver to a large hotel right in the city.

"You can walk or take the metro to the embassy tomorrow morning. We have meetings starting at 10:00. Remember to bring your passport and medical papers. There is a reservation in your name when you go to the reception desk. See you tomorrow."

"Spasiba, do svidaniya." (Thank you, bye in Russian)

I hoisted my bags on my back and shoulder. I knew about 30 words of Russian but intended to learn more.

When I was finally escorted back to the inner offices of the embassy and met my Russian contacts, my inner alert system was triggered. Maybe I was hypervigilant after my Human Terrain System training, but it was more than that. It seemed like my boss was completely out of the loop and his local Russian staff knew it. They ran the office. They were to the point and brusque.

"Welcome. Ah, you are dressed nicely...not like many Americans who come to work here. Do you speak Russian? Understand?" She spoke a few phrases in Russian. I shook my head "No."

"The RSO (Regional Security Officer) will sit in on this meeting. We have arranged a conference call with your host university in Novosibirsk. Dr. Melenka speaks excellent English."

I was ushered into a large meeting room with a large, oval-shaped wooden table. There were no windows. We introduced ourselves and the RSO started:

"We don't have any other Americans on official business in Novosibirsk. There is one young man who is a Fulbright Fellow. You should meet him in the first week. He speaks, reads and writes Russian. We placed him at the same university, but he lives in a different sector of the city. I recommend you keep in constant contact with each other."

"Yes, will do." I wrote his name down.

"We advise you not to take public transportation. I advise you not to go out at night alone either. You'll be living near to the university and local shops. You should be able walk anywhere you need to go. If you need transport to your other universities, I suggest you arrange it with them.

The weather is the most dangerous element there. I trust you packed clothing for sub-zero weather?"

"Yes. I'm prepared. About how far a walk is it from my apartment to work?"

The RSO turned to my boss. He shrugged his shoulders as he replied.

"I don't know. They told me it would be about a 20-minute walk."

"How long did it take you to walk, sir?"

"What me? I've never been to Novosibirsk. You'll have to report back if that's accurate."

I suppressed my surprise. When we had a phone conversation before I accepted the position he described Novosibirsk *as if* he had been there.

He had been riffing on second or third hand knowledge.

"One other thing." The RSO cleared his throat. "You'll probably notice you are being monitored by the FSB. That's the new name for the old KGB.

Don't worry, they're not going to be knocking on your door to take you away. They just know you'll be there. You'll be a person of interest for them."

As a matter of fact, in 1973, the KGB did knock on my door and stood by while I packed. Two men drove me right to the airport where they had me flown out of Moscow to Krakow Poland. That was my first visit to Moscow back in the days of the Soviet Union.

He grunted. "It's a fragile time with Secretary of State Clinton's 'reset button' diplomacy, regarding Russia. Do you have any questions?"

We went over the tasks I was assigned, the protocols for reporting in each week and the names of my contacts there. I filled in several forms, next of kin notification included. My boss and my CIED col-league who was posted to a university in Moscow, suggested we go out for lunch.

"Have you seen Red Square? Let's go there first. There are some good restaurants around and shopping if you need to get anything before you leave for Siberia."

The last time I was in Moscow, in Russia, was 1973 at the end of my Circumnavigator's Fellowship tour. It was summer and the lines were long to get any type of goods or food. GUM originally opened in 1893, and after World War II expanded. However, the first time I was there it was very basic and sold only items made in Soviet Union nations. By 2011, GUM was entirely renovated. It included western upmarket brand stores including Louis Vuitton, Dior, Swatch, Prada, Omega, Cartier, Calvin Klein and a number of cafes and places to eat. Every floor was filled with shops. They had a large cinema and internet cafes. It was extremely bourgeois.

Figure 51. Red Square, Moscow, Russian Federation 2011, photo by Toni

Our boss chose a contemporary café serving hot food. He showed off his halting Russian by insisting on ordering our lunch, although my colleague had been married to a Russian musician for over ten years and knew Russian quite well. We listened as he gave us his perspective on life in Russia.

From time to time, I let my attention focus on our surroundings and the people coming in and out. This was a tourist and upper crust section of Moscow. People were fashionably dressed, walked with purpose and were energetic. The Autumn weather was brisk here, but not terribly cold.

After four days of meetings, more paperwork and preparation I boarded a Russian airline for Novosibirsk. Next to me sat a large, friendly man who saw me reading papers in English.

"Excuse me, do you speak English?" He asked me.

"Yes, why?" I responded.

He took out his business card from his jacket pocket. It was in Russian on one side and English on the other. His business was based in Uzbekistan.

"Do you speak Russian, too?"

"No, not yet."

"You're going to Novosibirsk, and you don't speak Russian? Do you want to die?"

"Certainly not." I smiled. "Why?"

"They don't like Americans there or most foreigners. Don't speak English in public. Learn Russian. All the signs are in Russian, too."

I sighed. I remembered I had asked my boss before I arrived about learning Russian. He had said it wouldn't be a problem in Siberia. I would have an interpreter assigned to me at my home university and he swore, "Everyone is learning English here." Now, I understood he'd never been to Siberia. How would he know? Mentally I prepared to adapt again and lose all preconceptions of what to expect.

I accepted his business card as he told me a little about his business and life in Novosibirsk.

"It's a shithole. I don't know why you want to go there." He exclaimed.

I let him talk until we were served an airplane meal and drinks.

"Give me your phone number, I can show you Novosibirsk." He offered.

"That's kind of you, but my work colleagues are meeting me at the airport. I don't have a phone yet. They will be taking me around the city I'm sure."

I said farewell to the Uzbek man, gathered and double checked my belongings before I departed. There was already about two feet of snow on the ground. I breathed in a blast of cold air as I descended the steps from the plane. There were only two flights a week to Moscow from Novosibirsk in those days. I planned to be there until the summer of 2012.

A young woman with copper red hair and a friendly face approached me after I collected my two large suitcases.

"You must be Miss Joanne?" She had a charming accent.

"Yes, pleased to meet you. And you are?"

"Irina." She took one of my bags and then stopped for a moment. She looked around the airport and then turned to me directly.

"You believe in God, don't you? You talk to God."

At this moment I had a serious choice to make. I wasn't sure if my honest answer would offend her and ruin our possible relationship or if hedging the question would deny her what she needed to know. I decided to be open and truthful. Quite risky to do with a stranger in a hostile country.

"Yes, I do."

She clutched her heart.

"Oh, thank God. I have someone I can talk to. But we have to be careful here. Most people are still strong atheists. We go outside to the car now. I am so happy to meet you. We go first to your apartment."

We drove on icy roads to a series of concrete apartment buildings by the Ob River. They all looked the same. A few children were sliding down the snowbank when we hauled my suitcases to the back entrance. Fortunately, I was on the 4th floor. There were ten floors and no elevator. There were three locks and Irina fiddled with the keys. The halls were grey concrete with graffiti phrases spray painted in black on the walls. At least the building was warm.

The apartment was spacious and had all the modern conveniences. Gas stove, refrigerator, toaster, kettle, washing machine and dryer. It was simply furnished with two large windows overlooking the river. There was food in the refrigerator and an assortment of tea, coffee and sugar. A full set of dishes, cutlery, linens and pots and pans were in the cupboards. They had prepared it well. I thanked Irina and we made arrangements for her to pick me up the next morning and have my first tour of the university.

They provided a radio/cassette player. I tuned into a news and music station. All the stations broadcast in Russian. It was my 'companion' in the months ahead. I saturated my house with Russian programming to ingest the language in whatever ways I could. I had a Russian/ English dictionary with me. There was no internet in the buildings in 2011. I was told there was reliable internet at work. I used the time to learn the Russian alphabet and practice their Cyrillic letters. As per my usual routines in a new country, I tried to stay up to adjust to the new time zone.

One advantage of working at Novosibirsk State Technical University as my base university, was that it provided all faculty and staff with hearty meals in their cafeteria. Breakfast, lunch and snacks were served. All buildings were connected by underground walkways. The only buildings which were not connected were the large gym complex, the Radio Engineering Department and the police office. Irina cautioned me.

"You cannot take photos here without permission. This is very serious. You must ask the guard or police officer if you may take a photo. Me, too I have to ask. Please let me know when you want to take photos."

I promised I would abide by their rules. I knew she was the person considered to be "responsible for the foreigner." I didn't want to get Irina into any trouble.

Irina showed me the maze of tunnels then escorted me to the police office to register. We waited there for over an hour so I could get my official papers and passport stamped. Anyone moving to other cities in Russia had to officially register within 48 hours. There still wasn't real freedom of movement, even for Russian citizens.

My other new Siberian colleagues were not quite as friendly. Understandably they were suspicious of me at first. They scoffed a little at the fact I didn't know any Russian. Some of the first slang I picked up were the words translated as "awesome, cool" (krutah/ klasno) and "clueless"(nevezhestvennyy). I was clueless when I first arrived.

They also impressed upon me that they were "Siberians" first. Siberia is very different from the tourist cities of Russia. They have their own accent and idioms. There were over 500 Siberian tribes whose presence predated the Russians by thousands of years. I had no idea Russia was also a country with tribes and tribal history.

Figure 52. Campus of NSTU, Novosibirsk, Russian Federation 2011

The word Cossack is derived from the Turkic word, "kazak" meaning "free man, adventurer, independent one." They were reputed to be great warriors. The Russian aristocracy permitted them to exist on their lands in exchange for their able-bodied young males to devote twenty years of military service to the ruling families.

This started in the 15th century and continued for over 300 hundred years. However, with the revolution and rise of Communism, the Cossacks actively rebelled. They were Orthodox Christians, who lived in their own semi martial communities with their own rules.

Cossacks were and are strictly anti-Communist. Under Stalin, thousands of Cossacks from the areas of the Soviet territory from the Black Sea through northern Russia were arrested and deported to gulags. Many of those who survived and who were eventually released remained in Siberia and Kazakhstan.

In time, a few of my Cossack colleagues warmed to me and included me in their family events. They put me on the spot at a birthday celebration in our department where everyone had to sing and dance solo. I earned grudging respect by being reasonably good at both, then joining in to learn Cossack dance moves and singing along in a Russian chorus. I soon learned to recognize Cossacks by their distinctive hair styles (both women and men had long hair) their clothing, their reserved and confident way of conducting themselves in public. They have their own dialects, traditions, songs, dances, and ways of rearing their children.

I had a few Mongolian and Tartar colleagues and various mixes of nationalities of the recently created and disbanded Union of Soviet Socialist Republics. (USSR) Most of the time everyone was professionally courteous but different ethnicities did not often mix outside of work. As I was told, most of my colleagues came from families where at least one member had been hauled off to the gulags in the region in the previous generation. They were descendants of the unjustly imprisoned. During and after World War II, prisoners of war were transported to Russia from Finland, Germany, Poland, Ukraine, Italy and even the British Isles. They languished in prison for years. Some married local women or fathered children and the result was a population of astonishing beauty. I saw all variations of hair color, eye color, facial features, height, and hardy dispositions.

It was very difficult to leave Siberia if you were born there. You had to have the State or government's permission and a job or family invitation and support. If you had these prerequisites, you could move but not necessarily your family.

As my colleagues explained to me, "You can't just choose what you want to study or where you want to live and then change your mind. You pass exams for entrance to study, the government pays for your degrees, but then you must continue in that profession and work where they tell you to. Here is not like in the west."

They had a similar saying in Russian as we have in America: "Don't trust the government." They have other more poetic and poignant sayings as well. Roughly translated, "let go your arms" and "you can't escape destiny" which provide a glimpse into the Russian mentality. They don't say "there is the easy way and then the hard way to do things." They say, *"There is the hard way and the harder way."*

After a rough start literally falling on my butt on the ice (they don't plow the roads or shovel the sidewalks, they let the ice grow layers); I began to gain traction on my feet and with my co-workers. The Head of Department approached me about their "problems" with the only other American sponsored by the US State Department. He was a young Fulbright Fellow, a smart Russian speaker and budding writer.

He wrote blogs in both English and Russian, but he was from the East Coast and lacked some of the more formal, interpersonal skills the Siberians expected.

"This boy," they commented, "He doesn't greet us, he doesn't speak to us except to ask for something. He doesn't come in and say, "Good Morning or Good Afternoon, he just opens the door and walks to his desk. He is rude. He even speaks Russian. What is his problem? What does he contribute to us here?!"

My position was one of a bridge and cross-cultural interpreter in this situation. I spoke to him privately, enlightened him on the importance of these "niceties" which in their culture were actual required rituals and not optional. He understood and changed his way of relating within the week. My colleagues were pleased. He also joined the university orchestra. Leo was an accomplished violin player which gained him additional respect.

In addition to NSTU, I needed to make myself available to nine other university departments in the "academic gulag" that was the chain of technical and scientific universities in Novosibirsk. This meant more travel and it necessitated me using the metro and buses from time to time when they didn't have a car available. Taking public transport in any country lets you see more of how the local population lives, dresses and interacts.

It's also necessary to use the local language. I was prodded to use my beginning Russian.

One of my primary tasks besides teaching in the graduate departments of Languages/Linguistics and International Affairs was to be the coordinator for their first International Scientific and Technical Conference. The aim was to steer the direction of this conference and convince them to have sessions in English as well as Russian, German, and Mandarin. Mercifully they were onboard with this idea. Otherwise, meetings and negotiations would probably have taken months.

The set date was in January 2012. The universities insisted my boss, as a representative from the US State Department, attend in person. He was not thrilled at the idea of having to come down to Siberia for a few days, but he really had no choice once the invitation was officially sent to the American Ambassador.

For Christmas and New Year's, we had off from our duties, but my social calendar was full. I was invited to parties, celebrations, out to restaurants, to my colleague's humble apartments and to events at the Novosibirsk Theatre, a magnificent building formally known as Novosibirsk State Academic Theatre of Opera and Ballet. Less formally it was called the "Siberian Coliseum." It is the largest theatre in Russia, larger than the Bolshoi Theatre in Moscow. It had a remarkable history starting construction during World War II as both a morale booster and a place to store weapons in its bowels should the Nazis advance. The government had renovated the theatre in 2005. Performers and shows from all over Russia and Europe were presented there.

Figure 53. Gorsky Adeen bus stop, Novosibirsk, Russian Federation 2012

My hosts had done their research on me. They knew I had been in the performing arts professionally and was also a published writer and poet. Russians support the arts and poetry passionately. They gave me tickets to ballets, plays, concerts and poetry readings. Two or three colleagues would accompany me, explain the programs, and watch for my reaction. I was delighted as well as rapt with the high standards of all aspects of these performances. The theatre itself was a work of art. I loved going there and they knew it. They were gratified I could admire Russian proficiency in these areas. They were justifiably proud of their national heritage in the arts.

The American Council Library in Novosibirsk was permitted to remain open in 2011 and 2012. It was closed in 2013, after the fiasco of American interference with their thinly disguised launch of the "White Revolution" in Moscow. As my Siberian colleagues commented, "What, the American government thinks we Russians don't know how to start a revolution if we wanted to?!" They openly mocked the obvious American influence in the street protests and the US government support of the "Pussy Riot" which resulted in the desecration of Orthodox Christian church altars.

The Siberian woman in charge of the US American Council Library asked me to do a series of talks on aspects of American Culture Russians may not have been exposed to. As part of my scope of work, this was encouraged. I had the freedom to choose my topics. I asked her what her audience of mainly young, university students might be interested in. She replied, "American Indians, American Artists and American Pop culture." These were subjects I was familiar with and had particular connections to. I prepared presentations on "Pow Wows", the artist Georgia O'Keefe, American/ Russian contemporary artist Mark Rothko and New York artist Jean- Michel Basquiat, the band SOAD (System of A Down) and country musician Johnny Cash.

My audiences grew for each of these talks and slide shows. I also noticed an elderly man sitting in the back of each of my presentations who fell asleep for most of them but woke up as I was finishing. He clumsily followed me at a distance. Irina accompanied me to many of my lectures. I asked her about this man and if I should be concerned since he seemed to be stalking me.

"Oh, he is FSB. He is just here to watch you. I doubt he understands English." She laughed. "He looks harmless."

He trailed us to the Nicholas Roerich Museum. There were less than 10 other visitors on the day we went. Irina had never been to this museum. She brought her eldest daughter with us for a tour. Denali and I had viewed this great Russian artist's painting in a small museum placed in a New York City townhouse when we were there in 2010. This was on a trip together before I left for Pakistan. Denali was inspired by Roerich's paintings and his adventurous life. I couldn't wait to send photos to both my children. They would both appreciate this painter's works.

Figure 54. Denali at the Nicholas Roerich Museum
in New York 2010, photo by author

However, as an American I was charged $20.00 for each photo. I decided to spend $100.00 to support this museum and share these treasures. My FSB "minder" skulked behind us. However, afterwards, he didn't follow us to Irina's daughter's folk-singing practice. I was grateful we could listen without his lurking presence. That was one way to shake my tail.

My boss decided that I was to accompany him and the other Americans from various programs around Russia, to Turkey. We were to present professional development sessions for a week-long conference in Antalya. This was the second week of January, and only two weeks before the International Conference was to start. It made no sense to me since we already had a number of American teacher trainers placed in Turkey, but it was a paid trip during the coldest part of winter to beaches on the Mediterranean Sea. This was our taxpayer's money going to paid vacations for State Department employees.

The Foreign Service officers sat by the pool or the bar chatting with each other and the various escorts who were hovering around them. There were plenty of Russian tourists there for winter holidays and clandestine affairs. Turkish men lurked trying to get the attention of our younger female and male team members. There was a sleazy feeling to this place.

I was happy to get up early and jog on the sandy beach barefoot. It was much warmer in Antalya than in Siberia. I soaked up what sun I could.

One of our last mornings as I was coming back from a jog, another State Department woman approached me. I was startled to see her there so early.

"Joanne, if you don't mind I'd like to talk to you."

"Sure, what can I do for you?"

"How would you feel about staying another year in Novosibirsk? We've had good reports about your work, you're building rapport there. We'd like you to continue."

"Oh," I said as measuredly as I could. "Don't ask me now in warm Antalya. I might just say yes," I joked. "May I let you know after the International Conference is finished, say in mid-February?"

"Yes. That timing should work for us."

"Okay, I'll let you know soon." We returned to the hotel for the wrap up sessions with our Turkish counterparts. I genuinely missed my Siberian colleagues.

My boss announced he was coming Novosibirsk for the conference. Before he turned up, the university went into high gear with their preparations for the "American official." This was the first time they had such an esteemed foreign visitor to their campus. They ordered food from outside to be catered for conference meals. Every area around the main hall and lecture theatre was cleaned.

The Russian presenters rehearsed their speeches, microphones were brought in, and the staff photographer was to be the official recorder for all our events. They even put toilet paper in the restrooms near the conference hall where he might use them.

On the day of his arrival everyone was dressed and made up to create a favorable impression. We were functioning smoothly as a team.

He arrived in a hired car with a driver, and we walked out in the frigid January wind to greet him. Within the first fifteen minutes I sensed my colleague's discomfort.

My boss had a naturally loud voice and could be accurately described as a flamboyant individual. He gestured boldly, needed to be the center of attention and did not possess a poker face. My Siberian work mates were polite but reserved. The head of the International Relations department gave me a look and indicated she needed to speak to me privately. I excused myself for a moment and followed her outside the main reception area.

"Joanne, this is your boss? This is who the American State Department sends us?"

"Yes, that's him. Why?"

"Why? Why they do not send us a traditional man! This is insulting."

It dawned on me I didn't describe his sexual preferences when preparing them because I didn't think it was important nor their business. But I had already learned Siberians are very traditional and family value oriented.

"He's the only man in direct charge of my program here in Russia. He's at the highest position."

She clicked her tongue and gave me a look of sympathy.

"You do not have an easy job, Joanne."

We returned to the reception and gave instructions for how to begin the opening session. Delegates from other parts of Russia, North Korea, Mongolia, Ukraine and Kazakhstan were seated. My boss and I were placed at the main dais panel facing the audience of over five hundred people. After a long, glowing introduction in Russian, my boss approached the podium. He opened with a few words of Russian, then proceeded in English. An interpreter translated using a microphone placed to the side so as not to distract from the main speaker. The official photographer started snapping photos. The entire conference sessions were being videotaped. This would prove a useful tool for our final review and evaluation.

Although there were a few misunderstandings by having four official languages, the conference provided all the participants with a chance to network and hear scientific papers first-hand. I was in charge of the Radio Engineering sessions. The engineers were happy to show me their department, their equipment and their research projects. It was a productive week.

The last day was one of self-congratulatory speeches, gift giving and handing out certificates. My boss was pleased with how it all went. My colleagues were pleased that he was pleased. He asked for a few photos, and I took responsibility for picking out suitable ones then having them sent to him in Moscow. We collectively breathed a sigh of relief when he boarded his plane.

The after-action evaluation was a lesson for me. When I proposed we have a meeting to review the conference, what we observed, how we felt our plans were implemented, places for improvement and so forth-my colleagues said it was a "great idea." They set up a microphone and the Head of the Language and Linguistics Department went first. She strode up to the microphone and said proudly.

"This was a wonderful conference. We achieved what we needed to achieve. We should have another one next year." People clapped vigorously as she returned to her seat.

The next person was a professor from the Engineering department. She walked up to the same microphone and said somberly. "Yes, this was a wonderful conference. I too, believe we achieved what we needed to achieve. We should have another one next year." She nodded her head and returned to her seat.

For over 90 minutes I sat in astonishment as every participant essentially made the same movements and parroted the same phrases. No one apparently dared to deviate from the script or criticize any part of our efforts. Everyone seemed quite pleased with the "great idea" of having an after-action review…their way. It was a hangover from the soviet times. No one wanted to return to the "self-criticism" sessions or any resemblance to the "party meetings" that this evidently conjured in their minds. This was my miscalculation about what could and could not be stated in public.

There was no "freedom of speech" yet, no matter how earnestly they may have yearned for this right. I learned another hard lesson.

It was 40 below zero and 3:54 am when Leo called me in March. He was in agony. He knew I was a TCM practitioner and might be able to help him. I asked him his symptoms and they sounded serious. The metro didn't run for another hour. He lived across town. I asked him if he could hold on for another hour and he said he could. I got dressed quickly. He was about my son's age, 24. He was the only other American in Novosibirsk. I was concerned.

Figure 55. International Conference NSTU team, Novosibirsk, Russia 2012

When I arrived at Leo's apartment building he was shaky with shallow breathing and very pale. After a preliminary examination and listening to his medical history and seeing the scars on his abdomen, I was convinced he should never have been medically cleared for Siberia. There were few clinics here and the standards were questionable. I called one of my colleagues who I knew had a car. I was going to call in many favors over the next 48 hours.

The hospital my Siberian colleagues took us to was considered the best one in Novosibirsk, but it was miserable. Sick people were waiting for treatment. There weren't enough chairs. People were sitting, moaning on the floor. The halls smelt of every vile human emission you can think of. The place was filthy.

My colleagues insisted Leo be seen right away and slipped the attendants money. Leo asked me to call his parents and took out his new model "smart phone." No ordinary citizens in Novosibirsk had one of these yet. I asked him to put it away since it drew immediate attention to us. I needed to wait and see what the doctors said before speaking to his family and to the embassy in Moscow.

It was very serious. Life or death they said. They needed to operate right away. I looked around at the conditions of the hospital. Would I want my son to be treated here and have to recuperate here...definitely not. I called his parents. His father, his brother and his sister were all medical doctors. I explained Leo's condition, the doctors in Novosibirsk's diagnosis and my assessment. They agreed he needed to be flown back to New York asap.

There were only two flights a week to Moscow, I explained. The next one wasn't until tomorrow. His parents thought the State Department would send a plane. After all he was a Fulbright Fellow. I had to relay the truth to them. This was not a Hollywood movie. No one was coming to rescue him. We would have to get him out. I tried the embassy, but my boss was on vacation and the Russian secretary told me to just stay in Novosibirsk to get him treated. The PAO couldn't be reached either. The RSO office number went straight to voicemail. It was up to me to make a decision.

I told his parents I would take care of him and call them after I made arrangements on our end. They said they would arrange for an ambulance to meet him at the New York airport. I got on the phone to my Moscow contact to meet him at the airport and make sure he got on the plane to the States. Because of his condition Leo couldn't eat anything or drink anything but filtered water until he got to New York. This would take extreme discipline and monitoring. He was already weak.

We thanked the doctors at the hospital, piled into my colleague's car and drove to my apartment. I called in sick for the day to care for Leo and make sure he was well enough to board the plane. We had to buy his ticket. There was no online ticketing possible from Novosibirsk then. My colleagues went to the airport. All this was done before 9:00 am.

It was a long day and night, but Leo slept while I coordinated. I was in contact with his family. When Leo arrived in Moscow, my friend met him at the gate, stayed with him until he boarded the plane to New York. In New York he was immediately rushed by ambulance to a hospital where doctors were waiting for him. His surgery was successful. His parents called me after to share the good news and thank me. I was cheered to know I had made the right decision. The doctors in New York said if he hadn't had surgery when he did, he wouldn't have made it. It was literally life and death for him.

I let my Siberian colleagues know and passed on Leo's family thanks. Not many American colleagues would have responded so quickly being called at 5:00 in the morning in minus 40-degree weather.

When my boss returned, he gave me and my Moscow friend a tongue lashing and "slapped our hands" for not following the Russian's advice.

He said there were "repercussions" to disregarding their instructions to keep Leo in Novosibirsk.

I countered by pointing out that if a young American man had died in Novosibirsk there would have been far worse "repercussions for everyone both American and Russian."

The training program with the US Army was being resurrected. Sequestration was about to end. I was emailed with an offer, but I would have to go through training again back in Kansas starting in May 2012. This meant I'd have to leave Novosibirsk a month early. I'd be breaking my contract and there would be a financial penalty. I decided it was worth it.

I made plans to ease out of my responsibilities at NSTU, take a final trip to Kemerovo and the other universities. No American had ever been to Kemerovo since the Soviet time. It was the site of the worst mining gulags. Prisons which required "hard labor." It was an epicenter for Russian criminals and identity theft. My Siberian Krav Maga coach gulped when I told him I was going.

"What, you want to die? Anyone who can *escapes* from Kemerovo. You must tell your boss "Nyet."

I let the Washington office know I wouldn't be returning to Novosibirsk once I departed from the "New Siberia."

My boss was not pleased.

Figure 56. Kemerovo State Agricultural Institute, Kemerovo, Russia 2012

14. VALLE DEL OMBRA – ITALY

L et me backtrack a little. After my work in Siberia, I started a new training class back at Ft. Leavenworth. That class was paused due to funding. We were told it would resume in September 2012-as the "September Class." After Kansas, there would be a short training and testing at Camp Atterbury, Indiana and not Ft. Polk (Louisiana) as with previous classes. Deployment to Afghanistan would proceed with greater speed. We would be assigned our in-country postings at the very end of training.

During training I met a woman who would become a good friend and teammate, Lisa Marie Akbari. For both of us, it was the second full training class we completed. Lisa had already served two deployments to Afghanistan as a DAC (Department of Army Civilian), but with a new contractor we were all required to go through it again. There were more politics with this new company and newbie class members. After completing the course, we were both called into the contracting office for a meeting the following morning. We rode to the office from the basic overnight quarters we were assigned. I had a feeling what was coming next.

Just outside Ft. Leavenworth, we had to sign our final papers and non-disclosure agreements (NDAs). We were not going to deploy with our class.

We were both in shock but also angry. We knew it was not a question of our competency that we were cut. As we drove back to the overnight barracks to pack up, Lisa waxed philosophical. She was ever the optimist.

"You know, if we're meant to work in Afghanistan, we will. It may not seem possible now, but we'll work together again. I believe that."

"Can't see how, Lisa. The only positive thing I can see at the moment, is that I'll be able to spend time with my son. I can be there for his graduation. Thank God, I already paid off all his college tuition. Meantime, I have to get another job quickly."

"You will." Lisa reassured me. "You always do, right?"

"Need to start searching today. What about you?"

"I turned down a job before this program started up again. It's possible they still have a spot open. It would be back in Africa with an NGO. I'll stay here with friends for another week while I plan my next moves. I've got some money saved."

Lisa drove her truck to the parking spot in front of our temporary accommodation. She looked at me.

"Their loss!" Lisa said.

"Right." I took in a deep breath.

We hopped out of her truck and got down to the tasks at hand. I was mostly packed anyway. Instead of going on to a CRC (Conus Replacement Center) I was going back to Texas. I hoped I could see Sequoia, and then onto California to see Denali. I'd already turned in my keys, ID cards and shredded all my 'products and papers'. When you were "done" you were done quickly in these types of programs

Lisa and I returned from dinner and found few of our training class colleagues waiting for us. My flight was the first one out the next morning.

"This isn't right. You should be coming with us. We should all be deploying together."

One of my closer teammates was an active-duty Army Sergeant First Class. He had invited us to his family home just a few weeks before. There we met three generations of his kin. He voiced the frustration we all felt. Then the cussing started.

"Fuck this isn't fair. You know who it was who wanted to cut you?" Another friend from another team chimed in.

"Yeah, I know" I assured him.

"Skanky's very ambitious." He remarked.

We all had or were given nicknames. "Skanky" had earned hers early on in training. I was given a few over the years at my posts. They included: Gypsy, Desert Rover, Hermione Granger, and my favorite... Ice Dancer (a joke about me falling on the ice my first weeks in Siberia). There were many nicknames in our training class. Some were more descriptive than others: Green Teeth, Nut Crusher, Prima Donna (PD for short), Professor, Porky, Beady eyes, Cruiser-those were the more charitable monikers.

I was going to miss the quick banter in our close-knit group. We carried on together over the months and this was a blow. But it was best not to linger on what 'could have been'. We stayed together for a few minutes exchanging parting remarks and strong hugs before shuffling away to complete our packing, call family and get some rest.

The van came to pick me up and take me to the airport at 4:00 am. The driver knew me from the three different training cycles since 2011. He was a staunch Christian. He gave me some counsel on my last ride out.

"God has a different plan for you, you know. You and Lisa shouldn't be treated this way but later on, you may realize it was for the best."

He kept nodding his head as he spoke and didn't expect me to respond.

"Thank you, Joshua. I won't forget you."

He handed me my two bags and waited till I was inside the terminal. It wasn't a large airport, and this flight wasn't crowded. I had a couple of hours to think, get on my laptop and send out my CVs.

Figure 57. Lisa Marie Akbari on deployment in Afghanistan 2011

It was the worst time of year to try and get a teaching or training job which I figured would be my best options. The best I could hope for was a short-term summer position and work on getting a longer-term contract starting in the Fall. I felt I was done contracting with US government departments. The last few with both the DOD (Department of Defense) and the DOS (Department of State) left a bitter sensation in my gut.

I called my son, who was supposed to fly out the next day to join me for my pre-deployment celebration and told him to cancel the ticket. I was going to be able to be with him for his graduation. Denali was surprised but very sympathetic when I told him I was "cut from the program" and lost my job. He also sounded excited when I informed him, I was coming to California.

"There is good news though because I will be at your graduation. We can spend time together in the next few weeks before you go to Pakistan."

"Cool, mum." Denali said with genuine enthusiasm.

"When can you come out here?"

"Give me a week to sort things out in Texas. I'll call around to find a place to stay since I know your place is small and you'll want to be with your friends after you finish exams. I'll call you when I get to Austin. I should know more in a few days, son."

"Mum, you can stay here. I know you really liked that job and were ready to go to Afghanistan, but you helped me so much. I'm glad you're going to be here for my graduation. Anyway, it looks like you'll be my only family who will be there. Dad's not coming. Sequoia won't say one way or the other, but I don't think she'll come."

I decided to email Sequoia, then try to call her later.

The reality of no longer having a job, a specific plan, purpose and soon an income, was beginning to hit me. Quickly I hopped on sites advertising for summer teachers. Browsing through listings before my flight was called, I found an interesting job working at an equestrian center in Italy. They needed a native English teacher to work with their riding students and special needs clients. It wasn't much money at all, but they provided room and board and it was in a beautiful part of the country-Umbria.

They needed someone very soon, the first week of June. I sent through my CV and a cover letter, then took a deep breath.

Within 48 hours I had a response from Italy. The family managing the school and the stables, wanted to Skype with me. We coordinated times. I was cheered when I saw the two sisters who ran the program, on screen. They were sitting at a table together in Italy. Both spoke

English quite well. It was as if we had known each other before or came from the same family.

Our interview went smoothly.

They verbally offered me the job and said they would send a contract the next day. I was to book my ticket and they would reimburse me upon arrival. Not only was I relieved, I was energized. While both my paternal and maternal sides of my family were from Italy, I had only visited and never worked there before. This was a chance to improve my Italian, relax in the countryside, eat delicious food while planning my next career moves. Maybe Sequoia would even want to come visit me, in Italy.

In the back of my mind was the terrible gnawing feeling that if Denali went to climb K2 with his father, he would never return alive. Over the year I had many dreams warning me of Denali and his father's death. I wanted to be in a place of peace during his travels and expeditions just in case my premonition proved true. I had a sense of the anguish and pain to come. I didn't want to be around anyone I knew, if and when that happened.

Lesser known than Tuscany, Umbria has its own style, beauty, cuisine and tourist towns such as Perugia and Assisi. It was one part of Italy I had never visited with my family or on my own. Shadows, shade, darkness, obscurity-these are the words used to translate from the original Latin-ombra. The region where I was to work derived its name from this Latin root which upon reflection, was a prophetic sign. Shades and shadows are also another way to describe ghosts. Ghosts were present when I arrived in Umbria. More shades congregated by the time I left.

My summer position was at a horse camp for children in Umbria. It was run by an Italian woman, her father, her sister and her son. I would be teaching English to their students and privately tutoring their son, Edo for his final exams. My start date was in early June 2013, just before Denali was to leave for Islamabad. We spent as much time together and with his girlfriend, as we could.

The last chance we had to spend time together in Oakland, we missed each other. We spoke on the phone a few times in the States before we would never speak again. His father would never permit Denali to use his expedition phone to speak to me while they were in Pakistan.

Figure 58. Denali at CCA (California College of the Arts) graduation 2013

The train from Rome stopped at a small local station near the town Citta di Castello. The elder of the two sisters picked me up. She spoke perfect English with a British accent. We embraced "Ciao" and chatted on the way to their rural property in the nearby hills. When we drove up the long driveway to a large country mansion, I knew I had made the right choice.

The family rented this estate because it was across from two large stables and horse paddocks. There were farms on neighboring hills and trails for hiking and riding connecting the properties. The air was clean and fragrant. Luxuriant green grass carpeted the entire area as far as my eyes could see. All colors of flowers bloomed, and the majestic oak, ash and hornbeam trees were in their full glory beside the tall cedars and pine trees. There was a large swimming pool, tennis courts, an underground pool, a commercial kitchen and dining areas. This was a resort turned into a horse camp for the summer. I was relieved it was even better than the photos and more than I was promised. I could unwind here. A year of competitive army training programs at Ft. Leavenworth and recovering from injuries from a hit and run accident had taken its toll.

My room was spacious with two large windows. Beautifully embroidered linens were placed on the dresser. There were Holy pictures and paintings above the bed and on the walls. Everything was tastefully placed with care.

I met the rest of the family at dinner. The elder sister Francie was mother to Edo, a fine young man who helped teach all things horses but needed tutoring in English to pass his high school exams. The younger sister, Vitoria had just finished university, spoke English well and helped run the camp. She was preparing to leave for Australia after the summer. Their father was a handsome man in his seventies with a stentorian voice. He didn't speak any English and he was the overall boss, but his eldest daughter really took care of the daily routines and communications.

The whole family spent most of their life with horses, training, showing, competing, and providing therapies. Their father had been married twice. His eldest son had been killed in a motorcycle accident seventeen years prior. He was Francie's elder brother. She was pregnant with Edo when that happened. Her mother lived in town with another brother who was considered "handicapped."

Edo's father was a police officer but lived with his new wife in another part of Italy. They all seemed to co-exist in a tolerant albeit vivacious harmony. All family members were welcomed at some point during the summer. It appeared they were able to experience love, joy, suffering and loss together even if they couldn't all live together at one time.

Other local staff did the cleaning and most of the cooking. There was a large wood fired masonry oven for pizza, industrial gas ranges, sinks, refrigerators and storage bins. Francie and Vito prepared breakfast and lunches for the campers and guests once they arrived. It was my job to provide practical English lessons which incorporated vocabulary for horse related activities. I found out they also operated horse camps in Ireland and did exchanges with children from Ireland and the UK to Italy and vice versa. We had two days to prepare for the children and their parents to arrive.

My work was busier at first. When you work at a residential school or camp you are never truly "off" since you eat, teach, recreate with the students. My Italian was quite rusty and having to find vocabulary and strain to understand the accents and slang could be tiring at times.

On June 6th I received my last communication from my son by email. My prayers were more fervent as I envisioned him travelling with his father and other climbers into the Karakoram mountains. There would be no further contact until he descended safely.

Figure 59. Horse riding with Francie, Edo and campers, Umbria, Italy 2013

My first night I settled comfortably in my bed falling asleep easily for a few hours when, at about two o-clock in the morning I heard the two young pizza cooks fighting, cussing each other out (I knew some of the swear words) along with clashing pans. I heard one of them say "Smetto-basta" (I quit-enough, in Italian) and stomp out. I hopped out of bed and peered out the window. Sure enough, one of the men was mounting his motorbike and starting the engine. I supposed they would have to find another cook by tomorrow night.

But, when I mentioned the spat the next morning, Vito laughed and said they did that just about every night. "He'll be back, don't worry." She continued making breakfast for all of us. I asked if I could help setting the long tables. I needed to keep occupied.

The campers were mostly young girls from families outside of Umbria. There were a few who were driven in each day from town, but they came after breakfast and shared lunch with us.

Edo sauntered in dressed in casual riding gear. He was always cheerful. He easily commanded their attention. The father strode in and held court with a group of parents who had stayed overnight before returning home without their children for the summer. A few of the children already spoke some English or peppered their Italian with American slang. A couple of the parents made it a point to come speak to me to practice their English as well. My halting Italian was patiently received. I understood much more than I was able to express despite the fact they spoke very quickly-especially those families from northern Italy.

After breakfast, parents bid affectionate farewells and all the campers walked down the hill and across the road to the main pad-dock. The other large adjacent property held stables with only white Arabian horses. I paused to watch them train the Arabian stallions. They were owned by a wealthy sheik from Dubai but apparently, he hardly visited. These horses were left in their stables except for once-a-day exercise. I didn't realize from early on they were forced to be fitted with "tie downs" which kept the arc of their neck and heads low. Tie-downs were created to keep the horse from raising his head above a certain level. Bonnet style tie downs go over the ears and around the crown of the horse's head. Others go over the nose. There is also a combination of both in the headstall style. Then there is the 'head-setter' tie-down that tightens. They are called tie-downs because they were created to tie the head down and prevent it from going up above a certain point, but it's cruel.

I kept thinking of how women in the Arabian Peninsula are also "tied down" in physical ways by having to wear hijab and niqabs (hair and face coverings in black) and are not permitted to travel without a male escort, or to drive on their own as well as many other "bowing down" restrictions to men.

In contrast, the horses this Italian family owned and stabled were often ridden bareback in free time or with English saddles during instruction time. They were groomed at least once a day and given lots of loving attention by the campers and the family.

After lunch was my time to teach English. The campers were lively, so we played "games" as much as possible to learn vocabulary. There were varying levels of English, but the children helped each other. I didn't blame them for wanting to be back on their horses or horse playing in the pool, but it was my job to entice some study and learning. On breaks, I put on songs in English. They requested a few they liked to dance to and dance they did.

Figure 60. Campers at Vacanzequestri with author, Umbria, Italy 2013

Every night we had delicious, fresh wood fired pizza and fresh salads. After dinner they would play Italian games like "L'Assassino"and English games like "Charades" and "Scavenger Hunt." Most time spent was outside on horses, walking, swimming, and sports. The campers had phones, but the internet was weak and only worked in certain spots on the hotel grounds.

In July the serious climbing in the Karakoram began. There were sites for climbing enthusiasts, family and friends of climbers to follow the progress of expeditions on all the major peaks. I searched the internet late at night when the signal was stronger. The first news was ominous. Eleven climbers on international teams had been ambushed and executed on the mountain Nanga Parbat. This evil and horrific act was the first time a terrorist attack happened in altitude, and for no apparent reason except to draw attention to themselves. The Taliban claimed responsibility for killing and robbing the climbers.

Denali posted a strong, condemning comment on a website. I wondered if he remembered my caution to him about the Taliban, before he left California. It bothered me we couldn't speak about this or email each other. I intensified my daily prayers.

The next news was positive. Denali and Marty were recognized as the first climbers of the season to summit Broad Peak. They and their climbing mate, Chris Warner descended safely. Marty called in to his media sites to post their success.

I felt as if I could catch my breath until I heard they were going to attempt a rescue for three Iranian climbers who were stranded on Broad Peak. This meant they would have to ascend in high altitude again after the arduous summit they had just achieved. Now, I was worried.

Marty had already been injured − he had a rock thrown at him during a skirmish on Everest in Nepal, a few of months before. He suffered a concussion at altitude. He didn't have much time to recover before Denali met him in Pakistan. He wasn't thinking right. They were going up a second time into the 8,000-meter danger zone then descending. Marty now intended to go up a third 8,000-meter peak when they tried K2. All in one month. This was madness.

Figure 61. Denali climbing Broad Peak in the Karakoram, Pakistan 2013

But he had an obsession. We had photos of K2 in all our houses, every place we lived. This was Marty's third attempt at K2. It was like his "Moby Dick." Sadly, Marty always put his own desires and needs first throughout his life. It did not bode well when I read that Marty, Denali and Chris decided to ascend up from base camp even though *all the Sherpas advised against it.*

The reports from Pakistan sites indicated Marty and Denali had pushed to camp 2 and were heading up to camp 3, but Chris Warner, their climbing partner from Australia, had turned around. He was heading down to base camp. Everyone at base camp was waiting for Marty and Denali to report in at the end of the day and then again in the morning.

I felt a dreadful heaviness in my body and spirit all day. I was in terrible pain and collapsed in my bed in the afternoon. I felt Denali's body for hours. This was so painful that I passed out for a little while.

Very late, after midnight, I heard Denali calling to me.

I heard him say, 'Mum, Mum, over here.'

I woke up and went to the window. The stars were out. I opened the door and went outside following his voice. I continued walking down a path into a forested area. Denali's voice was stronger now.

'Up here, up here, mum'.

I looked up and saw the glimmering stars and I knew. Denali was no longer alive. He has crossed the threshold from this world to the next.

Then I cried, alone, surrounded by trees, gazing up at the sky, pacing in the forest, trying to find my son…somehow.

I moaned, "Oh no, no Denali, no…please…don't be dead."

Figure 62. Denali Schmidt at K2 base camp after failed rescue attempt for Iranian climbers in the Karakoram, Pakistan 2013, from video by Adrian Hayes

The next morning, I waited in my room for the news to be official. Francie came and knocked on my door.

"Ciao, Joanna…there is a phone call for you at the office."

"Yes, I'm coming." I knew only a few people knew where I was working. Cell phone coverage was unreliable in the hills. The landline phone was used for business dealings, reservations, important conversations.

Francie and Vito were making breakfast and listening. We looked at each other as I placed the phone to my ear.

"Hello?"

"Is this Joanne? Denali's mother?" I didn't recognize this voice.

"Yes, who is this?"

"This is Chris Warner. I was with…

"Yes, I know who you are Chris."

"Look, the Sherpas have gone up to where Denali and Marty were last heard from. They didn't find them, but their tent was torn, there was evidence of… an avalanche. We could possibly ask them to try again.

I'm afraid there wouldn't be much chance of them surviving. The conditions are …We consulted with a doctor here at base camp. His opinion is there is no way they could have survived."

This news confirmed what I already knew. Denali and Marty were dead.

"No, I don't think risking any more lives is necessary now."

"We have Denali's things he didn't take with him. We can bring them down and I can make sure you get them? It will take days to walk out, but I can call you when we sort out Marty's things. His wife has already been notified. Your daughter has, too. I'm sorry."

"If there's any money in Denali's wallet, please give it to the Sherpas. I would like a few of his clothes, his notebooks, all his identification and his computer. Anything else…please give it away to those who need it."

"Yes, I can set them aside. No worries. We'll hold a ceremony for them when we get to the Gilkey memorial site."

"How are *you* doing, Chris?" I asked. I desperately wanted to end this conversation and get off the phone.

"It's a shock. I keep expecting them to walk back into camp. I still can't believe they're…gone."

"Yes." It was all I could reply. "Thank you for ringing."

"Alright then…"

"Bye for now."

I hung up feeling sick to my stomach. I didn't know what more to say but felt I should have asked him more questions. There was so much more I yearned to know about my son's last days.

Francie and Vito came over to me and gave me a warm hug. They told me to rest and go back to my room and not to worry about anything. They would screen any further calls.

When I returned to my room my cell phone was ringing. I had left it on the dresser.

"Hello?" I waited to hear the voice on the other end. When I heard the sound of my son's landlord and her tone, I knew what would come next.

"Joanne. I'm so sorry to have to tell you. We didn't know how to get in touch with you earlier. Denali and Marty were lost in an avalanche on K2. I'm sorry. Denali is…they both are presumed dead."

"I know. Thank you. I'll try and call Sequoia. Thank you for calling."

"Oh, Joanne." She continued. "I am so sorry."

"Thank you. Ok. I need to call Sequoia now."

The BBC news already started broadcasting the "story." I watched one clip and decided not to watch anymore. They had so many facts wrong. Who was feeding them this misinformation? They didn't even get Denali's birthplace right. It was disgusting. This was my family they were publicizing.

More phone calls came through. Francie and Vito were considerate and protective of me. They made sure to ask who was calling and then come tell me. They told news reporters I wasn't going to speak to anyone except family.

"Would you like to go to the church in town?" Francie asked me after lunch.

"Yes, I would." I felt unsteady but I forced myself to change before we drove down the hill. I kept seeing Denali in my mind and trying not to believe he was dead. I felt he had suffered terribly before he finally expired. I was furious with his father, too. Perhaps, that energy kept me awake. I knew I had to make arrangements and try to find out more about what happened from climbers who were there.

The small church was dimly lit by candles even during the day. We each lit candles. I worried about my daughter. I hadn't been able to speak to her yet, just my father and my brother. They told me she was distraught, of course, but she wasn't with them. Where was she? I prayed earnestly for guidance. This was going to be a harsh blow to her at such a young age. Only 22 and losing half her family. Denali, her older brother who loved her deeply and tried to encourage and protect her throughout his life, was her greatest constant for her twenty-two years. This was going to be a harder road for us to travel from now on. Denali's girlfriend Larisa hadn't contacted me, but I felt sure she had heard by now. She was already a fragile young woman. She would be knocked back mightily by this news.

We left the church and spoke a little on the way back.

"I can help you with the ticket and take you to the airport in Roma, don't worry." Francie and her family were life savers.

"Grazie, encore."

"We can bring your dinner out to you. You don't have to see anyone right now. I know how it is."

I knew she did know. It must have been wrenching to have your brother die at the same time you were pregnant with your first (and only) child.

There was a small table and chairs near my room. They faced the rolling hills and expanse of light blue sky. I sat there gazing at the sky, in a maze of memories and future planning swimming through my mind.

Edo came over. He didn't say anything but placed a white rose on my table. He looked sad, himself and said, "I'm very sorry." He bowed a little, paused for a moment then slowly walked away.

A white rose. They are unusual. I had seen a white rose in my unconscious state after being hit by a car seven months before in Texas. Inexplicable images raced through my mind before I came to consciousness. One of them was of Denali silently handing me a white rose as if it were a sword. He bowed and I bowed and accepted it. It was a sort of martial art ritual. In this 'scene' Denali said to me, "Swear you will never shoot a gun. Never kill." I nodded and said, "Yes, I swear." This was in November 2012. Now in July 2013, Edo hands me a white rose and bows. I thought how much his kindness and good-naturedness reminded me of Denali.

That evening there was a lightning storm. It was spectacular to see across the open Umbrian sky. The horses were restless. The campers were exhilarated. The energy was literally electric. I was despondent.

I returned to my room with the white rose. The phone rang again. This time I recognized the voice. It was from one of my Gumbaynggirr family.

"Joanna…that you?"

"Yes, Trish?"

"Oh, Joanna…we're so sorry!"

"Oh, thank you. I'm so glad to hear from yous."

"They both went out at the same time."

"Yes, Denali and his Dad."

"No, oh…you didn't hear yet did ya? My dad…Uncle Ken, he passed away yesterday, too."

Another loud thunder roar cracked outside.

"Oh, Tricia. That's a mighty loss. I'm so sorry, please let the other family know you all are my heart and in my prayers."

I looked out my door in time to see a zig zagged lightning bolt illuminate the sky. I don't remember what else we said to each other, but I know we tried to console each other. Memories of Uncle Ken and Denali when they were both younger flew through my mind. Uncle Ken was a huge influence on both of us. He was one of the few 'clever men' left. His death was a loss to their whole tribe.

The last few days with the family and campers are still a bit of a blur. I handled numerous phone calls from many parts of the world. No one really knows what to say, do they. A few family members I hadn't heard from in years mostly wanted to talk about themselves and their beliefs. A few friends thought I might have more details about their deaths. I didn't accept any phone calls from the press or people wanting a "story" and were circling the online waves like vultures.

I realized that for the most part I would be on my own. I felt like a thin shadow of myself but needed to push myself to cope before I saw my daughter. I called my father. He would know where Sequoia was. I steeled myself.

"Dad?"

"He's dead Joanne. Well, that's what you get for marrying that man. Some father he was!"

I knew my dad was angry. Righteous anger masked his other

emotions. People respond differently to shock and grief.

"Dad...is Sequoia with you now?" I was starting to tear up and could hear my voice tremble.

"No, but she's not alone. When are you coming back?"

"The day after tomorrow I'll fly to Texas. We plan to have services in California and Texas so both sides of the family can come. I'm not sure of the arrangements yet Dad."

"You just get back here and then we'll discuss it."

"Alright, Dad."

"Good night Joanne"

"Good night."

My mother sent a short email. It was the first time she had contacted me in years.

"Black Day...Mother."

That's all she wrote about the death of her only grandson. She never signed "love." The most affectionate word she used for decades to me was "fondly" but most often she stated "Mother." She never called. The few times we ever spoke by phone I called her.

Her coldness sucked out more of my diminishing life force. How I missed my own grandparents and their affection at this time. I was feeling fragile, unguarded, drained.

Edo came over to help me with my bags the following morning. He was sunny and solicitous. From over the road in the paddocks I could hear their father shouting instructions to the campers on horseback.

"Spalle, spalle!." (shoulders, shoulders). "Piedi, piedi!" (feet, feet)

Life continues. Work must go on. Love is still present with grief.

I said my goodbyes to the staff and the students at breakfast. There wasn't much more to say except to sincerely wish Edo "good luck" on his English and other exams and to assure him he had the capability to pass.

Francie drove us down the hill joining the road out of the Valle del Ombre. The shadows of death joined the shadows cast by the Umbrian sun.

Allora, ciao e basta. Da oggi in poi, questa e la mia vita. Dio me aiuti.

(Well then, goodbye. From this day on, this is my life. God help me.)

Figure 63. Larisa Original Painting by Denali Schmidt

15. PRINCESS NOURA – SAUDI ARABIA

Before boarding the last stage of my flight to Riyadh from Doha, I changed in the Qatar airport restroom. I wasn't the only one. Young women dressed in western style jeans, short sleeved blouses and t-shirts dug out rolled up black abayas and shaylas (long headscarves) expertly donned them while rubbing off at least some of their makeup. A few girls stood near the hand dryers and spoke on the phone. They used their position and the noise to cover their conversations in their last few hours of freedom.

My abaya was a parting gift from my colleagues when I taught in Bahrain years before. It was black but had an inlaid silver embroidered pattern down the front. It looked conservative but elegant. I was glad I kept it. It was not so long as to hinder my stride as many abayas do. I felt shielded and ready to embark.

There were many reasons why I resisted going to this part of the world before 2013. However, my life circumstances changed so completely that what I once considered obstacles to working in the Kingdom of Saudi Arabia, would now become advantages.

The anguish I felt inside and the black hole I experienced at some time every day when I thought of my son killed, was best expressed by black. Draping myself in the obligatory black abaya would make me more anonymous and maybe less vulnerable. I supposed I would be surrounded by pillars of privacy by being in a cluster of women during my time of mourning. Strangely the thought of being in a group of women, all of us wearing black, comforted me.

But I forgot, or chose to forget, what I had already learned in strict sharia law countries like Pakistan. There, all women experience at some time almost every day, the ceaseless restrictions, and the continual compromises they are forced to make just for being female. The Wahabism of Saudi Arabia spreads its tentacles over many parts of the world, but its center is in "The Kingdom." I underestimated its force at the vortex.

The airport in Riyadh is serviceable, dingy brown and beige with throngs of men milling about everywhere. I searched for a placard with my name on it and finally found a "Mister Bashir" who was supposed to meet me. His face matched the email photo I was sent, so I approached him.

"Salaam..." I began but he finished my greeting for me.

"Alaikum salaam Ms. Joowan. Let me take your bags, please."

He easily carted my two large bags to a six-seater van and opened a door for me. This was one benefit of countries in the East, even older women were helped and often given a front position in line. I surveyed the interior for a moment before stepping up into the vehicle. I did not see one woman 'uncovered'.

"We go first to the office, then you will see your room and rest. How was your flight?"

"Fine, thank you. What is your name, sir?"

"Mohammed. I am one of the drivers. You will see me in the mornings."

The windows were covered with black mesh screens. I took in as much as I could given these filters. This was a city with architecture much like most of the Gulf Arab countries I had worked in: the UAE, Bahrain, Qatar and Oman. It was flashy, modern, clean, and rectangular. There were few variations in the colors which mirrored those of the dry sand colored landscape. Like other Gulf countries, they planted rows of palm trees as median markers and outside most large commercial and government buildings.

The existential sun was already beating down and the mirrored glass in tall buildings shimmered, exaggerating the natural light.

We stopped outside a modest three-story building with the sign 'British Council of KSA' mounted on the roof toward traffic. Mohammed showed me in and up the stairs to the main office. My heart sank when I saw the set up.

As in other education programs and recruitment offices I had seen in the Gulf, this one was all for show. While they advertised the name "British Council" they were Jordanians and Pakistani nationals working in the KSA who appropriated the 'British' name and logo. International copyright laws were not honored here

They took my photo for an ID, gave me a copy of the 'new contract' to sign which had fine print stating they would only issue an iqama after a year (a type of visa which allows for exit for a woman on her own)

and they would loan us the money for the first two months since we did not get our salary deposited until the third month. In addition, I would be lodged in 'temporary housing' with two other women and not in my own apartment as stipulated in our original letter of agreement.

The men processing me did so as if on an assembly line, with civility but no real welcome. I was too tired to argue and realized they had me as they planned. I was trapped, along with the other female teachers, as a solo woman in Riyadh.

It was late August, and the temperature was in the high 40s (Celsius) or about 118 degrees Fahrenheit. Thankfully, the offices and transport vehicles were air conditioned. Another of the drivers took my luggage and shut me in without speaking. I found out later he only spoke Urdu and a little Arabic, but no English.

We pulled into a quiet neighborhood. High sand-colored walls faced the street; therefore, it wasn't possible to peek into the inner courtyards or homes. The van rounded a corner and I saw two mosques close to each other and a few small stores, one with large water bottles at the entrance. The driver honked his horn and the gates opened onto the compound. We drove in. The gates were quickly shut behind us. I wanted to remove my black head scarf but there were still men around. The driver opened the van door, took my luggage and escorted me to the office. This was a large residence.

I heard they had almost 200 female teachers lodged here, but it was a workday, and most were at the university. It was quite tranquil.

A tough looking, tall woman who I guessed was from Somalia by her features and accent, explained the rules and obligations to me. I had to sign more forms before being led to my two-story villa. I was told I would be sharing the kitchen, washroom and dining room with another professor who would be back later in the afternoon. She had a bedroom on the first floor, and I was to be on the second floor. The villa was air- conditioned and I could purchase an internet plan. They supplied basic kitchenware. As long as we were not alone, we could walk to a mall very near which was open until ten at night.

She showed me the swimming pool and a room that was supposed to be a gym, but it only had a few yoga mats, several jump ropes, and a large exercise ball; certainly not enough for 200 women to work out. There were no weights or machines for strength and endurance train-ing. No pull up bars either.

A room set aside as a 'prayer room' contained nothing but a measly pile of prayer rugs and one hanging prayer from the Koran written in calligraphy.

There were no other communal spaces and only a few patches of grass.

Men patrolled the grounds at a leisurely pace, watering the few plants and cleaning the walkways. This surprised me since I thought there would only be women inside the compound. These men were dressed in the *shalwar kameez* clothing styles from Pakistan, Bangladesh, or India not the thaubs the Saudis or other Arab men wore.

"There is a shopping shuttle bus every day except Friday. Today you can go at 5:00 and buy things you need. Here is 500 SAR. This is your settling in allowance. I suggest you rest from your travels. You start work tomorrow and need to be dressed completely and in the bus by 6:30 am. Any time you go out of the compound you must be sure to wear your abaya and headscarf, no exceptions. Do you understand?"

"Yes, ma'am I do. Thank you."

She turned and walked back to her office. I went upstairs to my room to unpack and take my first shower in "the Kingdom." I opened the curtain on the only window in my bedroom, but the compound walls shut out any view of the street. I could however look up to the grey blue sky.

At about 4 o'clock I heard women's voices and doors opening and closing. My villa mate had returned from work. I went downstairs to introduce myself.

"Hi, I just arrived. My name is Joanne."

"Oh, hello. Welcome. Nice to meet you. I'm Nadia. Where are you from?"

"America... and you?"

"The UK, but we only moved there when I went to high school. I was born and grew up in Algeria."

Suddenly we heard loud and strident electrified voices calling for prayer.

Nadia excused herself and went into her room. She was young, I thought maybe twenty-four or twenty-five. She had large, soulful brown eyes and a very sweet looking face. Her voice was high pitched and easy to listen to. She wore at least four rings on her hands, but I got the impression she was single. When she returned to the kitchen, she had taken off her head scarf and abaya. Nadia looked even younger.

"Please excuse me. You must have a lot of questions. I know I did. If you wish, we can share food costs and cooking. I 'm going on the shuttle this afternoon and can show you around the mall, if you're not too tired?"

"Please, I would like that. I want to switch over to this time zone so it's better if I stay awake. I'll be ready at 4:45. We can walk over to the shuttle together."

"That's perfect. I have to change and charge my phone. See you later then."

"Ok, I'll be upstairs unpacking."

When we were both clad in our obligatory black coverings, we walked out joining the other thirty wholly black robed women who piled into two buses. There wasn't much talking during the short ride. Nadia nudged me gently to disembark.

"If you don't mind, let's go to Marks and Spencer first. Then we can go food shopping. They have a well-stocked Carrefour here."

"You lead the way, Nadia. The only thing I really need to get tonight besides food, is a local sim card. "

"No problem, there's a kiosk right near Marks and Spencer. This way."

It was a fairly large mall and not too crowded. Every female over the age of about nine years old wore a black abaya and hijab to cover their hair. They were of different materials. Some had embroidered designs or other decorations on their head scarves. More than half the women also had niqabs. These were mounted on thin metal over their noses. Their faces were fully covered except for their eyes. I reckoned it must be extremely uncomfortable to wear these for any length of time.

Most of the men I saw wore the white or beige colored, long thaubs and many wore the traditional head covering for men as well, called *shemaghs*. Shemaghs were held in place with black or dark colored "agals." Only Arabs were permitted to wear traditional fashion. Other men wore western style pants and shirts or South Asian style shalwar *kameez* in various colors.

I was told once that Shiites often wear western style clothes, no head covering and no beard. but Sunni men wear more traditional clothing and usually do grow beards. I overheard some men speaking

English and wearing western clothes but averted my eyes since I was with a Muslim woman and in KSA. There are sharia law enforcers policing in every major public place in Riyadh, and many of them are women. Speaking to strange men is haram (forbidden).

We paused in the lingerie section of Marks and Spencer.

"Look at this! "Nadia giggled as she showed me the packages of women's underwear, bras, thermals and stockings that had the illustrations or photos pasted over with white labels so none of the female form could be seen. Someone had taken time, labor, and money to cover up all these items for fear someone could be aroused by them. It was almost surreal.

"Over there is the place you can get your sim card. You do have your phone with you, right? "I dug in my purse and plucked out a turquoise Nokia flip phone I had purchased in Pakistan a few years before. It was hardy, reliable and had a long running battery. It wasn't flash, but it had a camera and easy to use keys.

The man at the kiosk was from the Philippines, spoke English well and was very friendly. He changed out my sim card then adjusted the settings. I felt more secure knowing I had a way to contact my daughter, other family and friends if need be, and they could contact me directly. When I pressed the power button on, my contacts appeared. I still had my son, Denali's name and phone number on my list. I felt a sharp pain and gasped seeing it, knowing even if I dialed it I would never hear his voice again.

After we purchased some food Nadia suggested we walk back since the shuttle wouldn't come again for another hour.

"It's safe here even at night, but you shouldn't ever walk alone."

"I'm up for it. This way I can see the route back to our villa."

The contrast between the over air-conditioned mall and the thick, dry heat outside was striking. I had to get used to walking in an abaya again and cope with the temperature. After only a few minutes I was sweating profusely. The sand and dust from the city caused me to start coughing. Nadia offered me a bottle of water.

"It's important to always have some water with you. Dehydration can be dangerous."

Most North Americans and even most westerners would not offer a stranger their water bottle. I wasn't worried about germs and accepted her offer gratefully.

"Thank you. I'll remember to keep my water bottle with me at all times, and have it filled."

As we approached the gate a taxi pulled up ahead of us. A few young women in abayas swished out of the back seat. They signaled the gate guard and we caught up to them as we were guided into the compound. As soon as we were inside the other women started shedding their shaylas and undoing their abayas.

"You new here? I'm Chrissy and this is Kate, Paula and Sarah."

We all greeted each other and shook hands. Chrissy had an Aussie accent, and I guessed the other women were from the UK.

"We'll see you tomorrow." Chrissy smiled, winked and walked with her friends to another part of the compound. They looked like they had already found a way to be more independent in Riyadh. These were women I hoped to get to know better.

It was dusk and the static drone of the evening prayer over loudspeakers started again. Nadia quickened her pace. We entered our villa and put away the groceries. Once again, Nadia excused herself for prayers.

I filled up water bottles for my room and for work, ate some fruit and rice though I wasn't really hungry, then lumbered upstairs to take off my abaya.

A mechanical hum blanketed the buildings. The din created by the sound of hundreds of window unit air conditioners covered almost all other noise. I felt flat and knew I needed to rest. My trusted travel alarm clock was still ticking inside my luggage. It was easy to find. I placed it on the small dresser beside my bed and set it for 5:30 am. Getting dressed for work in the KSA meant planning for at least an additional 15 minutes to put on all the required clothes.

I placed my laptop computer on a table at the foot of the bed and plugged in an external hard drive with hours of music from Hildegard de Bingen entitled: Voices of Angels. It seemed somewhat incongruous to do in such a strict Muslim country, but her music was mystical, uplifting and a beautiful way to drift into slumber. It also reminded me to pray in my own manner at the times I felt forlorn.

The next morning, I woke to a 'thump, thump, thump' outside on the pebbled walkways. Pushing back the curtain I saw two women jogging in running shorts. They were blonde and red headed and evidently didn't care about covering up. My alarm sounded. I felt a familiar rush of nerves and tears. It was another 'first day' of work in a new situation. It was another day of coping without half my family, without my son. I reached for a bottle of rescue remedy.

By 6:20 am, over a hundred women in black were standing, talking, texting, drinking coffee from their thermoses and waiting for the shuttle buses to Princess Noura University. I could already see certain cliques of women, mostly by country of origin and native language. There were a number of Somali women, Maghreb Arabic speakers from Algeria, Tunisia and Morocco; a few from Pakistan, about ten from South Africa, a few Australians and New Zealanders, not too many of us from the USA, and a few who were difficult to place.

Nadia explained that many of the Somali women had Canadian passports. She and others from Northern Africa used their British passports. There were also two Palestinian women who had British passports. We were all here as single women since we were 'unaccompanied'.

In the totem pole of power hierarchy in the KSA (and in many other countries), as single women over 21, we were in a very low position. Those of us who were non-Muslim/infidel women, were considered to be the lowest. You would likely not be promoted or be designated as head of department, and you would never be invited to even apply for an administrative position at the university. This was an unwritten rule I learned from working in sharia law nations. If you converted to Islam, you might have a better chance.

At this stage in my life, I simply wanted to teach in as non-demanding environment as possible while I struggled to recover at least part of my spirit and capabilities after feeling as if my skin and soul had been stripped off me with the death of my son and his father, a man who was once my husband of many years as well as the father of my two children.

If I had to get out of bed every morning because there were literally a hundred or more female students waiting for me to teach them during the day, it would ground me and perhaps even begin to transform the numbness and anguish I felt continually. I knew I truly was a shadow of my former self.

This was a new place, with no previous associations with any of my family and no memories of being or even speaking with my son, Denali. There was less of a chance to be triggered back to the past, to searing pain; at least that is what I presumed.

The drivers and their cattle car vans arrived. I felt as if we were herded wherever they wanted us to go. Most of the younger women put on their headphones/earbuds and drifted into their own worlds. Some women were grading papers en route, others chatted and at least a few tried to get some sleep on the long ride to the outer section of the city where Princess Noura University was still being constructed. I was keen to try and look out my window. The roads looked newly paved.

We were passed through the first of two checkpoints then unloaded at the grand front entrance. Nadia was my guide and ushered me through to the escalators up to the administrative office floors. This was a huge campus in various stages of completion.

"There are no men here. We joke not even a male cat is allowed to put his paws on the campus. The monorail is controlled automatically since women can't drive here. Any repairs are supposedly done at night. "

Nadia paused at the glass door of the Human Resources office. I noticed many of the girls and women took off their abayas and headscarves once inside the buildings, but not this woman.

"Sorry, I have a class now, but she will show you around and take care of you. It takes a few weeks to sort this place out, but you'll manage I'm sure. See you at the villa, later then."

"Can't thank you enough, Nadia." She waved her hand as if this were nothing and stepped lightly back down the corridor.

"Come in, please."

The young head of HR had an American accent but definitely looked like a Saudi or Emirati woman. "You arrived yesterday, is that right? How were your travels?"

"Yes, yesterday. They were fine, thank you."

"You are one of our very experienced teachers. Welcome. For this semester we will be putting you with our advanced students in the pre-med courses and one writing class for intermediate students. We don't have the computer labs ready yet, but next semester, ins hallah, then you will be teaching the research and writing class. Here is your schedule. You only have twenty-five hours with students and the rest are for administration and mentoring. Any questions?"

"Excuse me, but you realize this is three different levels and three different courses? I was told I would only be teaching one level for the different courses five days a week."

"Yes," she sighed. "We wished to do this for our faculty, but we are very short staffed and have many more students at the beginning and intermediate levels than we planned for. You will notice your contract states '*and any additional duties as assigned and/or necessary*'. You'll figure it out and the department heads can help you as well. Do you smoke?"

"No, why?"

"That's good. We've had some difficulties with faculty sneaking cigarettes during breaks. Smoking is forbidden anywhere on this campus. We set examples for these girls and their families expect us all to keep to the rules and present healthy lifestyle choices. Remember it's still Ramadan. Please do not drink or eat in front of the students until after the Eid holiday."

"Certainly. I'll remember." Another young woman appeared at the door.

"This is Miriam. She will be taking you around and introducing you. If you have any questions about the campus, classes, or personnel, she can help you. Here is a map of the campus. I suggest you have it with you for the first few weeks. Good luck and once again, 'Welcome to Princess Noura University, the largest Islamic university for women in the world!' We are very grateful to you for choosing to come here and teach."

Miriam smiled and indicated she would navigate.

"Here is where we are." Miriam pointed to the office labeled on the map.

"We must go over to these buildings. We'll take the monorail. Come."

In some of the corridors and at each monorail stop there were large screens mounted with a continuing loop of scenes from Mecca and imams speaking or chanting in Arabic. Apparently these were the only men permitted to be seen on campus.

After a morning of meeting my students and going over the curriculum, I noticed a surprising state of affairs. Most classrooms did not have enough chairs or desks and girls were sitting on the floor. They didn't seem to mind. This was repeated throughout campus. Students were seated on the stone pathways, small patches of grass, studying on the stairs.

Figure 64. Inside Princess Noura University (PNU),
Riyadh, Saudi Arabia 2013, photo by author

The library was very impressive as a building, but there were almost no books on any of the shelves and no students present. I asked the librarian, who was from the UK, when they were going to have books available. She laughed.

"Ins hallah, as they say. I've been waiting for six months already. In a way, it makes my job a lot easier but it's so boring here, I prefer to have work. Every book in any language has to be approved by a panel apparently and this takes ages. There was an incident recently, tragic... smart, beautiful girls. After that curriculum and reference books were pulled on all the science subjects, and they had to start the process over."

"What do you mean by a 'tragic incident' with books?"

She motioned me into a back conference room which was empty as well.

"The books used for biology and anatomy contained both female and male illustrations and information, of course. This was for the nursing and pre-med curriculum. In two different families, daughters were studying these subjects here. They lived at home, so they brought the books with them to study. One of the neighbors in one case, and one of their male cousins visiting the family in the other, saw their books. They considered the subjects and presentations 'haram'- forbidden. They said these girls had dishonored their families and tore out the pages they thought were 'haram'.

"Oh no. How are we going to teach either subject without any photos or illustrations let alone videos to show the inner body systems?"

"Much worse than that, these two top students were stabbed to death by members of their own family. After that we pulled the books out of circulation. The pre-med course is on hold for now."

'Barbaric and ignorant. Poor girls!' I was getting angry. I could feel these emotions churn in my solar plexus.

"One of their sisters still attends classes here. She's in the Business department but teachers say she no longer speaks in class. She's listless and doesn't seem to care anymore. She's still in shock but must live with her family. The same family that killed her own sister. That's the mentality we have to contend with in Saudi."

We walked out of the conference room slowly. The librarian bit her lip.

"Need the paycheck, you know. Couldn't get a position in Sussex, but I won't stay long. Don't have the stomach for the life here really."

"I might not either." I said confidentially. "Thank you, I'll come here again, books or no."

"One more thing. The only place open to buy food on campus during Ramadan is right near the library. There's a kiosk with tasty sandwiches and strong coffee. Reasonable prices, too. It's run by Phillipinas and they can show you where to hide while you scoff whatever down. One saving grace being way over here. Try it."

"I shall. I didn't bring a thermos, just my water bottle and jet lag is getting to me."

The librarian pointed out directions on my map and since Miriam would not meet me again for another two hours, I was free to wander as well as eat and drink.

The young women at the kiosk smiled openly.

"Hello Ma'am. How are you today? Your first time here?"

Possibly it's a stereotype, but every woman I've had the good fortune to meet, spend time with and even live with—who was originally from the Philippines—has always been warm hearted, kind, and generous. These three women were gracious, genial, and helpful. They made delicious coffee and were teasing each other as they worked in such a playful way the whole atmosphere was illuminated.

"Where you from, Ma'am?"

"Texas. America. And you?"

"Manila, you know it?"

"I've never been there but I've had a few friends from there. All good people."

"Thank you, ma'am. You teach here?"

"Yes, just started today. It's a big campus and has a beautiful library."

The faces of all three women suddenly changed to a more somber expression. They looked uneasily at one another.

"Many Philippine men died building that library, ma'am and this university. Sorry ma'am but we don't think it is beautiful. They never found all the bodies and families back home never get those bodies to bury as Catholic men. "

"So sorry! How did that happen? Building accident?"

"They are going so high to build the dome and it crashes down on top of 18 men one morning. Then they get others to go up to try again and another accident. When we ask for them to dig and find the bodies, they will not."

"That's not right."

"No ma'am. Sorry, too. No one tells this story, no one here cares about Philippines people. We are just slaves to them."

"We are not much better than slaves, here either…just a different kind of slave." I said, then paid them for the meal. I ate my food behind a partition.

My heart was heavy with this news, however at least my heart was registering feelings. Oscar Wilde was reputed to have said once, "It is not terrible that a heart is broken, it is meant to be broken. What is terrible is if a heart turns to stone."

He also wrote: "Pleasures may turn a heart to stone, riches may make it callous, but sorrows cannot break it. Hearts live by being wounded. "I was already beginning to see the wisdom in working here. My emotions were not completely dead, they starting to be re-awakened here.

Figure 65. Author in front of main library PNU, Riyadh, Saudi Arabia 2013

At the end of the day the reverse rituals began. Miriam led me to the front entrance where hundreds of girls and women were re-robing, twirling their hair atop their heads, placing the shayla over it care-fully, some adjusting niqabs over their noses, fastening abayas closed, changing shoes, checking their bags and passing through the female 'monitors' who made sure we were covered sufficiently before exiting. It was a humiliating protocol for adults. I took in deep breaths of air once outside and found Nadia waiting for me.

"Sorry, I realized I didn't have your mobile number so we could text. How was it today?"

"Full on. Here's my number. Can't wait to get back to the villa."

"Tomorrow is only a half day. It's Thursday and still Ramadan. That might cheer you?"

"Sure does. Friday's off, too. Peace and quiet."

"Not really." Nadia quickened her pace back to the bus as she spoke.

"Fridays are not quite peaceful in the afternoon. Our compound is near four mosques, with loudspeakers. Friday afternoons the imams can be quite loud and long. Personally, I put on my headphones or try to go out. You might want to do the same."

"Thanks for the heads up, Nadia. Here we are, eh?!"

Boarding the bus after work was quite different than early in the morning. Women were livelier, some were speaking in low tones over their phone, some were less discreet. I pondered all I had seen and heard. With three different courses I would have hours of prep to do on Friday. At least I had a breather before a full week began.

"You Joanne?"

A woman I figured to be in her early forties dressed in black and pink track pants with a pink short sleeved T-shirt was at my door on Friday morning. I had never seen her before. She had a beach towel on her arm.

"Saw you on the bus and someone said you were from Texas? I'm Val from Texas. Pleased to meet you. Want to go swimming? This is the best time for the pool before it gets too crowded."

"Wow, yes. Just let me change and meet you by the pool, ok?"

"Great, see you there. The water's warm."

Val was right, we were the first ones by the pool at 7:30 am. There were a few women jogging and some doing a kind of stretching class in the makeshift gym. It was Friday so most of the staff were off duty. There was a pause in all the usual activity. Swimming is one of my most favorite ways to relax. We both dove in and swam to the deep end.

"Where are you from in Texas?" I asked once I came up for air.

"Tyler...you know it?"

I did know where it was though I had never spent much time there.

"Yup, I have a friend in New York City who is originally from Tyler. Small world. I'm based in Austin. I went to high school in Houston and left as soon as I could. Some of my family still lives there."

"Don't care much for big cities but I end up working in them most of the time. Never thought I would end up here, but I needed the money to pay for my Masters."

"How long have you been here?" I asked.

"Too long, honey. Three whole years. I thought I could work on my PhD, but I'm not getting much done. I keep telling myself this is the last year though I am saving money. There's nothing much in the teaching field back home unless I want to go way out in north or west Texas, which I don't. It's not even great money at Princess Noura, but the cost of living is lower so I can save…and no taxes. Crazy all these Arab countries are hiring us infidel women teachers and paying us decent salaries, but our own country won't."

Figure 66. Author and colleague outside PNU entrance, Saudi Arabia 2013

"Completely agree with you. What's even worse to me, is all the aid and financial support in the billions of dollars going to countries that work against us, are corrupt and pocket the money. The US government even funds their teacher training. Yet our government doesn't provide enough money for better public education or teacher training because of the excuse 'there's not enough money in the budget'. Messed up."

"You married, Joanne? Have kids?"

I inwardly clench at this question. It's a normal one for getting to know someone but it was so soon after the death of my son, only two months. For me, having to articulate, to vocalize that Denali was dead, is a dagger through my heart every time I have to say it aloud. I responded as best I could to Val, hoping my tone would indicate I didn't want to speak any more about my situation.

"I was married with two children, a son and a daughter. My son and his father were killed in July. We were already divorced, but I never remarried. My son was 25. My daughter is 22. She lives and works in Houston near my father. I saw her right before I left for Riyadh."

"Oh, my God. I'm so sorry. That's so recent. Was it a car accident? Did they die together?"

Most people are taken aback by the mention of the death of someone young. Yet at the same time they have a morbid curiosity if they don't know *how they died.*

"No, they died in the Karakorum mountains of Pakistan. We don't know exactly how or even when, but many have died trying to climb and return from K2. It's called the "Savage Mountain.""

"Oh, Lord. Did they ever find them up there?"

"Not yet. Their bodies are buried …. somewhere." I was starting to shake inside and couldn't keep speaking about their deaths much longer.

"Oh honey, we don't have to talk about it if you don't want to. I can't even imagine the pain you're feeling because I never had any children."

"I can't imagine that myself." I replied softly.

"Could you tell me the scoop here and any heads up I need to be aware of….that would help me a lot."

Val looked around as if to make sure no one was listening.

"Well, if you follow the rules here, living is routine and predictable. If you somehow rub one of the other Muslim teachers or heads of departments the wrong way, they will find a way to get rid of you or make your life miserable. Careful of some of the Saudi students, too.

Just one complaint can get you in trouble and some will try and bribe you to change their grades. Fact of life here. It's not really a university, it's the appearance of a university. Something about elevating Saudi Arabia's status for trade agreements if they showed they were raising education standards for girls."

"Any other tips?"

"Most of the ex-pats who aren't Muslim hang out together in different groups. There are some who go out and seem to know where all the parties are, but they are mostly in the under 40 age range and have to cover for each other because drinking and sex—without being married—are against the law here basically. Of course, there are 'temporary marriages' many enter into for financial support, as well as companionship. Most of the time the authorities seem to look the other way. Some women have been caught and punished. Remember the penalty for adultery is death! As an American you would probably only be deported and put on their list so you couldn't ever come here or work here again. Other nationalities are not so lucky."

"What do you mean?"

"Have you heard the nickname for our street yet?"

"No."

"This is the "Butcher Block"…as in… this is where they carry out punishments as dictated by their Koran laws. This is the place where they slice and dice."

"Are you sure? Have you seen this?"

"Not seen, heard. If you're outside on Friday afternoon you can hear the hours of preaching, shouting and then screaming. They executed a young Philippine girl a few months ago. She came here as a babysitter for a Saudi family with nine children. At the time she was only sixteen herself, and they left her in charge of at least five young children and one little baby, who was sick. The parents were gone for hours and didn't answer their phones when she tried calling. The baby died. The parents only knew after they returned home. They had the babysitter charged with murder. She was held in prison for two years until she reached 18. There was an appeal from the Philippines, and even churches, but she was beheaded right in the square, in public, down the block. I felt I should be outside as a kind of witness, even though I couldn't see…I could hear. I remember her cries, her pleas, the screams."

Val lowered her voice.

"Just know, many of the women here do not disagree with these laws or punishments. Lots of the teachers in this compound came here to marry a rich Saudi. They want to appear as followers of Wahhabism. We need to be a very silent minority to exist here."

We kept swimming as we continued our conversation. The sun's rays were getting stronger. The water was refreshing and soothing.

"Have you been able to travel out during the holidays? Do you go back home or other places when we have a break?"

"Yes, but only after a huge argument about my iqama. It took me a year to get it. Whatever you do, don't give them your passport again once you have it in your hands. If you are even thinking of skipping out, you'll need it, or you could get arrested at the airport. You can stall the first three months but after that you'll have to hand it in to get your visa updated. You have 86 more days to decide."

Val gave me a serious look, then dove under water. A few more women were out walking toward the pool.

As I stroked the water and pulled my body forward, plans began appearing in my mind. Plan A, Plan B and Plan C for Saudi Arabia.

First, I would have to be sure and retrieve my passport as soon as the personnel office opened on Saturday. Then I would have to find the least expensive ticket out on a late-night departure, preferably on a Friday night. I couldn't leave until I received at least the first paycheck, which wouldn't be for sixty days. Maybe by then I would find a way to adapt to staying here longer…or maybe I wouldn't.

More women were lounging by the pool or starting to do laps. I did four more laps of backstroke then joined Val by the walkway. She set down a large blanket so we could spread our towels over it. There was no shade.

"This is the last week of Ramadan. Next week the hash starts up again if you are up for hiking?"

"Sure. Do I have to join or something before next week?"

"Naw, I'll let you know on Wednesday when I know where this one will be. I have a couple of friends who have a car and they come and pick me up here. Keep this quiet, though. Not many from our compound know about it or go. It's a relief to be with people who we don't work with, even if only for a few hours."

"Can't wait." I exclaimed. Val lay down to sunbathe. I followed her example.

"Wait." I said, "How do you manage hiking or doing hash trails in the heat, in the desert in your abayas?"

"We don't." Val shifted so her back could get sun.

"We drive away out of the city and into the desert. There are some Saudi, military and law enforcement types, even some Jordanians.... who are really Palestinians, and Syrian guys. They come along for security and for flirting with the young expat women. After we finish the hash, we cover up again, drive back to the rendezvous point and separate into taxis to get back to the compound. No one is the wiser."

For the first time in months, I started to feel animated. The water and the possibility of hiking out in the desert with a fellow Texan stirred a deeply buried sensation of 'hope'.

If I was frugal, I could still save money even after paying my own ticket out. Finding another job as back up would be a priority. I would start this evening.

Being in danger of harm to my emotional and spiritual well-being is just, if not more important, than being physically harmed. My feeling was that staying here would make me a target.

This was a place of danger to me as an individual. I needed to escape...to travel off this "X."

Flgure 67. Author on the "hash" outside Riyadh, Saudi Arabia 2013

16. SEARCHING IN SERIAN – MALAYSIA

As I drive over the rural roads, passing the checkpoints near Tebedu and the Indonesian border, I take care to be mindful of the field workers walking on the side on the road bent over carrying their baskets full of crops. They hang shiny CDs on makeshift clotheslines over their fields to warn off predatory birds. Some of their villages still display their ancestor's and conquered enemies' heads. They know where their loved ones are, and they revere them.

Denali, my son, would be fascinated by this land and people here. In fact, I reflect, both my children would find this place to their liking.

At times the young children I see in the Bidayuh district schools, smile down to the earth and are full of mischief, running, swimming, laughing and singing. This is one of the few schools which have not been 'selected' by the Ministry of Education offices. The principal is himself Bidayuh and involves the neighboring communities as much as he can in all school activities. He values his young students and speaks four languages fluently: Bidayuh, Malaysian, English and Iban.

One of the youngest boys sits drawing on a small chalkboard during the breaks. He is content and concentrated. He reminds me of my son at the same age. I try not to cry. It is less than a year since his death.

There is much to cry about where I work in this jungle region. What is happening here to the Iban people and especially to the targeted Bidayuh families, is tragically similar to what happened to Native American and Aboriginal children in North America and in Australia. This time it is the Muslim run government who contrives to take children away in the guise of 'educating' them. They must board at schools away from their families and villages, starting as young as six years old. They are put 12-20 in a room in bunk beds. They must hand wash their own clothes, clean the rooms, and help make their own food. The youngest ones are given plastic baby bottles of chocolate Milo drink to suck on at night to quiet them.

They are not allowed to see their parents except twice or maybe three times a year and their parents are not allowed to come onto the school grounds except with permission. If they try at other times, they face penalties, fines and even the threat of imprisonment or their children will be made wards of the government.

Figure 68. Lobang Batu school, Sarawak, Borneo, Malaysia 2014, photo by Lisa Marie Akbari

One day every week I work here training teachers. It is one of my five schools. I can see some of these parents walking across from the barbed wire fences, trying to gain a glimpse of their child or some child they know. It is heart breaking for all except those wishing to capture the hearts and minds and convert these children from their Indigenous beliefs and customs to strict sharia laws and the Muslim religion. If they convert they are given more free time to attend the school mosque, special 'training' and the family is given money. Sometimes the older children are given special 'trips' to other countries and other 'benefits'

Figure 69. Arabic writing on Kampung school, Sarawak, Borneo, Malaysia 2014, photo by Lisa Marie Akbari

and incentives. It is a terrible bargain, and the parents often feel they have no choice.

The Bidayuh and Iban teachers in the school are the only connection to their families and languages. I work with a number of them who deliberately requested to teach in these schools. These teachers have enormous strength, courage, and heart. They need to be able to put on a mask in front of the government designated administrators and imams. They must endure insults, harassment, and unjust treatment in order to be

the touchstone and hope for their Indigenous communities. I admire these teachers and I pray for their success. They have to serve in silence.

One of my colleague's daughters is training to be a teacher. She comes to me with her lesson plans and ideas for a library reading club. This means she will have to spend her own time setting up the books and chaperoning the children, but she is still single and is eager to try. I encourage her and will act as a sponsor when she has to ask for authorization from the principal.

Her mother thanks me and invites me to a weekend celebration of food, music and dance in their village as an Easter celebration with their Seventh Day Adventists church. I accept and cherish the time I will have away from this boarding school and children held as prisoners. These villages have a sad history of being held prisoner by the British, the Japanese and now the Malaysians.

Figure 70. Tebedu school staff, Borneo, Malaysia 2014

Sequoia will be here soon to share the soothing sounds of monsoon rains and view this bold beauty. It will be her first time to be with me in my workspace overseas and her first time to Borneo. I hope she will be re-energized by the exotic landscapes and these remarkable people.

I also hope we can ease some of this deep fresh sorrow we both bear from the loss of her brother, my son and his father...her father. I ponder this all as I drive solo past the checkpoints back to my little house near Serian.

It is raining, as it does at some time every single day. We are right on the equator and the days and nights are equal in time. You can count on it raining and on it being very hot and humid. I am required to wear long skirts and tops as per the Muslim code to cover my whole body down to my ankles and wrists. There is no air conditioning in the schools where I work, but I have fans in my house and can open my car windows. My car is a little Proton Saga, and it sputters as I pull into my drive. The grasses have already overgrown my front steps and lawn.

No one uses lawnmowers or other machines to cut the grass here in rural Sarawak. We use large hedge clippers and squat down to clip the slithering vines, wildflowers, and tall grasses. Since they are watered daily and the sun is strong here for at least half the day, everything grows rapidly in Borneo.

As I uncover the earth, the bricked border early the next morning, I pull out weeds around a cement slab with a drain cover in my backyard. I pause sweating. The clippers and the flora are still wet, and the task is more difficult unless I wait until later in the day when both are drier.

I step back into the kitchen to wash my hands. Glancing out the window to view my progress I catch sight of the narrow, rectangular, horizontal slab framed by the lush green grass and hold my breath. Suddenly it reminds me of a tomb. I think of my son, Denali, and how he has no real resting place. I think maybe this year his body will be found on the mountain K2.

But can I help to bring his body down?

Tomorrow is Palm Sunday in the Christian calendar and Passover in the Jewish tradition. This is a time to reflect on the histories of both the Old and New Testament, on stories of suffering and miracles. There are so many types of suffering. There are countless stories of human endurance as well as Divine support and guidance.

Then I recall those people I have met and worked with in numerous parts of the world, including here who need prayers, guidance, and protection. The suffering so many of us feel is almost unbearable, yet we continue to be guided and protected from physical death. I can still breathe, move, eat, sleep, write and remember. I wonder why?

I remember last year at this time was also a time of pain and loss for my son. His best friend, Zach, was killed suddenly. Denali drove in a haze of grief, hundreds of miles to be with Zach's family, to see for himself. He was exhausted from the demands of his best friend's tragic death, the final semester of his undergraduate years and the logistics of planning for his future. Denali was pale and thin by the time his twenty-fifth birthday arrived, his sister Sequoia visited him, and his last papers were due.

When I flew in to see him just before his graduation, I saw the deep pain in his face and sensed his sorrow when I hugged him. He held himself tightly for the first time in a way that I had never felt from him before. He wanted to show me he was brave and prepared to show only his 'happy face' to others. Denali had so many obligations to various different people on that weekend.

The ceremony was regal with traditional music, red carpet, gowns and mortarboards, as well as inspiring speeches. It was a truly celebratory event. Denali was spontaneously full of joy for much of the day.

After the processions were finished, came the awkward minutes of meeting his father's relatives. His father was not there, nor was his sister, but his paternal uncle and grandparents attended. We paused together to have some photos taken and then dispersed. I stayed with Denali and his girlfriend then posed for more photos.

I remember a station wagon pulling up to the curb. In my memory it is black, but maybe it was Denali's grey car. The back hatch was lifted, and garlands, leis and flowers were laid behind the back seat. Then Denali placed his own leis and flowers on top. For a moment I shuddered and saw these flowers as part of a hearse and funeral procession. We were both dressed in black.

Denali was wearing his black cap and gown. I had a strong premonition of his death but fought it back since it seemed so incongruous with this joyous event. Inwardly I shouted "No, don't take him!" as if I were already speaking with Death.

Eidetic images of death in the mountains kept returning to my mind and filtered into my dreams. I was born with the gift/curse of Cassandra.

In the twelve days that followed the CCA graduation, before I had to leave for work overseas again, I tried to warn Denali. We met for lunch and walks. He was relieved I had recovered from my injuries after being run over by a car a few months before.

"You look great, mum" he said. "It's better you're not going to Afghanistan."

Denali's former landlord offered to host a party to celebrate

Denali's graduation and to farewell both of us. We had participated in many dinners and parties over the years at this house. A party there seemed a way to close a life chapter and part in friendship. I helped prepare the feast. Denali and his girlfriend brought flowers for the table. After the main meal, people started asking Denali questions about his future plans.

The landlord tried to steer the conversation to 'lighter' topics but the comments concerning possible dangers in Pakistan were repeated. At one point we spoke about the Taliban. Denali said he understood they weren't anywhere near where his father and the climbing expeditions were going to take place. I decided to speak up and warn him not to underestimate the reach of the Taliban, or the cruelty of their methods. My direct experience with the Taliban was drawn from my own work in Pakistan in 2010.

Underlining my warnings, I told my son, "I don't know why exactly, and I cannot tell you how, but I know they will strike in the mountains this year. You need to be prepared for this possibility."

There was quiet for a moment; then someone made a joke and people continued drinking, eating and laughing. We took our last photos together. Then it was time to go.

Denali, his girlfriend, and I headed out to the street.

We were chatting all the way to his car. Denali and I stood outside speaking for the last time, face to face. I warned him again about not climbing K-2. We had spoken of this before. While he wanted to go travelling and see the exotic landscapes of Pakistan and the Karakoram, he had trepidations about climbing K-2.

"It's the most dangerous mountain in the world, you have to respect that, of course I'm scared, but Dad would never put me in a risk situation where I would lose my life?!"

I wanted to point out that his father insisting that he climb both Broad Peak and K-2 without any previous 8,000-meter peak experience or strict training was irresponsibly risky. It was not like climbing in Alaska, Switzerland, or New Zealand.

There was always tension when we had to speak about something concerning his father. He had told me he "hated it" when anyone spoke badly about either of his parents or his sister. He said he told his father the same thing. Our family had enough troubles over the years; he didn't want to hear about them anymore.

I looked at his earnest blue eyes and his youthful face and decided that if it was the last time I saw him, I wanted to cherish this time together. I would hold my tongue. So instead of warning him one more time I replied,

"I hope you're right, son. Take good care."

I hugged Denali longer than I usually did for our farewells and followed on an impulse to ruffle his thick head of hair which made him smile. We expressed how we loved each other then, agreed to speak on the phone the next day and see each other again before I left. As Denali pulled out from the parking spot he waved. I waved back to him for the last time.

The next few days Denali was busy selling, storing, and giving away most of his material possessions. He lost track of time. We were supposed to share a meal just before I left but he couldn't get back to Oakland that day. Denali had left his phone by his bed and didn't have it with him when I called. Over the years I witnessed him doing this since he wasn't one to be concerned about not having his cell phone with him. He was different than most of his peers in this respect.

The next day he rang me to come over, but I had already flown back to Texas. He was stunned when I reminded him I had a ticket for the day before and he had forgotten the date. I heard the disappointment in his voice when he realized we could not meet in person.

We spoke again and I warned him once more. "Denali, you are going to find yourself in a situation where in order to survive you are going to have to say, 'No' to your father. You have to be strong to do this. It's important for you to see this and be prepared for it. "Ok, mum," Denali said finally. He changed the subject by asking me about my job in Italy.

Denali was waiting on his New Zealand passport to arrive. It had his visa for Pakistan, and it was imperative they use their New Zealand citizenship for security and political reasons. If it did not arrive in time, Denali would miss the connections in Pakistan and the climbing in the Karakorum.

When I asked him about this, Denali didn't seem concerned or upset. Even if his passport didn't arrive in time, he said he could just be with his girlfriend, and they would go over to Berlin since he had a job lined up there starting in August.

His father was supposed to send him the ticket to Pakistan, but at the last minute he instructed Denali to buy it promising he would reimburse him after the climb on K-2. Now Denali was spending the money he had saved for his internship in Germany to buy and send supplies over to his father. He spent thousands of dollars getting himself and the gear to Pakistan. Money was getting very tight. This worried Denali. He decided to sell all his possessions including his car.

We had an agreement that whenever Denali earned a 4.0 grade average in his university courses for the semester, I would give him $400.00 as a gift and incentive. He never received a mark below an A. He graduated with a 4.1 tying for top of his class at CCA. I remembered this and asked him if he would like me to deposit the money plus a bonus into his account as a graduation gift. Denali paused and said over the phone, "Mum, better wait till I come down to deposit it." It was the first time I sensed he wasn't sure he was going to climb down safely.

Denali had a simple cell phone which only worked in the USA. There would be no skype once he was in Pakistan, and probably no possibility of private internet time until he was down from the mountains. Marty had various sponsors he promoted. He made constant updates via the net. His father loved the media attention, grasping every opportunity to promote climbs and the products he used on his expeditions. He used the *'father and son'* hook as a means to gather more interest. "First time father and son attempt to climb K-2" was repeated to all media who would listen, print, twitter, blog, text or broadcast his ambitions.

Denali's job was to assist his father in all aspects including archiving for a film his father had in mind to market. Denali was the filmmaker as well as the logistics supporter, packer, shopper, diplomat, photographer, climber, expedition partner, morale booster, rescue partner and even team leader at some points in all the climbs and at the end. His father, Marty was already in his fifties. He had several health problems including arthritis in his hips which caused him continual pain and discomfort, however stoic he might have appeared in public. Marty's ego was always his priority and his downfall.

Denali's final email to me was on June 6, 2013, to let me know he had safely arrived and was about to meet his father in Islamabad. We were never able to have technological communications in any form again.

However, we did have another type of contact. Communication

that few people may understand but which we continuously used during our lives together from the moment of his inception—continuing even after his physical death. We 'knew' when we were in trouble, we possessed a kind of deep telepathy in addition to dreaming of each other. I had this with his father years before SAT communications phones and Skype. I experienced it with his sister, my daughter, in a different way-usually a precognition of what was going to happen.

When we finally received the few possessions Denali had, that were able to be returned from K 2, I paused and wept holding the shirt we had bought together at a thrift store. He wore it when we were together, and I saw him wear the same shirt in photos from Pakistan. It still retained his smell. I packed it and have it with me in Borneo.

I read later in his journal about his own private struggles. I poured over his last sketches, observations, poems, and dreams. He jotted down his thoughts, his fears and in places the ink was blurred on the pages.

Denali had many premonitions and thoughts about his own death.

One of his final paintings was of K2 with a modernesque smiley face very near where they probably perished.

Figure 71. K2 Original Painting by Denali Schmidt 2013

I was grateful to have his final written words before they climbed up from K2 base camp. In hindsight, much of his artwork at California College of the Arts years before hinted at the way he would die-in the cold, on a mountain, under the ice.

Denali was fascinated by sculpture for most of his life. For some reason it bothers me that the memorials others constructed for him are of tin and metals—not etched in beautiful stone. Denali doesn't have his own tombstone; he is listed together with his father. No one ever asked me what he would have wanted. They pressed their own wants, ambitions and issues repressed for decades onto a grotesque, cold monument with no bodies buried beneath.

Denali was full of love and loved both his parents, but he was definitely his own man by the time he was killed. He shouldn't be paired with his father. They were completely different in almost every respect.

I am still searching for more tangible evidence of my son's death a year later in 2014. I will resume my chores in my little jungle suburb of Borneo amidst the grasses, fruit trees and multicolored flowers; amidst a people who lovingly display their ancestor's skulls so all will remember them.

The sun is out. The grasses are dry enough to trim now. Fortunately, my next day at work is at a village school that is still controlled by the community and not residential. It is the farthest drive right up to the Indonesian border.

I won't have as much time to prepare for my daughter's visit. I need to arrange everything ahead of time. My wish is for her to feel this place is inviting and not overwhelming, as the jungle here can be to outsiders.

Maybe by creating new memories in new places, my daughter and I will be able to come closer to each other. Denali would have liked that for us. He will be with us no matter where we are. He knows where to find us.

It is we who are still searching.

Figure 72. Sequoia and author in Serian, Borneo, Malaysia 2014

17. KABUL-FIRST CONTACT – AFGHANISTAN

Expats, nationals, and personnel who can afford to, are leaving Afghanistan as I arrive in the late summer of 2014. The installed leadership coalition tries to steer a new Afghan government after the elections, but it is fragile and the factions adversarial. The new coalition has yet to be officially decided, but most predict it will not be a smooth transition. They mistrust each other. Fighting escalates between the two factions to be joined in ceremony and political marriage. The recount begins and friction escalates. There is a sense of dread in the atmosphere. Tension is part of the dust, the winds, the birdsong in Kabul.

Yet there are still birds flying most places I look from my limited view on an outdoor third floor balcony. We are placed in the closely guarded southern suburb of the capital city. Dwellings built into the stark hills, communications towers or trees serve as temporary perches for the flocks of the swift flyers. High walls, bushes, grass, and rubble provide nesting places for the more earth-bound creatures including a solitary male peacock who arrived a few hours before I did. He continues to grace our presence every day parading the grounds and casting his discerning iridescent blue crest and ebony eyes on all who tread within his territory.

Many years ago, I was told by an Aboriginal elder of the Gumbaynggirr people, that every place has their own energies. If the place is still 'alive' then birds and other creatures will be there. If ever you notice there are no birds in sight-this is a *dead zone.* Going or staying there "will make you sick."

Fortunately, many living creatures continue to exist here, even in what is a "conflict zone." I reckon the place I am guided to is still "alive." But am I? Is the place I inhabit between the living and the worlds of those passed on a "real" place? How long shall I continue to love my family so intensely even though half of them are now ghosts?

Figure 73. Peacock at AUAF villa, Kabul, Afghanistan 2014, photo by author

This morning, Saturday, is my day off from teaching at the American University of Afghanistan (AUAF). I am excited to hear the "call" of the peacock and run to the window. We haven't seen him since the fire-fight near us a few days ago. I hope he returns. He adds such beauty, wildness and grace to this compound. In the courtyard adjacent to our guesthouses, the off-duty guards play a vigorous game of volleyball on this Saturday afternoon. It is hot and there is no breeze, yet they jump, sweat, shout out to each other, laugh, and probably curse, though I am still ignorant of the common swear words used here.

Last night, from about ten thirty until morning the sounds of live music filled our balcony. Drums, stringed instruments, tambourines, lots of whoops, clapping and a man singing continued all night under a waning bright moon. We speculated that it must be a wedding. We could see the garish flashing lights of a commercial wedding hall right near our villa, but the music was further north.

Sometimes being around so many people here all the time in close quarters makes me long for the solitude of Borneo. I cherished that time to reflect privately, meander in my memories of our family life when my children were young. In my mind I could review my life, my actions, my words and my love with my son, my daughter, their father, and my aunt Lauradele. She died a few months after my son, creating an ever-larger cavern in my heart. She was the only family member I could call no matter what time of day or night if need be. She would find the time to talk with me. She gave loving, wise counsel. I miss her.

For some reason today I saw at least three different flocks of animals being hustled along the streets. Ruddy colored goats, wooly sheep, shepherds on donkeys or walking along with large poles herding, hurrying them across the side streets. They were adept at guiding their animals in the midst of traffic, motorcycles, bicycles, buses, vans, cars, other beast drawn carts and pedestrians. Their antics made me smile.

Here my thoughts are of necessity, occupied with situational alertness, other people's issues, new curriculum demands, my student's needs, my neighbors, and always with the mood of those who drive us, watch, and monitor us. One has to be focused here, and always on guard.

I have a bit of a quandary today-*to sign or not to sign*-the 'death waiver'. This piece of paper permits us to be able to go out and about Kabul to certain non-expat sites. If I sign it, the University will have no liability or responsibility for what may happen to me. I decide to sign.

It is providential that one of my Afghan colleagues is a Georgetown University of Doha graduate. We know some of the same people from both campuses. This colleague also has a car, knows the local languages fluently, as well as English. He offers to take another colleague from Eastern Europe and myself to "see some of Kabul" starting with the zoo.

Figure 74. Kabul zoo with AUAF colleague,
Afghanistan 2014, photo by Sarwar

It is a sweltering August day, but the streets are jammed. We chat easily in English on our way. He points out sites of interest, recounts history, stories and recent events at certain places while giving us advice about local customs we should pay attention to, and situations to avoid.

Incredibly, for a conflict zone the zoo is packed with families ambling about and street vendors selling sweets, drinks, and food. We spot some anemic-looking lions, many different birds, monkeys and lots of people staring at us, as well as the caged animals.

"Would you like to see the famous 'Chicken Street'? We can go there and to the mall after if you wish?"

"Oh yes, I heard a lot about this street. Do they really sell chickens there?"

"No, mostly carpets, jewelry, things for tourists really. We can just have a look."

He parked the car and gave some money to a man who would look after it on the street, a common practice in many large cities in the world, not just Kabul.

The three of us walk a few blocks to Chicken Street, which is more like three intersecting streets. There were a few touristy looking folks, us and a number of Afghan men promenading. My Eastern European colleague is a tall, very pretty young woman who attracts heaps of attention wherever she goes. She is also bright, sweet and quick to learn. She knows at least three languages fluently and completed two years of her undergraduate degree in the USA.

She is a focused individual. Right now, she is on a mission to find a ring which matches her earrings. We stop at every shop displaying jewelry. There are quite a few on this famous street.

Our male colleague is patient as well as helpful. He spoke to the shopkeepers whenever she desired to see a ring in the display under glass and vigorously negotiated prices. Eventually she chose one resembling multicolored opal which reflected a prism of colors. Her delight at this purchase carried into the rest of the afternoon.

"Do you want to see the mall?"

She asked me as we turned the corner to the block where the car was parked and guarded.

"Really, there is a mall in downtown Kabul?" I was incredulous.

"Not a large mall like in Dubai, but they have stores and a cinema"

Sure enough, we entered and had our bags checked at a four-story building which served as the mall. It was practically empty, the lighting was dim, but some stores were open. A restaurant and café on the fourth floor were serving customers and a Bollywood film was running in their movie theater, which I imagined was only filled with men.

We decided to have a drink (non-alcoholic of course) and something sweet at the restaurant. Our colleague did the ordering. He also insisted on paying. It almost felt like an outing in any other country except we were still in a conflict, or some would say 'war zone.' There is a danger in using other peaceful countries as a point of reference in Kabul. It is a unique place and has its distinctive threats. No day is an 'ordinary day' in the same respect as in a country where IEDs and VIEDs (vehicle borne improvised explosive devices) and kidnapping are not a common occurrence. Planning an excursion or movement needs to account for quick changes. Our colleague grew up in Afghanistan, knows this city, it's moods and its dangers.

"Time to go." He said suddenly.

We are guided back to the car. Our colleague opens and closes the doors for us. He drives back to our guesthouse/villa. As an Afghan national, he cannot enter these gates. He drives the car as close as possible to the check point and nods at the Pashtun guards.

"Thank you both so very much."

"You are very welcome. I hope you see Kabul is not all destroyed, or a place where fighting and death are the only features of our life here. We can go out from the city next time. Somewhere safe."

My female colleague added. "The weather should be cooler soon, too."

"I'd like that. Let' see how this week goes. See you on campus tomorrow."

We stepped lightly into the courtyard. The guards looked stern and disapproving. We slid our headscarves off as we opened the door to the villa. Part of our routine was to sign in and out on the whiteboard. We moved our colored magnetic markers to "In."

"Why don't we make dinner together? You can come up to my room. I have lots of food."

"Sounds fine. Let me change and make a phone call."

I was grateful for her invitation. I enjoyed her company. We entered our two different entrances to our separate villas. Our small compound consisted of two guard houses and a turret like structure in the front garden and two living quarters for American University of Afghanistan (AUA) faculty. Each building has a "safe room", but they are located on the second floor. Both of us have rooms on the third floor. We would have a better chance if we could get to the top balcony. Instead, we are supposed to go out to the main hall of our level, go down a flight of stairs, open the second set of doors downstairs and run back to the "safe room." We wouldn't have much of a chance should we be attacked. Moreover, we aren't allowed to have weapons. Only our Afghan guards have guns. But we do have knives.

Figure 75. Neighbors AUAF villa, Kabul, Afghanistan 2014, photo by author

We live in the same neighborhood as one of the two Afghan Presidents. This makes our accommodations vulnerable. There is hostility in the air.

Our transport to work is basic. Our vans have no extra shields or "armor", no bullet proof glass and no extra locks. Our Afghan driver has no weapon. There are only three possible routes from our compound to the university. These are used in rotation every week. Our transport schedule is changed daily so as not to make us predictable, but the schedule is posted in our villa and in the university transport office. It's too easy to snap a photo and text it around. We do it ourselves.

Up on the balcony I spot the large, grey torpedo-shaped helium balloon which is a feature of the Kabul sky. It drifts over Bagram air base in the distance. Over our heads a few kites spin in the wind as the sun starts to descend. My children used to love running kites, watching them dip and rise in the air. Even here, in Afghanistan I cannot stop thinking of Denali's death. I wonder how he would respond to the nuances of light I see in this evening sky, to the rough mountain arms, the peacock and to my sorrows. Here, where there are no memories of us together, I am in constant psychic pain missing him, his laughter, our conversations. The Irish poet, priest John O'Donohue once wrote, "Oh, I am lonesome for the conversations we never had." That is how I often feel when I let myself think of my son.

Somehow, being closer to Pakistan, where he and his father perished is irrationally comforting. His body is not that far away from where I stand.

Weeping is part of my life now, though I am in a city where more tears are shed than in most places on Earth. Denali believed in destiny. I suppose it is my destiny to be in Afghanistan. I wonder what my daughter's destiny will be.

The next Friday I accompany some women expats for brunch to a place outside Kabul near the city dam. It is run by an American family. They came years ago to set up a farm, residence, restaurant as well as shelter for female survivors of violence and a base for the Afghan girl and boy scouts to have meetings, camps and conferences. They started cottage industries onsite including handmade linens, crafts and clothing for sale. They named their place Parsa. Women from their shelter prepare a weekly brunch which costs $10.00 US per person. It's served buffet style and seating is outdoors on low tables with cushions laid upon the grass, under weeping willow trees. They advertise on their website and by word of mouth. During warm weather they open every Friday to outside visitors. So far, they've never been attacked.

They don't allow weapons on their grounds.

Parsa has no visible guard houses but is set far back from the main road. The expats who patronize Parsa come from all different sectors. There I met contractors, NGO and medical personnel, foreign government workers and intel connected individuals. This is a breathing space, a place for informal networking and a chance to spend money to directly fund a worthy enterprise.

Figure 76. Parsa outside Kabul, Afghanistan 2014, photo by author

I ask permission to take a few photos as some of the scouts set up tents for a long weekend camp. I inquire of one of their leaders who speaks English, where they will go hiking. "Up there in the mountains." He points to a high hill on the perimeter.

"Isn't it dangerous?"

"We know the trails. The city is more dangerous...really."

He instructs one of the young scouts how to stake down the tent flaps. This something I know well. Our family trips always involved camping and since my husband was an expert adventure guide, he taught us all the most effective and efficient ways to set up camp. These scouts use large canvas tents with metal poles and hemp ropes. It takes more effort to erect them in the wind.

We stroll around the farm smelling the lemon gum and other fruit trees, watching the livestock, and soaking in the sun on a peaceful afternoon. I don't want to leave but we must. We hired a "Gold Taxi." We can't keep the driver waiting. We make plans to return every Friday Parsa is open.

Figure 77. Afghan scouts at Parsa, Afghanistan 2014, photo by author

The next week on AUA's campus I am scheduled to start additional night classes. During the day I train teachers and staff at the Afghan Ministry of Finance. I team teach with another American woman. She was one of the original founders of the American University of Afghanistan in 2006. She also trained teachers in Iraq. She is a vibrant powerhouse of a woman, tall, blonde, and bold from the Midwest. She knows her way around Kabul. We complement each other in training styles. She is also named Lisa. Together we find a way to navigate the murky male politics of both the University and Ministry departments. Travelling to Ministries puts us at risk. We become more visible to more people and once again we have no weapons, nor does our Pashtun driver.

The American University of Afghanistan (AUAF) is located on grounds which formerly housed the Russian intelligence services. The dreaded KGB had their main headquarters on this block of land.

Figure 78. NIMA (Ministry) with Lisa R. Kabul, Afghanistan 2014

The night classes are students who have other responsibilities during the day. I am given intermediate level classes. 70% of my students are male. Overall AUAF is about 80% male across departments. Most students are provided scholarships paid for by US agency funding. One of my students comes over to my desk to proudly show me his new 'smartphone'. He slides through his photos in front of me stopping at a screen shot of my photo. It is my US passport page with all my details visible.

"Look teacher, I know you. You see?" He points to my passport scan.

I am jolted, shocked and angry all at once but try to keep my expression neutral and my voice steady.

"Oh yes, that's me alright. Where did you get this photo?" I ask sweetly.

"My friend. He works here in the office. He text me. I have more teachers…see."

"I see." I comment as I view a number of my other western colleague's passport pages from Canada, the UK, America and Australia. My breathing quickens.

"Listen, Ghazan. Would you please delete my photo and not send it again. Do you understand? I am very old, you know. I don't want anyone to know my age. As a woman it's not nice. I think the other teachers would not want their photos or ages sent around either. Please delete all these photos right now."

"Oh, okay teacher. See, I delete." He presses a button on the screen, but I know he probably has more in his phone gallery. It's possible he copied them and can retrieve them.

"Thank you, Ghazan." I nod affirmatively and he goes to find a seat in the classroom.

"Alright, let's begin, shall we?"

In my mind I calculate exactly how long it will be until the first break for evening prayers. Someone should be in the administration office during the break. I need to report this to the security officer, too.

Five minutes before the established interval I let my students know they will have a little extra time tonight. While they are filing out the door, I make my way toward the administration building, but then decide it will expedite the process if I can find the Head of Security first. He is a British, ex-military officer. He is the only non-Afghan security hire, and he is a contractor to AUAF. He'll be able to contact the right people and alert the administration discreetly. Evidently someone is copying, disseminating, and maybe even selling our information from the inside.

The Head of Security smiles when he sees me approaching then furrows his brows when I tell him what happened in class.

"Do you have the name of the student Jo?" He takes out a small moleskin notebook to write it down.

"Yes, here it is and his student ID number."

"Right, I'm on this straight away. Do you have his cell phone number?"

"Not with me, but I think I can get it for you."

"Text it to me ASAP. I'll get back to you about this. Please keep it quiet for now, would you?"

"Will do. "I assure him. It may be a longer night than I anticipated. I run by the café to grab a coffee before they close.

While I'm on break, my phone rings. It's my good friend and former HTS colleague from Kansas, Lisa Marie Akbari, whom I haven't seen since we were together in Borneo. She is based in Kabul working for a non-government organization called World Vision. She was right, we both ended up working in Afghanistan.

"Hey, how are you?" We purposely keep our phone conversations and text messages brief.

"Good, I'm good. Can we meet soon? Be great to catch up."

"Sure, Lisa. Just email me the time and place. You know my days off, eh?

"Yep. Got your email. Check yours later, okay?"

"Okay, keep safe."

"You, too."

Lisa cheers me. She has a musical, gentle voice and she laughs easily. She will understand the gravity of this situation. I can't confide in any of my AUAF colleagues.

Hurrying back to class I notice a group of students hovering around Ghazan. He was showing something on his phone to some young men. I steady myself for the final hour. This is going to be one of the longest classes I've had to teach in years. I force myself to focus.

"Goodnight, Khuda Hafiz. See you next time."

I did manage to get all my students phone numbers. I texted Ghazan's number to the Head of Security before I packed up.

It was pitch black, no moon and only a few lights on campus. It was past 9:00 pm. I made my way to the back transport lot where we waited for our van ride home. Other colleagues stood around, some smoking, some silent until our van driver started the engine and signaled for us to climb in.

Some of our faculty members were nervous. It was true, you never knew if you were going to make it back safely. Some chatted constantly, annoying the driver and other seasoned passengers. One or two were indiscreet enough to discuss their students or their weekend plans. I tuned them out.

My mind was laser sharp tonight. I kept sorting through possible scenarios. How did someone in the AUAF office take photos of our passports? Did he do it at night? Someone would have seen him during the day. Was it a he? Did he or she have an accomplice? Did they take our passports out of the office? Did they sell our personal information? Would they find out who uncovered their scam? Would they be disciplined?

Would there be retaliation?

The caffeine infused my thoughts. We were approaching our guest-house. I would be awake for hours. Now I just had to wait patiently and see what the administration and security decided to do. I trusted the Head of Security would get back to me. It was only a question of when.

Figure 79. American University of Afghanistan author at gate, Kabul 2014

The next morning the Head of the Language Department called me in. He was incredibly tall. Six foot seven. I looked up as he spoke since we were both standing.

"I heard about last night. Nasty business. Listen Joanne, this is timely really. We are going to open a new branch of AUAF in Mazar. I think you would be best to go up there and get everything set up. You will be coming back to Kabul from time to time, but Mazar will be your home base."

"Wait, my contract was for Kabul. I'm quite sure."

"Well, actually it is for wherever we choose to place you. Don't worry it's safer than Kabul. General Dostum is supporting this expansion. He's offered a large villa on his compound just outside the city as a place for you to live and have classes for the female students."

"Is there anyone there to assist me. I've never been to Mazar. Are there any books, resources, computers, classrooms and furniture?"

"Yes, General Dostum's nephew is there and there is a car with a driver for you. You have a budget, too. We can keep in constant contact. It will be fine."

"Who do I live with?"

"Um, his nephew lives on the first floor and you have a private room and bathroom on the third floor. There is a woman who comes in to clean and do laundry for you both. I believe she cooks, too."

I didn't like the sound of this situation. An Afghan single young man living in the same house spelled trouble. No other expats nearby was a security issue, too.

"What about security?"

"General Dostum will provide us from his own security detail. They will be guarding the neighborhood 24/7 from what I understand."

"Alright, please let me think it over."

"Our only other alternative is to let you go, Joanne. We are moving all our female teachers out of Kabul after this...breach. There have been more kidnappings and the administration feels it's a matter of your safety."

My stomach lurched. I couldn't lose this job. I didn't have another option and I was still paying off medical bills from the hit and run accident injuries I had. Insurance had only covered 80%. Besides, I was just getting to know people in Kabul. I rather enjoyed my life on the main campus.

Once again, I packed my things, said farewells to my new colleagues and prepared to go further north and west.

It was coming on winter. Mazar-i-Sharif is in a spectacular spot surrounded by a range of the Hindu Kush mountains. The air was fresh, and it seemed much safer than Kabul. There was a large military base near the airport known as Camp Marmal and a UN headquarters that hosted parties for expats and locals at least once a week.

For the first week I was hosted at a hotel in town. Two of the AUAF local staff picked me up from the airport and made sure I was settled in. They brought me Indian food takeaways and took me on a tour of the city. We went over to the UN compound at night. I did notice the local guards waved their friends in while giving only a cursory search of their bags. When we were inside those bags were opened and provided drugs to various expats who worked in the UN mission.

There were children brought in from Skatistan or some name they gave to a skateboard playground. It was touted as a great recreation outlet for both girls and boys, but it also proved to be a place for choosing and grooming children for sex trafficking. Sadly, there is almost nothing that is offered by "humanitarian programs" for free. There's always a price—visible or hidden. Bacha bazi boys euphemistically known as "dancing boys" or "playing boys" is an endemic part of Afghan society. Boys are dressed as girls, trained to act, dance, and perform sexual favors for older men. Warlords, law enforcement, military, politicians, wealthy businessmen and landowners participated in this "practice." In Pakistan there is something similar. In many parts of Central Asia there is a saying: "Women are for breeding and men are for love" ...or..." boys are for love and girls are for making children." The fact that homosexuality in any form is condemned by Islam doesn't enter into the conversation.

Corrupt expats eager to try out sexual perversion away from their home country, spouses and families-participate here, too. They pay the local "providers", and the children are brought to compounds and private villas.

Figure 80. Afghan men and bacha bazi boy in Afghanistan 2014

It is criminal, despicable, and evil but there was nothing I could do about what I saw. Many Americans and western country citizens don't realize how much child sex exploitation goes on in their own countries. Often law enforcement, lawyers, politicians, and judges are involved. It is a terribly rewarding business. Children are considered commodities, products, packages. They are used and sold over and over again. If you get in their way and try to stop their commerce, the traffickers will not hesitate to take you out of their way by any means. You can't fight them alone.

In my opinion, the Global War on Terror should have been a war against the terrors committed against children…worldwide. The most innocent and vulnerable are the ones most attacked, especially in conflict zones, places of poverty and where natural disasters strike. It is easy for children to go "missing."

The two men working for AUAF were from Dostum's family. General Dostum and his family controlled Mazar. They were also known as ruthless warriors. They drove me out of Mazar at the end of the week to a large, lonely compound off a dirt road. It was not a safe situation for me as the only expat, single woman there and I knew it.

My room had a balcony on the third floor, its own spacious

bathroom which doubled as the "safe room" since it had steel doors and a sliding steel plate to go over the window. It didn't inspire confidence. There was a large kitchen on the first floor where villa rooms had been converted to classrooms. The offices were on the second floor. The young men lived in the basement. It all felt wrong. I called back to AUAF Kabul to report.

"Look," My boss answered. "Try it for a month and then we'll talk about it again. We need to make sure you and the other expat women are out of harm's way."

I didn't believe him. I heard from other colleagues there were only two of us expat women who were moved out of Kabul in our department. We were both older women. One of my male colleagues from the UK was eager to trade places. He wanted to leave Kabul.

"How about we check with each other every week. The security situation is questionable here."

"Alright fine, Joanne. Call me at the end of next week. Good luck!"

The few Mazar staff started bringing in women who were interested in learning English. They came in groups of three and four, some with other female relatives. I received them in one of the large classrooms and answered questions through an interpreter when necessary. They said they were excited to have a female, native speaker to come teach them.

After a few days, I decided to ask a couple of local women from Mazar who were English teachers and spoke English well, what they thought of my living situation. Did they think it was safe or proper for me to be living in a house with two young, single Afghan men?

They all shook their heads, "No."

"No, teacher. This is no good. You are far away here. These men.... They are no good." They confirmed my suspicions.

I asked them to walk with me a little outside in the courtyard. It was there they recounted a tragic story of one of their Hazara relatives who had lived not far from this compound.

"She was very beautiful, young and had two babies. It was winter when Dostum's men came to her house. They killed her husband and father and took her away. They hurt her. Wouldn't let her go for three days and then left her on the road. When she walked back to her house, her two babies froze to death. She wouldn't leave them. When we came to help her, she went crazy. We keep her with us now. Nothing more to do."

Most Afghan women I knew wouldn't ever say or maybe even know the English word for rape. They will confide someone "hurt them" and the implication, depending on the situation they describe is usually "hurt" means "rape." In their laws, women are almost always held responsible for being raped, no matter what the circumstances. *They are charged* with "adultery" or "unlawful sex outside marriage." The penalty in sharia law…is death.

The first weekend I stayed in the villa, there were men going in and out of the basement, loud raucous noise. I stayed up on the third floor. I called Lisa on Sunday night. She was in Badakhshan working for World Vision again. I described the scene.

"That's not a good situation. You should get out of there. If anything should happen, they will blame it on you."

"Yes, I know. It will probably mean I lose my job, but better being alive and having to look for work than the alternative."

"Are you in your safe room?" Lisa asked me.

"The safe bathroom…yes. Luckily there's an electrical outlet here so I can keep my phone charged. What about you?"

"I'm not in a much better situation than you are. I came here with two Afghan women, but they went to stay with their families. I'm holed up in the safe room here but it's a joke. I don't trust the two Afghans assigned as my PSD (personal security detail). I only have two more days for this monitoring/evaluation report before I'm done here. Then I head back to Kabul. If you want to…we can keep talking…about anything. We should check in on each other every hour anyway."

"Good idea. I have internet here, thank God. I'll go get my laptop."

"Ok, barricade yourself in your room, too. Have you got your whistle…not that it will do much good if you're not near any other people."

"It might pause them for a nano second." I laughed. "No, this is bad."

We spoke throughout the night and the next morning more prospective students were brought in. Some brought food to share with me. The week was uneventful until Friday night when I heard more men come in, to party with the Mazar boys. I emailed AUAF and told them about the situation.

Saturday morning at around 4:00 am I decided it was all clear and I could go down to get some tea. I put on my black abaya and tip toed downstairs. No one was around. I started the kettle, had my cup, spoons and teabag ready. The kettle stopped whistling and I poured out some of the boiling water. Then I heard a key being turned in the front door. The door opened.

I couldn't see the front door from my position back in the kitchen. There was no way out and to get to the stairs I would have to run across the front foyer. I looked for a large kitchen knife. There were none out on the counter and opening a drawer might be noisy. I grabbed the kettle of boiling water. A tall man in shalwar kameez with a turban-like headdress approached. He was reaching into his front sash, a place where Afghan men often kept their special daggers—kukri or pulwars. I stood ready to throw the boiling water on him.

He stopped when he saw me. We both looked at each other for a brief moment, casing each other. Then the man showed me both his hands, placed one over his heart and bowed slightly. He pointed to the downstairs bathroom and made a washing motion with his hands. I kept looking at him while holding the kettle. He backed up, then turned and went into the bathroom and shut the door. I heard the door lock click.

I ran upstairs with the kettle and barricaded myself in the room. I listened to hear the toilet flush and the man walk to the front door. He opened it, closed it then I heard a key turning in the lock from the outside. I momentarily breathed a sigh of relief. But evidently this man had a key to this villa. Who was he? I'd never seen him before.

I waited until 6:00 am and called my Mazar staff. He was grumpy. I had woken him up. I told him what happened.

"Don't worry. There is a mosque across the street. He was probably coming too early for prayers. He needed to wash."

"But why does he have a key to our place?"

"Oh, we leave a key outside in case someone needs to come in."

"What?! That's not safe, not secure. Please, you need to bring it inside. Who else has a key?"

"Maybe a few men who deliver supplies. I can't be here all the time. Don't worry this is General Dostum's house. No one makes problems for us. I swear."

I waited another two hours and called the Head of Department. He was not happy to hear of the situation. I told him I needed to return to Kabul until it was sorted out. He agreed. I started packing.

He arranged a ticket and told my Mazar staff. They drove me to the airport, apologizing the whole way and asking when I could come back.

"The women want to study with you. They tell me this. Please come back soon. Everything will be ready for you. No problem."

I didn't say much. I doubted the situation would be remedied anytime soon. It looked like I would be leaving Afghanistan shortly. AUAF would probably give me no choice.

When I got to the airport, I called Lisa.

"Call me when you get back to Kabul. Maybe we can meet. You're almost out, Jo."

When I boarded the plane, I saw my seat was taken. I tried to reason with the man by showing him my ticket. He and his companion brushed me aside with their gestures and spoke loudly in Dari.

A young Afghan man in western jeans, shirt and jacket started speaking to them and then to me. He spoke English, too.

"Sorry, Miss. They will change seats. This is your seat."

"Oh, it's alright if they want to sit together. I can find one in the back."

"No, Miss. It's not alright. They have to learn. They cannot push women because they want something. It's not right. They didn't know you were a foreigner."

The two men got up, bowed slightly, and moved to the back. I was surprised. I thanked the young man behind me and settled in the seat near the window. No one else said anything. I had the row to myself.

As the plane flew over the Hindu Kush mountains I was spellbound with its beauty. I thought again of my son dying in the mountains, in the snow and ice. There are worse ways to die. There are worse ways to live.

Figure 81. Mazar airport on tarmac, Afghanistan 2014, photo by author

18. AFTER MAIDAN – UKRAINE

Throughout time, people and nations have used touchstones to describe events which pivoted the course of their lives and/or their nations and their histories. "Before the war" or "After the flood" or more recently

"Since September 11th" and now, "in the time of Covid" and "during the pandemic." By the time I arrived in Kiev at the end of July 2015, Ukrainians already had their own new marker, "After Maidan... things will never be the same."

In my personal history, I marked everything "after their death" and I supposed my daughter did as well, though we never discussed it. 2015 was another tumultuous year starting in Kabul working at the American University of Afghanistan, exiting quickly for a short contract in Florence, Italy.

In Italy I was hired to try and revive a Waldorf high school which endeavored to be a bilingual school. In addition, I hoped to obtain my Italian citizenship based on my father's heritage. But once there, I was told I would have to return to the United States and pay a considerable sum of money for an Italian passport. This made my decision easy. I would have to leave Tuscany.

I planned to visit Francie in Umbria before I left. A few days ahead of my trip south, I received a phone call letting me know that Francie's son, Edo had been killed in an accident on the same road her brother had been hit on his motorcycle and killed twenty-one years before. My heart sank. Edo has passed his exams, then gone to work in Australia with his Aunt Vito. He had returned to Italy for a short holiday. Now, this fine Italian boy who was the treasure of their family...was dead. Edo was even younger than Denali was when he was killed. I was stunned and in grief for my Italian friends. Edo was Francie's only child. He too, was their family's only grandson.

I sent Francie and her family a message. I knew she wouldn't want to speak on the phone. The funeral was to be held in Umbria. Regrettably, I couldn't change my outward ticket. My visa was about to expire. I was unable to attend the funeral. I expressed my deep condolences, spoke to Vito over the phone. She was already in Umbria.

Vito told me she was in Australia when she had a sudden thought that she *must go back home to Umbria right away and not delay.* It was such a strong feeling that she didn't question it. She bought a ticket and flew to Italy. It was very expensive to leave right away but she followed this "calling." When she arrived in Umbria everyone was asking, "What happened? It's good to see you but why are you here?" She said, she wasn't sure, but it was great to be with everyone. Edo was there at her welcome home dinner.

The next day Edo was killed in an accident. Vito knew why she was "called back to Umbria." It was important to be with Francie and her family for this heart-rending life event.

"You know, Jo…I never believed in destiny. Il fato (fate) But now I do."

I promised I would keep them in my prayers. We had another bond of grief. I felt terrible I would not be there to support them as they had supported me. Our Lady of Sorrows had come to visit us…again.

I needed to get back to the States for two reasons. First, Sequoia was organizing an exhibition of Denali's artwork in San Francisco. Second, the day after the art exhibit opening, I was to leave to work in Ukraine. I had been selected for a brand-new Peace Corps Response program at the Ternopil State Medical University. The timing was right once I found out I couldn't obtain an Italian work visa and would have to leave the country. I accepted the position.

Sequoia had never consulted me about taking Denali's artworks or how to display them. Even when Sequoia visited me in Borneo, she never mentioned her plans or her actions. I was still too mired in grief to resist, though legally she had no right to his works. Her disregard wounded me deeply.

Sequoia also gave some of Denali's paintings away to people *she* thought should have them. This was a constant point of friction just before the opening of the show. Sequoia told me she was giving one of my favorite paintings of Denali's works entitled, "Buried" to a friend of Marty's. An interloper in our family over the years.

Denali's art show was entitled, "Peak Inspirations." The afternoon before the exhibit opening, I happened to be scrolling to Mike Horn's facebook site. (Yes, I prefer to call that site facehook). Mike had been with Marty and Denali on the mountain Broad Peak, and at base camp on K2 in 2013. He was originally from South Africa, a former military man who moved to Switzerland. He is still known as an "extreme adventurer." Mike was a driven man whose wife died of cancer a few months before this 2015 expedition to try once again to summit K2 in Pakistan.

I was following his attempt because it was possible that my son and his father's bodies, or parts of them, might be found. Sometimes it happened after a thaw that bodies slid down and were exposed, even after many years. The only people who went up K2 were extreme alpinists, climbers, and Sherpas. I wrote and requested anyone who might be climbing K2 to please contact me first privately, if they thought they found his or his father's body or body parts. I didn't want to find out on social media or through the press.

I was watching a short video clip on Mike Horn's site. Suddenly I saw an image which made me gasp in horror. It looked like my son's head. The face was distorted, the mouth contorted in what looked like a cry of agony. It was a severed head, laying in the snow with long dark brown hair. Often hair and fingernails grow for years after death. I rewound the clip and paused it at the frame where the head was displayed. It definitely resembled Denali. I felt like a knife went through my heart and stomach at the same time. How could he post this online? No matter whose body part it was. He displayed it like a trophy. Revolting, despicable, crass, and cruel.

I debated whether to call Sequoia. It was only a few hours before the exhibit was to open to the public, but with the speed of the net and facebook posts, by now it had tens of thousands of views. I felt it was better I tell her before someone else sprung it on her or mentioned it at the show.

"Hi Mum, what's up?" She was already at the gallery.

"Sequoia, you'd better go outside and sit down before I tell you. This is serious."

"What, ok Mum, I'm going outside. Ok...what is it?"

"Sequoia, have you looked at Mike Horn's post today on facebook?"

"No, why?"

"Watch the short video clip and at about one minute 25 seconds tell me what you see."

I waited, holding the phone away from my ear in case she screamed.

She swore and then came back to me.

"Oh my God. It *could be Denali's* head. Ok, I've got to hang up and call some people Mum. We'll talk later. See you soon. Love you."

I didn't know what Sequoia would do. As quickly as I could I walked to the metro station in Oakland and boarded the train for San Francisco. I wasn't used to walking in high heels and a dress. Fortunately, there was still an hour before the official opening.

Sequoia greeted me along with her friend from Greece she hired to help set up the show.

"I called some friends to post online, Mum. I posted a comment, too. Let's not talk about it right now. We just have to wait and hope he takes it down."

"Alright Sequoia. Is there anything I can do?"

"No Mum. What do you think of the exhibit?"

I felt overcome with both sadness and pride seeing my son's art displayed. It seemed wrong that Denali was not physically there with us. I felt uncomfortable and annoyed that instead of placing plexiglass over his original painting of "Buried" as he had directed, they were placing the dry ice directly on the painting. This would fade the paint and definition over time. It was careless.

Figure 82. Buried painting by Denali Schmidt being covered with ice at the White Walls Gallery, San Francisco, California, USA 2015

I couldn't stop thinking about that video of a head and face that looked so like Denali. It was looping in my mind.

People were starting to arrive. People from my past, people I knew and didn't know. Denali's friends. Art critics from the San Francisco papers came, too. It was a swirl of people, colors, and emotions. It had been two years since Denali and Marty were killed, but I still kept expecting Denali to come in the door at any moment.

Sequoia knew I was leaving the next night. We stayed at the gallery until everyone had gone. The show was to continue for a week. She didn't mention her plans to me, but we had lunch together before I left for the airport. The video was still up on facebook. Neither of us spoke about it the next day. She didn't tell me she was in the process of securing a visa to go to Pakistan by herself and trek into the Karakoram.

At the Kiev airport we were met as the first group of Peace Corps and Peace Corps Response to be integrated back into Ukraine after all the previous volunteers had been hastily evacuated due to the violence and an escalating civil war.

One of the Ukrainian national staff looked very much like my ex-sister-in-law, Doris. It was uncanny. Seeing her continually reminded me of Marty and my "outlaws" (ex-in-laws), an uncomfortable sensation. We were driven to a grungy hotel within walking distance of the Peace Corps office in Kiev.

Kiev is a synthesis of a contemporary European and former Soviet city. There were modern shopping areas, parks, a variety of good restaurants, cafes, churches and public transport. There were remnants of Soviet architecture, statues and offices. It's an easy city to walk about and people are friendlier than in Russia. I mention Russia because recent events have tied these two countries together again…though they are quite different. In fact, Kiev comes from the original name of this city area, Kiev Rus in the Middle Ages.

Ukraine is a country of Slavs. Most Ukrainians speak Russian. Most medical and technical books are in Russian. Most of the generation over 35, who are professionals in medicine and science studied in Russia or with Russian professors using Russian textbooks. The Crimean's, as I learned, want to be part of Russia. They were for most of their history. It is outside forces from Europe and the United States who want to punish Russia and set their own "buffer zones" in Ukraine. Outsiders are stirring up civil "unrest."

Ukraine has a history of being fought over by greater powers. The Mongols, the Cossacks, Ottoman Turks, The Austro-Hungarian Empire, The Russians, and the Germans. After the people of Ukraine elected a leader, President Vitor Yanukovych, who the American and European governments did not support because he wanted to suspend the Ukraine-European Union Association Agreement and continue friendly relations with the Russian Federation in 2013; outside influencers contrived to create a "Ukrainian Revolution." Vitor Yanukovych had been elected leader numerous times since 2004, but they implemented a coup which ousted the elected President. They installed the corrupted Petro Poroshenko, a puppet beholden to both the USA and the European Union.

In 2014, Petro Poroshenko was "elected" President of Ukraine. He immediately signed the EU Association Agreement while Russia started their annexation of Crimea after a referendum in Crimea indicated citizens there were overwhelmingly in favor of keeping closer ties to Russia.

During 2014, protests and "separatist movements" increased, culminating in the massacre in Maidan Square in Kiev. Initially this was blamed on "Russian influenced separatists" but later proved to be hired assassin mercenaries. Who provided the money for these disrupters is still not entirely clear. The whole situation in Ukraine was and is complicated by many competing "interested parties." Dive further into John McCain, the Biden family and Pelosi family to follow the money ties from the USA to Ukraine. For some reason the Peace Corps sent over 300 "volunteers" in various fields from: building civil societies, education, medicine, agricultural assistance, and English language training to Ukraine. Ukraine had more Peace Corps representatives working in their country than any country in Africa, Asia, or South America. Yet, the Peace Corps boasts it is non-political and humanitarian. Judge for yourself after doing more research.

After the checkpoint we were ushered into the Peace Corps headquarters. By the first stairway was a poster of President John F. Kennedy. I paused.

Figure 83. President John F Kennedy and Sergeant Shriver greeting first Peace Corps Volunteers at the White House, Washington, D.C. 1962

There were only two of us in the specialized Peace Corps Response team. We did not have to go through the long in-country orientation, language training or more onerous Peace Corps political training. We were specialists who already had years of experience in our fields, and we were older than the majority of Peace Corps volunteers. Our training was only ten days in Kiev and then out to our sites. My Peace Corps Response teammate had been a Navy Seal and with Naval Special Warfare for over twenty years. He had definite ideas for our training. We managed to get through with some practical strategies for life in Ukraine.

After a few days in Kiev, I spoke to my daughter on the phone. She informed me she had obtained a visa to go to Pakistan and arranged for a trek with a guiding company into the Karakorum. She was going to look for those bodies seen at K2 base camp. She was going by herself, and her Aunt Doris and Uncle Charlie were paying for this dangerous adventure.

She was going to leave soon.

To say I was shocked and horrified is an understatement. This was a reckless trip from my perspective. It was only two years since her father and brother were killed and going alone as a young, attractive, single women into Pakistan with no known family or contacts there was rash.

Her mind was made up. The Schmidt side of the family supported her. I was extremely concerned.

I called my father. Her grandfather was the only person she usually listened to and heeded his advice. He was also worried and furious. My father told me he warned her he would not pay her funeral expenses, and should she go he would not support her financially in any way. He loved her too much to approve of such an expedition. I thanked him and I agreed with him. Love needs to be tough love from time to time.

I confided in my teammate. He suggested I contact anyone I still knew from Pakistan and someone who might be able to provide over-watch. I did this right away. One of my contacts agreed to help me. Sequoia promised me she would keep in touch by SAT phone and by email when they had access. She sent me her itinerary and details of the guiding company based in Pakistan. I continued to pray fervently. She was intentionally travelling right on an "X."

We had to have another medical check in Kiev before I left for Ternopil.

The doctor who checked me asked me about my experience with Traditional Chinese Medicine (TCM). She asked me if it could help with insomnia and post trauma reactions. She explained she had been one of the doctors helping during the Maidan massacre. She'd been at the square that night and she had recurring nightmares. It was affecting her work, her family life and her health.

I brought my TCM med kit with me. I showed her the needles. She locked the door and lay down on the examining table. I gave her a treatment and placed ear point seeds in to give her more relief. We arranged a time for two more treatments before I had to leave Kiev. She reported these treatments helped. She wanted to learn more about TCM herself.

I boarded the train by myself. I journeyed to my post in the west of Ukraine with a heavy heart. My daughter's travel was constantly on my mind.

It was the first time the US Peace Corps launched a program at a medical university. I had heavy responsibilities in setting up a new program and representing the United States during this tense time in

Ukraine. I would be their first "face" for a humanitarian effort. The university set me up in one of their faculty dorm rooms and provided me with a lovely guide, who herself was a professor and knew four languages fluently.

After the first few days they took me with their faculty to a "camp" out in a rural area. This was the summer orientation for medical students from their own university and from the eastern areas embroiled in the civil war.

Figure 84. Demonstration in Ternopil with
Svoboda, Ternopil, Ukraine 2015

Medical residents, doctors and students from Donbass and Luhansk regions were brought in for the week. Most of their hospitals, medical universities and clinics had been bombed. Medical Universities in Donbass had to close. As many of the students and residents as possible were transported to Ternopil. They spoke Russian. My halting Russian came in handy.

My colleagues and most of the medical personnel from the East were upset. They openly expressed their disgust with US policies.

"America wants us to fight brother against brother. We won't do that."

America and a few European countries constructed the Joint Multinational Training Group at Yavoriv Combat Training Center

Ukraine in western Ukraine. Supposedly only "non-lethal" supplies were provided such as radar equipment, body armor and medical supplies although artillery shells, drones and weapons were kept in storehouses on base. The stated goal was to train over 250,000 Ukrainian soldiers. They also had a Psyops unit producing recruiting advertisements and anti-Russian propaganda.

My Ukrainian colleagues expanded my knowledge of Ukrainian history.

"We don't need outsiders telling us about the Russians. Holodomor is still fresh in our minds. The Soviets starved us to death by the millions. No other country came to help us. We had genocide here, in Ukraine. We will never forget. But Putin is different. Russian is not communist anymore. As you Americans say…move on!"

The Ternopil State Medical University was spread out over the city. Different departments were sometimes miles/kilometers apart. There was no intranet and not all buildings had reliable internet. Communications were slow and sometimes garbled. The head of the IT department was one of my students. We collaborated and were able to construct an intranet usable for all departments. It saved time, walking and helped with scheduling and translations. The university was in the process, as were many government departments, of switching the official language to Ukrainian. The university opened a new Military Medicine wing the first week I was there. They needed intranet access. There was so much need in Ternopil.

Figure 85. Military Medicine Department ceremony Ternopil State
Medical University, colleagues, interpreter and author, Ukraine 2015

All of my students during the week were faculty members, doctors
and professionals in a few fields including bio engineering and IT. I
volunteered to teach two Saturday sessions on "Information Literacy"
for medical students. We did these in a large computer lab.

My Ukrainian colleagues were helpful but distant for the first
month. I found out later one of the reasons they didn't trust me was
because of a US program which handed out vaccines to their children.
They were infected with HIV which they attributed to the "free vac-
cination" program.

"We never had problems with the vaccines from Russia. Our children didn't need to take so many vaccines. Then Americans came with
this project telling us we needed vaccines for Measles and other child-
hood diseases. They weren't a problem for us in most cases. We tried
their new polio vaccines. Soon after children started showing strange
symptoms."

I didn't want to believe our government or agency programs would
ever do something so evil intentionally. I thought it must be a mistake
or a coincidence these symptoms happened after the vaccines were
administered. But over time and with them showing me their research

I believed they were correct. My eyes were opened to more tactics used for "influence and control."

A few of my female, single colleagues were delighted I enjoyed the theatre. As faculty members we had discount tickets to the main theatre in Ternopil known as one of the most beautiful theatres in Ukraine, the Academic Drama Theatre of Taras Shevchenko. The first time we strolled through the square near the theatre I saw a few booths set up by the political factions, Privy Sektor and Svoboda. They are considered to be right wing groups. They are strongly supported in Ternopil.

Figure 86. Taras Shevchenko Academic Drama
Theatre, Ternopil, Ukraine 2015

There is a statue of one of the leaders of a far-right group started after the first World War. His name was Stepan Bandera. His statues stand proudly in the main park and in outskirt parks as well as in other parts of the country. My interpreter and her family are strong supporters of this movement. They invited me to what I thought was going to be a Slavic National Performance but turned out to be a huge rally. It was in the biggest stadium in Ternopil. As someone who is short, with olive skin and dark brown hair I stood out at this rally. The opening on the gargantuan screen was of a rite done outdoors with large kettle drums, bare chested men pounding on these drums, and roaring fires lit around them. The full house crowd went wild.

Images from history and recent events were flashed on the screen. One image was of President Obama and an American flag burning behind him. I felt extremely uncomfortable, even more so as I looked around seeing my colleagues and the crowd responding with enthusiastic sounds and clapping. Yet, it was important to attend a local cultural event and not just classical ballet, plays or musical concerts to understand Ukraine and Ukrainians in 2015.

I can't write much more about my time in Ternopil, the trips they took me on to L'viv, the sacred sites of their Ukrainian Orthodox church (where you must wear long skirts and head coverings) and hikes in the forests and up into the hills outside Ternopil. The reason is the university decided I needed to sign their own form of a non-disclosure agreement. I did.

Meanwhile, my daughter completed her 17-day trip and trek in Pakistan. She was guided safely and returned to Texas safely. I was relieved and glad to hear she had astute observations about a part of the world and a part of life she had seen. It gives people a greater appreciation for their circumstances in the West once they experience lesser "developed" countries, poverty, oppression, and danger.

My father was happy to receive her back in Houston, but he kept his threat about not supporting her as he did before. Sequoia needed to pay for all her expenses at the office space they shared and all the "perks." She decided to transcribe her journal into a book and her company could publish it.

My father commented to me briefly, "At least she can find a way to monetize the experience." She had caused us sleepless nights. We were still very concerned about her.

In November 2015, my right ear became infected. I wasn't worried. I worked at a medical university and there were competent doctors willing to treat it. However, as per protocol for the Peace Corps I needed to report this and get permission for a Ukrainian national to administer an examination and treatment. The main office in Kiev sent a Ukrainian woman to see how I was doing at the University and consult with the doctor I chose in Ternopil. It didn't seem necessary, but it was dictated to me.

When she arrived, she openly insulted my colleagues at a class she was observing. Just before I started my lecture one of the doctors asked how my ear was. I told him it was improving. This let the Peace Corps representative know I had already seen at least one doctor. She was outraged.

"No, no you cannot go to doctors here. We have *good* doctors in Kiev. You must go to Kiev and report in from there."

She may not have realized at the time how insulting she was. The doctors in Ternopil worked in challenging conditions with a meagre salary, but the ones I saw were competent and caring.

I was ordered to take a train back to Kiev. She said the insurance would not allow for me to ride back with her and her driver in the Peace Corps car.

The doctor in Ternopil had urged me to keep warm and slow down for a few days until I healed. Taking a long train ride to Kiev and running around the city in early winter was not helpful. To keep my mind off the pain in my ear I wrote during my journey. The following is a direct excerpt:

"I'm in the economy 'wagone' on the Moscow bound train which will stop in Kiev. It appears I am the only female in this cramped wagone, the only other one is the conductor who walks briskly with a "no nonsense" expression through the train checking tickets, delivering hot tea and handing out pressed white sheets for those who want to stretch out on the vinyl benches. At least the train is partially heated.

All around me are big boned, strong looking blokes and all of them proceed to change. They are taking off their shirts (very Slav thing and usual). Some strip to their bare chests, others to white ribbed sleeveless undershirts or plain T shirts. Many take off their shoes and some take off their socks. I smell tobacco and sweat. Most unpack plastic bags of various pungent foods including dried fish, fried pancakes of mystery meat and/or vegetables, hunks of bread. Some unwrap newspapers or cloth to create placemats. Most passengers, including me, produce a large bottle of water.

The man across from me takes out a bottle of beer (it is about noon) and offers me some bread which I politely refuse. Some begin chatting with each other, a few play cards, two play a portable chess game, some already spread out the white sheet and go to sleep. I cannot help but hear the snores, all different sounds-rasping snores, gurgling snores, heaving breathy snores. No one seems to mind, in fact there is a warm feeling of comradery created in just the first hour. I need to stay alert though because I am still a "stranger in a strange land"—evident by my features and my clothes. I am not from here.

The sight out of the windows is startling - such vibrant color contrasts.

Inside almost everyone is dressed in dark colors, black, greys, browns. Outside the trees and bushes illuminate the wet landscape with bursts of crimson, scarlet, orange, gold, lime green, bright browns, and yellows. Every hour of this chugging ride we pass a village where I have a glimpse of women (probably younger than I) walking on a dirt path, stooped over, wearing a headscarf (babushka) and carrying a large basket on their back or heavy bags in both hands. Every so often we pass a train station where men with bright orange work bibs stand aside on the tracks leaning on rakes, shovels, or picks.

After about five hours a vendor strides through showing his wares. He calls out in Ukrainian and Russian to buy his "cheap sim cards-good for Moscow", portable flashlights, phone chargers, cell phones, pocketknives-people can try out the phone chargers with his portable plugin and open the pocketknives…something that would immediately cause alarm in any western country.

Sitting near the window a damp chill causes the metal in my right arm and shoulder to ache unbearably. I try rotating my shoulder but after a few rolls I see the man across is looking at me, concerned. He takes out a bottle of what looks like vodka, pours some into a plastic cup he has and nods in offer. Very sweet offer, but again I politely refuse. He downs it and looks over at the other guys in the compartment who are still awake. Now I become a confirmed "invisible woman" i.e., a woman over 35, who doesn't speak the language well enough to maintain a conversation of interest, and who doesn't drink.

Another vendor comes by selling ice creams in a portable, insulated pack. He displays sweets, cold drinks and pours out juice into a communal glass, wipes it after, then proceeds to his next customers.

"Americans are obsessed with sanitation" according to many of my colleagues from various parts of the world. In some ways this is true of Americans. Fortunately, I have my own water bottle and don't have to share any drinking cups or utensils. Of course, vodka kills most germs and is often used in hospitals for patients, instruments and to calm a practitioner's nerves as well.

The lights have been off for about half an hour now-perhaps they will come on at the next stop-at least I have my own flashlight if I need to walk about. The conductor walks by with her torch leading the way. She shouts in Ukrainian that Kiev is the next stop. I realize I have made progress in three months here because I can understand almost everything she says and reply in basic phrases she comprehends. I can also read the signs at the stations, albeit slowly.

Finally, "Kiev" is announced. People change back into "street" clothes, put on their shoes, repack, comb their hair, phone their families or friends and stand at the door ready to push out into the dark. Me, too. I have learned by now not to be near the end of any line or "mob" at public transport stations.

I step down and another conductor offers a hand and right there is the Ukrainian doctor with her very tall, muscular driver who immediately takes my bags and protects us from the crowds. Dr. L welcomes me and thanks me for the treatment I gave her back in August. She accompanies me to a clinic with an Ear, Nose and Throat specialist with brand new equipment, the highest standard of hygiene I have seen anywhere.

Just to fulfill all the US government and Peace Corps requirements, he orders yet more tests and a follow up appointment. He speaks in Russian to Dr. L, and I understand a little more but need an accurate English translation which she gives me later.

I cannot hear too well because my right ear and Eustachian tube are blocked. Probably, I have a condition called labyrinth nephritis, blocked Eustachian tube and possibly an acoustic neuroma. My right ear hearing has diminished by 10% but it is not permanent provided I get the correct treatment very soon, if not right away. They have medication I can take.

The Washington, D. C. Physician Assistants for the Peace Corps insist the diagnosis is not correct (via long distance phone calls). They state that I probably contracted herpes on my hiking trip with Ukrainian nationals. I don't know what they thought we were doing beside walking in the forest, for me to "contract herpes." It was ridiculous.

They recommended medical evacuation. They also recommended a very risky operation with a more than 50% chance I would lose my sense of balance. The Kiev doctors thought it was absurd. They told me privately it would be best if I seek treatment right away back in the USA, with doctors I know and trust.

However, if I use my own doctors in the States, I will have to wait at least six weeks and go through another application process to return. I decided to send another email to my contacts and see if there is another job open they know of. This will be it for trusting the DC Peace Corps office for medical advice. I have an excellent TCM doctor in Austin. I send him an email, too.

I am permitted to return to Ternopil to close out, pack my belongings and arrange for someone to administer the final exams I've prepared. My colleagues at TSMU are sympathetic and hope the Peace Corps will have me return. Personally, I doubt it.

Within 24 hours my friend, Lisa Marie Akbari sends me an email. She needs someone to complete a team for a huge project back in Afghanistan. This will be on a contract for a subcontracting company called "C" working for USAID. It would start right away. She realizes I am still in Ukraine, but they need someone competent. They could be a little flexible on the timeline. Am I interested? She says we can Skype. She'll tell me the low down. She's still in Kabul.

Afghanistan…again. But it's Lisa. I think it over for a few hours and then I reply.

Figure 87. On "farewell" train in Ternopil with
TSMU colleagues, Ukraine 2015

19. INSIDE JOBS – AFGHANISTAN

Afghanistan. This would be the third time and my third contract in this country. I vowed to myself the second time I was in Afghanistan, that it would be my last. Lisa had helped me on a short contract at the beginning of 2015, with a girl's schools that I suspected was a front. I needed her judgement on what I uncovered. It looked like there was double accounting, suspicious movements of young "schoolgirls" to the Serena hotel for sexual favors, and connections with nefarious criminal networks based out of Afghanistan. A young Afghan woman supposedly ran the boarding school. The young woman's name wasn't even real. It was a created cut-out name to elicit sympathy and money from naïve, wealthy, liberal Americans.

Lisa was still based in Kabul. We were both living "outside the wire" in different sections of the city. Lisa came over to the "school" a few times. She met with the staff. We poured over the books. Lisa was an excellent forensic accountant among her other skills and talents. She confirmed what I already knew.

"They are doing double entries, padding expenses, handling tens of thousands in cash every week. They've created a dummy transport corporation. I agree with you. They're corrupt and this is a front."

If it was anyone but Lisa I wouldn't have considered going back to Kabul after that experience.

Normally, processing paperwork for USAID takes weeks if not months. They processed mine in less than 48 hours. It was curious. Lisa and I Skyped twice. She gave me a heads up about a few situations which could be troublesome but also said she thought *this was a worthwhile project*. She would be staying in a secure compound in a different section of the city. I would be staying at the company compound. She would explain more logistics once I arrived.

First, I flew out to be with Sequoia in California. She had moved there to try and expand her business to Los Angeles, as well as be more independent. My youngest brother worked and lived there as a touchstone. Her best friend from Houston lived down the street. She brought her dog Safi with her, too. She seemed happier there.

Figure 88. Serena hotel courtyard, Kabul, Afghanistan 2015

We went to see a new film which was screening about the American Suffragette movement. There was a panel discussion after with one of the main actresses. Sequoia was building her business network. She was doing well in a tough business-publishing-in a tough city-Los Angeles, California.

I was pleased for her that she was on her way as an entrepreneur and giving a platform and voice to those who may not have been heard or seen otherwise. The initial shock of our family deaths was easing and the hard reality of life without them was sinking in for both of us. We coped in different ways.

Sequoia was planning a "gala" to raise money and awareness of her newly founded *Denali Foundation*. She planned to use part of the money to bring art supplies to under-served schools including the Waldorf independent school on the Pine Ridge Reservation in South Dakota. Denali, Sequoia and I had been there when I took a Denver Waldorf High School group up back in 2000. We also went to a few Pow-Wows when we were there. This was something I thought was suitable to do in Denali's name. If the project in Afghanistan went smoothly, I might be back in time for the gala in Houston in 2016. We enjoyed ourselves, celebrated Thanksgiving dinner with her friends. We were on better terms by the time I left.

Figure 89. Sequoia Patti Schmidt and author, Los Angeles, California 2015

My ticket had me stopping in Dubai for a night. I was going to meet two other members of our team there before we all departed for Kabul. We were told we didn't have to worry about our visas. They would take care of them for us. We were all staying at the same hotel in the UAE. We each had received the same email. They sent the time for us to meet at the reception desk.

One woman was from the UK, the other was Afghan although she had a Canadian passport. Her family had been granted Canadian citizenship. She was to be the section leader for our portion of the large textbook Education project. She also spoke, read, and wrote Dari. She was quite nervous.

We greeted each other and went for a coffee in the hotel café. I sat by a large picture window and recalled how many times I had passed through this city since 2007. While we were getting to know each other, our phones simultaneously showed emails from the company. We were to stay one more night in Dubai. There had been a bombing diagonally across the street from the compound. The Spanish embassy, a Chinese restaurant and many other buildings were hit. They needed to check security and start repairing shattered windows before we arrived.

"Not an auspicious beginning is it." The British woman ordered a cocktail.

She asked me if I wanted one.

"No, thank you. I don't drink."

"Neither do I." The Afghan woman chimed in. We smiled at each other.

Actually, I hardly drank alcohol. I certainly didn't at work or just getting to know strangers in a Muslim country. I had resisted pressure in Russia and Ukraine by making it a personal rule not to accept alcohol except on occasion with American friends. After 2013, I knew I would probably get depressed if I drank on my own or become morose when with friends. I needed to keep my inhibitions.

I emailed Lisa and asked her to call me later. She would be able to give me an accurate read about the attack. Fortunately, Lisa lived in a different compound. She was out "in the field" when the bombs went off.

We landed at the Hamid Karzai International Airport the next morning. I noticed the Afghan/Canadian woman didn't wear a headscarf. The British women had blondish hair. Both she and I covered our heads. The company driver and one of their security guards were there to meet us. It was already snowing slightly. Kabul can be bone chilling cold in the winter. Few places I had lived in the city had adequate heating.

We drove inside the company compound garage where two other security guards opened our doors, took our bags and had us sign in and show our passports. We were shown the main office across a small field. There was broken glass all over. The windows on both the first and second floors were cracked. There was debris scattered all over the front yard.

The three of us were given room keys and instruction sheets. We met the Chief of Party (the official title for the in-country boss) and a number of Afghan local men who worked on this Education project. The Head of Security was from South Africa and his two main guards were from Croatia. The rest were local Afghans and we had Afghan drivers. This American company had obviously been cutting corners on their budgets and not hiring American contractors for security. This was not a good sign.

None of their vehicles were up armored either. They were "thin skins", Toyota four-doors and two jeeps.

We were taken across the street and through another checkpoint and gate to where our workstations and accommodations were situated. The whole street smelled of smoke, charcoal and burnt flesh. The drivers hauled our luggage up to the third floor. We each had our own room. I had to go out to the hallway to use the bathroom. We were given a quick tour of the few office spaces, a makeshift "gym" in the basement consisting of one treadmill, some weights, a pull up bar and a broken rowing machine.

We were taken up to the balcony on this villa-like structure. By the door was a coiled roll of what looked like barbed wire which we were instructed to roll down the stairs in case of attack. This was supposed to slow down the attackers. There was no "safe room." I paused to stay up on the balcony and get a clearer view of where we were.

Kabul did feel familiar to me. I crossed the balcony to gain sight of the interior of the compound when I glanced down at the side of the wall at what looked like blood. I bent down to have a closer look. There, on the balcony tile was a human body part. I best express strong events and emotions in poetry. Here is a poem I wrote.

Meat in the Trees

There is no ease
in describing these
bits and pieces of people
blasted high, spreading low

Landing on streets and balconies

children screamed at the meat in the trees
I saw the shattered glass
bent down to have a closer look

Burned flesh like striated bacon
Inspecting so I would not be mistaken
No, I was right
a thumb still attached to an index finger

I did not look up to the branches
It was not my day to take more chances
I had already smelled and seen
enough of macerated human beings

We were each issued body armor and a laptop. I arranged my small room, freshened up and then texted Lisa. She texted back. She was en route and would be there for lunch.

Figure 90. Checchi compound room, Kabul,
Afghanistan 2015, photo by author

The company's main compound contained a large dining room and kitchen. Everyone served themselves at the buffet provided with local Afghan food and sat down at a long table. If you were a female, there was another small room with a round table where you could eat without male company. Most of the local Afghan women went there for meals.

Lisa came up behind me as I was spooning saffron rice onto a large plate.

"Hey, how are you?" I was cheered to see her.

"So, you made it?" She smiled. "Join us down at the end of the table."

I excused myself from my new teammates and wandered over to where Lisa and another American woman were sitting. Lisa introduced me to her section leader. Lisa had just had her 37th birthday. Her section lead was showing her photos from that day and of the birthday cake. I did notice Lisa had put on more weight and looked tired.

"They've split up this project into three sections essentially. Two of them started last month. The one you're on starts tomorrow. Jo, you're on the curriculum, books section for K-12. We split up the country, too. Guess what-you are going to Jbad *(Jalalabad), Kabul city and back to Mazar. Fun, huh?!"

"Nice." I grinned. "Where do you get to go?"

"Bamiyan, Kandahar and other parts of Kabul. We can compare notes."

"How do you two know each other?" Her section lead was curious. I didn't know how much Lisa had told her. I let her answer.

"We know each other from working in the States and from the American University of Afghanistan programs." I nodded affirmatively and proceeded to eat my lunch.

"Have you worked with USAID before?" She asked me.

"Yes, I have in a few countries including Afghanistan." Lisa and I exchanged looks and kept eating.

My section lead came over to us.

"Joanne, we need to meet with our Afghan team in about thirty minutes alright?"

"Yes, Noorin. By the way this is my friend Lisa and her team lead...Karen."

We finished our meals and brought our dishes to the kitchen. Lisa showed me where the tea, coffee and hot water urn was. I poured myself a large cup of coffee and we stepped outside to the porch area. It was still snowing.

I put my coffee down and we were able to give each other a "hello" hug.

"Look, we may not be working together as much as I thought, but we'll be able to see each other at least once a day unless we're travelling. Even then you're welcome to come over to my apartment if you want to get away. We can talk freely there. There are too many "ears" here."

"What can you tell me? The Chief of Party seems out of it from the little I saw."

"He is. He's a desk jockey. He only goes out for socializing. We just have to make him look good. I did hear he's a lawyer and he has a side business. Something about getting SIVs (Special Immigration Visas). Under the table stuff."

"Lucrative." I said. "As I recall, the going rate was at least $10,000 cash per person. Probably more by now. He must have an embassy contact. If he "sells" only a few a month that's quite a bit extra to take home. No taxes either."

"There is talk that they don't fully honor our contracts. They find a way to send us home before the 89-day mark where our higher salary kicks in. They don't tell USAID though. They keep the difference. Have to watch our backs here. Sorry, Joanne. I'm finding out more each day. This time I need your opinion and fresh eyes on."

"You've got it. Any chance we can get away on Friday? I've got some friends in another sector I need you to meet."

"Not this Friday, but you go ahead Jo. Get some sleep tonight and tomorrow let's meet at lunch again. Let me know how your first day goes."

It was getting cold and almost time for our meeting. We hugged again away from the others then went back inside.

Figure 91. Training in Kansas Lisa Marie Akbari and author USA 2013

The first week was tough. Another Canadian woman who had worked for this company before, arrived. She was the "fixer" for our social science data. Noorin wasn't experienced as a leader. She and the British woman got into an argument. Noorin accused her of being prejudiced against Afghans. She went right to the Chief of Party and didn't discuss it. Apparently Noorin had given him an ultimatum. Either he fired the Brit or Noorin would resign. The British woman, in fairness was competent, knew USAID particulars and had worked with the same company in Afghanistan and elsewhere for a number of years. She was summarily terminated. She had a dry sense of wit, too. She sent us each an email which simply stated.

"I am poorer having known you." It was true. She had probably been counting on a decent salary and savings, as we all anticipated when we signed on. We were supposed to earn extra since it was over Christmas, New Year's, and winter holidays in the west.

Now we were short a team member. Moreover, while Noorin was an adept interpreter she was not a team leader, nor had she done such a huge project before. She knew almost nothing about school curriculum or textbook selection and procurement. She moaned about not having enough staff.

The company agreed we needed another American to assist since the Canadian woman was only on our team as a temporary loan. We needed someone for the duration. They told us to hold on, it would take another month for her to arrive. She was not an "expert", but she was living with a Pashtun in the USA and "knew about the culture." I was dubious about her actual skills.

I proposed interviewing a former colleague of mine from AUAF (American University of Afghanistan). He knew English, Dari, Tajik and Arabic fluently and a fair amount of Pashto. He graduated from Georgetown University School of Foreign Service in Doha and did his master's degree at Leeds University in the UK. I knew he was competent and would be an asset for Lisa and me, too. Noorin said to call him.

My Afghan friend from AUAF was interested. I invited him over to the compound the next week before his formal interview. When he arrived and was searched and vetted, he joined Lisa and I for lunch in the company dining room. We couldn't speak freely but we planned to meet outside the company compound later in the week.

Our small team of three women (Noorin, the Canadian and myself) three local Afghan men who spoke English, a driver and sometimes a security guard, went out into the city almost every day. We went to different school districts, Ministry offices, storage facilities and to interview teachers and administrators five or six days a week. Most schools were closed to students for the winter. This was better for us since administrators and officials were not as busy. It was also a pause in the "fighting season" in Afghanistan. It was a little less dangerous to continually be *outside the wire* in colder weather.

We drank liters of hot tea, sat around in frosty rooms, inspected inventories, documents, listened to complaints and accounts of materials, equipment, funds which were promised but never delivered. This was a $791.1 million-dollar project. Almost a billion US tax dollars were channeled into this project. The worst of it was this was the third time in less than ten years that a "textbook, education project" was launched in Afghanistan through USAID. Each time millions of dollars were allocated. Each time the project aims were somehow never achieved. This was money going down a sieve of sub-contractors, corrupt officials, and criminal networks.

Figure 92. Author with Afghan interviewees Kabul, Afghanistan 2016

As Lisa and I asked incredulously, "Are there no legitimate humanitarian projects left?"

From time to time, we went to meetings at the USAID rooms within the US Embassy in Kabul. The Embassy was a massive bunker above and below ground. Standing outside waiting to be let in at the checkpoint was hazardous. It felt like we were right on "the X." I never liked going there.

USAID personnel never went outside. They "came up with ideas" for research and reports. They contracted companies and teams like us to do their work for them. They just approved or required re-writes and editing of our "products." They sent these back to Washington, D.C. and published them thereafter.

USAID requires very specific forms and protocols. Technically, they never used real names of local assets or contractors in their reports to other national governments and/or ministries. However, they too hired local nationals. These workers did not live in the embassy compounds. They came for a few hours and then went back into the community. They received less salary than their American counterparts. They were a weak link and susceptible to corruption and betrayal.

Information and data from an American program can fetch high prices on the open market. Many of the USAID programs provided funding for over a decade to Afghan organizations, government entities and individuals. We were seen as "walking ATMs." They got used to the continual flow of funds. No one wanted this money spigot turned off.

A significant part of my responsibility was to submit a decision after all our research in the field. We would either recommend the project for further funding, or not recommend i.e., deny further funding. I needed to quantify and justify our decision…either way.

It was becoming clear to us that not only was the money not going to areas designated but worse, the Taliban were extorting money from teachers, administrators, families, and ministries. Trucks bought to deliver textbooks in rural areas were sold before or right after the delivery was scheduled. Book storage units were filled with other materials. We had firsthand evidence of all these manipulations and abuses.

The books were not printed in Kabul-which had a working printing company-but contracted to firms in Pakistan. The first shipment of books I tested fell apart in my hands. They had used cheap glue, paper, and packaging. A few containers had books on top and old newspapers underneath. They cheated on the numbers delivered.

In school districts which were supposed to provide free textbooks to families and teachers, the books were stolen and sold in market stalls.

The Taliban issued a fatwa (declaration) against any English books and any books using the "new curriculum." This was another excuse to sabotage deliveries, steal transport and materials and threaten teachers who had copies of these textbooks.

Schools for girls were targeted. The Taliban claimed responsibility for kidnapping teachers, torturing, raping, and killing them including during a teacher training sponsored by "Save the Children." They bombed schools, threw acid on young girls trying to attend schools and sent death threat letters to families sending their daughters to school or who were teachers in girl's schools. They poisoned their food and their water at the schools.

The Taliban infiltrated school systems, ministries, companies. They extorted money for positions. They were ruthless and showed no mercy.

Were these USAID and NGO (non-governmental organizations such as Save the Children) programs making it better or worse for Afghan society and specifically for the females in Afghanistan? It was/is a complicated question. Lisa and I wrestled with this question constantly.

Figure 93. Security, driver and author in Mazar before attack, Afghanistan 2016

We called or met each other at least once a day for the first three weeks I was there.

We compared notes and gave each other our honest assessments and observations. We made plans together for when we returned to the States.

Christmas was approaching. It's not legal to celebrate any other religion or religious holiday in Afghanistan. It must be done in secret. Lisa and I arranged to spend our Friday off on December 25th at her place.

On Sunday, December 20th we were both working with our teams at the company offices. We ate lunch with our sections but then went outside to talk privately. For some reason the two Croatian security guards followed us. I sat down to talk. Lisa came over. I saw dark circles under her eyes. She looked exhausted. Ordinarily Lisa moves steadily and is calm under most circumstances but Sunday she was agitated. Her voice had an urgency I paid attention to instantly.

"Listen. I've found something. We need to talk. I'm supposed to fly to Bamiyan tonight. Can we talk now?"

"Yes." I was just about to get up and go with Lisa when another American woman from another team came out in a rush.

"Joanne, we need you inside. I need to interview you now, okay?"

Lisa came over and took my hand between her hands. She looked at me intently.

"Alright, go ...but we *need* to talk!"

The other woman was impatient. I accompanied her inside to the smaller dining room. I turned to look outside once more and saw Lisa heading toward the company garage. For some reason I shuddered.

That afternoon we were doing planning for our next field visit. Noorin invited some of the other Afghan men on staff to sit in. They were in an uncharacteristically good mood, making jokes, sniggering. I was the only non-Afghan on the team that day. They kept speaking in Dari. There was something in the air.

I felt something was wrong. Something was about to go down. I'd had this experience before when I was unjustly imprisoned for a time. Inmates would be going about normal routines or be out in the exercise yard and suddenly there would be a shift. Imperceptible at first, but after a while you could sense when something violent or unusual was about to happen.

This situation felt similar. Something was off, but I couldn't be certain.

Lisa texted me to say the flight to Bamiyan had been postponed due to weather. She was going home a little early and would see me tomorrow.

One of my friends working for another company needed an acupuncture treatment. He asked if I could get over there that evening. I arranged for a driver to take me after dinner. I asked the driver to pick me up at 9:00 pm.

At 7:00 pm I was at the other company compound in their basement with two other people when we all heard a strange sound. It sounded like a heavy object being dragged across the ceiling and then a scratching noise. We looked all around and two of us went to an adjacent room when suddenly we saw a golden light at the end of the room which extended in rays up to the ceiling. I had just enough time to ask, "Do you see that?" when the light disappeared. Interiorly I felt a death. Someone close to me had died. I didn't say it aloud to my two companions.

I administered acupuncture and had taken out the first set of needles when my phone rang. The company driver had come early. He was ready for me to return to the compound. He didn't say why.

Quickly I put on my long black coat, my head scarf, said goodbye to my friends, apologized for not being able to stay and got in the car. The driver and security guard didn't say a word the entire way back. There was a thick, strained atmosphere in the vehicle. They told me to go right up to my room, Noorin needed to see me. I was confused.

When I got upstairs, I saw Noorin and two local Afghan women who worked for the company were standing outside my door. They had been crying.

"Joanne, we're sorry to have to tell you. Lisa's been shot."

"What? When? Is she in the hospital? I need to be with her."

They looked at each other before speaking to me again.

"You can't. Joanne...she's dead. She's been shot dead near her apartment."

"What?" I wanted to scream aloud but I stopped myself. I realized I was with Afghan women. I also realized I didn't know who I could trust.

"I still want to be with her. Which hospital is she at? Let me get the driver."

"Just a moment." Noorin said. She called the security guards. The three women formed a semi-circle in front of me. I was in shock.

One of the Croatian guards ran up the stairs to me and stopped in front of us.

"I'm sorry. Lisa is dead. You cannot go see her. She is at the police station. The US embassy will send someone. It's a crime scene. It is too dangerous for you to be with her. I'm sorry. Get some rest. We'll know more in the morning."

I was dazed but somehow also clear about what I had to do.

"Thank you all. I'll be alright. I just need to take a shower and then get some sleep. Goodnight. Please keep Lisa and her family in your prayers."

They nodded and said words I don't remember. They watched me go to into my room and shut the door. I put my face in my pillow and cried. Then I called some of my American friends in Kabul including some of our former classmates from Ft. Leavenworth who were still in Afghanistan. Lisa was loved and respected by many people over the years.

Friends were texting me reports of other American deaths. These were American soldiers. Within twenty-four hours seven Americans were killed. Six American servicemen were attacked by a motorcycle suicide bomber near Bagram Air base, and Lisa who was a Coast Guard veteran in addition to having served as a US Department of Army Civilian. They were all to be flown to Dover Air Force base and then have a "dignified transfer" to their families.

Somehow, the news reports came out within a half hour after Lisa's assassination. I emailed as many people as I knew to warn them. These reports were totally false. Major news outlets reported that Lisa was working for World Vision and was "proselytizing Christianity." It appeared as if this "report" was prepared ahead of time and disseminated widely. Yes, something was wrong. I thought back over the events of the entire day going backwards.

I mulled over who else knew Lisa had changed plans. The news already reported the shooter was an imam (holy man, Islamic cleric) and he had been caught running from the scene.

Worse, in some reports there were photos of Lisa's body with brutal captions and horrific celebratory comments. People were as cruel as they were about the young Afghan woman known as Farkhunda who was publicly lynched in Kabul in March 2015. She was falsely accused of desecrating a Koran. Her name was Farkhunda Malikzada.

It was December 2015 and dark by late afternoon. Who was there to take flash photos?

I couldn't sleep yet. I went down to the security office. The Chief from South Africa was on duty. We had gotten along well the weeks I was there.

He knew I knew Lisa. He knew why I had come down to see him.

"Tell me." I pleaded. "Please tell me everything you know about what happened. You were there weren't you?"

He closed the door to make sure we were not overheard.

"This is not official but yes, I was the first to arrive from our company, but we weren't called right away. When I got there, police and the Afghan press, and photographers were already there."

He turned away from me for a moment and then continued.

"Lisa lived at one of the most secure compounds in Kabul. There's never been any incidents there before tonight. What's more, in all my years in different parts of Afghanistan I've never seen them leave a body uncovered like that, especially a woman. The police hadn't covered her up. They let them photograph her. There is a video. Everything was caught on tape. The killer knew there was a camera. He planned it to be on film. I'm afraid it's already being posted on Jihadi sites."

"Did you see it? Can I see it please?"

"I saw it. I can't let you see it, but I can describe it frame by frame to you. I know you were good friends. She didn't deserve to die. Especially not that way. I'm sorry."

He described every frame, every movement to me in detail. The last actions when Lisa's phone rang as she came out of the container that served as a workout room on the top floor. She was outside holding her large bag in one hand and the phone in the other. When she placed the phone by her ear to answer, a man who'd been hiding in the shadows ran up behind her and shot her in the temple. She fell forward. He put the gun in his pocket and stepped over her body. The last movement Lisa was able to do in her life was somehow reach her hand out to grab her killer's leg. The gun went off in his pocket and wounded him. He hobbled away but left a blood trail. The police found him by tracking his blood.

"Who has Lisa's phone now?" I asked. It occurred to me whomever called her might be part of this assassination.

"The Afghan authorities. The US Embassy staff are with them now, I believe. They'll contact her next of kin as will our Chief of Party."

"What's all this rubbish on the news already. It's not true, any of it."

"Sorry, I don't know anything about that. I just made sure her body was respected, took the names of the Afghan police and the Embassy staff. After they took her away, I came back here."

"Thank you. I know it must be very difficult to have to see that and deal with it. Please, though…find a way I can see that last film myself. It would mean a lot to me and to her family."

"I'll see what I can do, Joanne. Goodnight."

I made it back to my room without collapsing. I felt as if the wind was knocked out of me. I sat on my bed looking over texts Lisa had sent me. I wished I hadn't deleted hers over the weeks. I only had the ones from Sunday, December 20, 2015.

The next morning, I went down to breakfast early. When three other Americans from another project came in, cheerful and bouncy, I couldn't bear it. It seemed very few people on the compound had been told.

One of the women said, "Good Morning. How are you today?" She smiled at me.

"Not too well." I replied.

"Oh, are you feeling sick? Adjusting to the food here can be hard on your stomach."

"No, it's not that. It's Lisa, my friend. Do you know her?

"Yes, we all know her. Lisa's great. She's been here for a while, why?

"Did you know she was fatally shot last night in Kabul?"

Then the two women started screaming. The American man stared at me.

"No, no, no, no, no. It can't be. Why? How? Are you sure it was Lisa?"

"Yes, I'm afraid it's true. Lisa was my good friend. She's the one that told me about this job and recommended me for this team. We don't know why yet. We just know it was an Afghan man who killed her at her compound."

"We have to do something. We need to have a company meeting.

We need to at least hold a service for her. Oh my God!"

Other people heard the screams and were running into the dining area.

"What happened? Are you alright?" Everyone started talking about Lisa and about the other Americans killed. They started discussing how to plan a service for her and how to send condolences to her family.

Then, Karen came in. She was fraught and almost hysterical. I knew Lisa didn't really get along with Karen personally, but they had worked together for over a month in Kabul. Karen was wringing her hands.

"She shouldn't have done it." Karen kept repeating. I didn't know what she was talking about.

"Lisa? What shouldn't she have done Karen?" My voice was stern now.

"She shouldn't have been talking about Jesus and the Bible. She shouldn't have been preaching Christianity!"

"What are you talking about? Lisa would *never* do that, especially in Afghanistan. Lisa knows this culture and its prejudices. Her father is from Afghanistan. He served in the Afghan military. I know Lisa very well. She would never do that! Who said she did? That's a lie!"

Karen started pacing. It occurred to me as I waited for an answer and saw her body language, that she may have been the one who reported or created a report to the press with this slander. Again, I wondered what her motive was…why?

More people were coming in to eat breakfast. Karen went over to the table with the two American women and one man.

"We should plan a memorial service for tomorrow. I'll get the flowers and talk to an Imam I know. He can say an opening verse. She was Muslim wasn't she…her father was."

I nearly lost my temper. One minute she was saying Lisa was a preaching Christian, now she was saying she was Muslim. I decided not to say anymore and left the dining area, went across the street and up to my room. I had to decide what to do. First though, I said a prayer for Lisa and silently spoke to her spirit. "Lisa…what really happened? You can see from where you are now."

I emailed my family and friends to let them know I was alright and not to believe what was online or in the news about Lisa. I would explain later when I was back home safely in the States.

Noorin came and knocked on my door.

"Joanne, if you want to, you can take the day off today."

"Yes, thank you. I need some time to myself and to help plan the... Lisa's memorial service."

A few hours later the Chief of Party wanted to see me in his office. I swallowed some Bach Flower Rescue Remedy and composed myself.

Flgure 94. Memorial service for Lisa Marie
Akbari, Kabul, Afghanistan 2015

"I'm sorry. I know you were friends. I didn't really know Lisa. We are sending one of the girls to get her things from her apartment. Would you be okay going through them? We'll send whatever you think she would want her family to have, back to the States."

"Yes, sir. I can do that."

"Now, you don't have to decide this week, but if you want to resign after what's happened, we'll understand."

This man had no compassion in his voice whatsoever.

"I will think it over, sir and let you know by the end of the week."

"Good. We'll hold a memorial service tomorrow. Nothing religious, no prayers of any sort. We don't want to offend any of our Afghan staff."

"Do you have any questions, Joanne? Any issues?"

I shook my head, "No."

"We are obliged to offer you counseling through USAID. You would have to go to them over at the embassy. Our insurance will cover the cost."

I knew, we all knew that having "counseling" on your record, especially for post trauma, was a career killer. In the contracting world it was a stigma no matter what was stated in their employee handbooks.

"No, thank you. I have my own ways of dealing with this."

"Okay, if you don't want to come down for meals just text and someone can bring food to your room."

"Thank you, sir."

"One more thing. I'll announce this to everyone at the memorial but first to you. There must not be any chat on social media. No talking to any press. No comments, no leaks. There will be severe consequences for any employee we find out has violated this instruction. Understand?"

I simply nodded. I didn't want to discuss this. There were already circulated press reports, facebook posts, opinion pieces, dark net chat. I left his office feeling drained.

People avoided me when I walked across the compound. I didn't want to speak to anyone if it wasn't necessary. I hoped Lisa's phone would be included with her belongings. I doubted that Afghan police would really investigate her murder. I doubted the US Embassy would press them either. Her father was Afghan after all. She used two passports, her American and her Afghan one. She had given up her security clearance to stay and work in Afghanistan on this contract.

I started to think about what poem would be appropriate since we weren't allowed to recite prayers.

Lisa's mother, Stacy, was Irish American. Stacy named Lisa-Lisa Marie. Lisa loved her and missed her. Stacy had a very tough life when she was married to Lisa's Afghan father. We spoke about her a few times. Lisa kept an old photo of her with her.

Her mother had supposedly committed suicide when Lisa was about twelve. When Lisa described the circumstances under which she was found, we both suspected she did not. I hoped they would be together now across the threshold.

The poem I chose was *"Do Not Stand By My Grave And Weep"* by Mary Elizabeth Frye. I think Lisa would have approved. She was definitely with us for her memorial service in Kabul, and with me throughout the rest of the time I stayed to finish our work in Afghanistan.

Lisa was there when we were under siege in Mazar for over 24 hours in January 2016. She was there as I gathered evidence. She was with me when I was forced to leave right at the 89-day mark, as she warned, and paid a lower salary to finish my report while I was back in the USA.

Lisa was with me for the next deployments to Afghanistan in support of the US Military over the next years. Yes, I returned again… and again.

Lisa is with me as I write about our time together and about our continued quest for answers and the truth…no matter where we are.

Do not stand at my grave and weep,
I am not there, I do not sleep.
I am in a thousand winds that blow,
I am the softly falling snow.
I am the gentle showers of rain,
I am the fields of ripening grain.
I am in the morning hush,
I am in the graceful rush
Of beautiful birds in circling flight,
I am the starshine of the night.
I am in the flowers that bloom,
I am in a quiet room.
I am in the birds that sing,
I am in each lovely thing.
Do not stand at my grave and cry,
I am not there. I do not die.

Figure 95. Photo of author on HKIA NATO base in front of barracks, photo by Shala Hammond, Kabul, Afghanistan 2017

EPILOGUE

My life continues. My work continues. My travel continues. We are all on an "X" while the restrictions and fears continue during the time reported as a "global pandemic." We cannot travel as freely physically but we may have more opportunity and time to travel internally. I am finishing this book from remote Alaska where I am working and living.

My next book is entitled: *The Path to Yun Tai Mountain.* As a preview, here are some of the chapters and the locations I write about:

Zumba in Ankawa – Kurdistan
Te Waipounamu – New Zealand
Co-ed Barracks – Afghanistan
Training with the Shaolin – China
Fight Clubs & Meditation – Thailand
Wiwayang Wacipi – USA
The Mosul Road – Iraq
Healing in San Miguel – Mexico
Negotiation Education – Israel
Moose and Mukluks – Alaska, USA

My website is: jopattimunisteri.org

There are more photos, blog posts, articles, and information on my website. You are welcome to contact me.

My thanks to you for your support.

LIST OF PHOTOS/ILLUSTRATIONS

Made in the USA
Las Vegas, NV
05 March 2022